Translanguaging as a Lingua Franca in the Plurilingual Classroom

BILINGUAL EDUCATION & BILINGUALISM

Series Editors: **Nancy H. Hornberger** *(University of Pennsylvania, USA)* and **Wayne E. Wright** *(Purdue University, USA)*

Bilingual Education and Bilingualism is an international, multidisciplinary series publishing research on the philosophy, politics, policy, provision and practice of language planning, Indigenous and minority language education, multilingualism, multiculturalism, biliteracy, bilingualism and bilingual education. The series aims to mirror current debates and discussions. New proposals for single-authored, multiple-authored, or edited books in the series are warmly welcomed, in any of the following categories or others authors may propose: overview or introductory texts; course readers or general reference texts; focus books on particular multilingual education program types; school-based case studies; national case studies; collected cases with a clear programmatic or conceptual theme; and professional education manuals.

All books in this series are externally peer-reviewed.

Full details of all the books in this series and of all our other publications can be found on http://www.multilingual-matters.com, or by writing to Multilingual Matters, St Nicholas House, 31-34 High Street, Bristol, BS1 2AW, UK.

BILINGUAL EDUCATION & BILINGUALISM: 137

Translanguaging and English as a Lingua Franca in the Plurilingual Classroom

Anna Mendoza

MULTILINGUAL MATTERS
Bristol • Jackson

DOI https://doi.org/10.21832/MENDOZ3436

Library of Congress Cataloging in Publication Data

A catalog record for this book is available from the Library of Congress.

Names: Mendoza, Anna, author.

Title: Translanguaging and English as a Lingua Franca in the Plurilingual Classroom /Anna Mendoza.

Description: Bristol; Jackson: Multilingual Matters, [2023] | Series: Bilingual Education & Bilingualism: 137 | Includes bibliographical references and index. | Summary: "This book explores the use of multilingual practices such as translanguaging, code-switching and stylization by speakers of less commonly taught languages. It investigates how students use these languages alongside English as a lingua franca to participate in classroom tasks and social interactions in secondary classrooms in Hawai'i"— Provided by publisher.

Identifiers: LCCN 2022046191 (print) | LCCN 2022046192 (ebook) | ISBN 9781800413429 (paperback) | ISBN 9781800413436 (hardback) | ISBN 9781800413450 (epub) | ISBN 9781800413443 (pdf)

Subjects: LCSH: Translanguaging (Linguistics) | English language—Study and teaching (Secondary)—Hawaii—Honolulu. | English language--Study and teaching (Secondary)—Social aspects. | Multilingual education—Hawaii—Honolulu.

Classification: LCC P115.35 .M46 2023 (print) | LCC P115.35 (ebook) | DDC 404/.2071—dc23/eng/20221220

LC record available at https://lccn.loc.gov/2022046191

LC ebook record available at https://lccn.loc.gov/2022046192

British Library Cataloguing in Publication Data

A catalogue entry for this book is available from the British Library.

ISBN-13: 978-1-80041-343-6 (hbk)
ISBN-13: 978-1-80041-342-9 (pbk)

Multilingual Matters
UK: St Nicholas House, 31-34 High Street, Bristol, BS1 2AW, UK.
USA: Ingram, Jackson, TN, USA.

Website: www.multilingual-matters.com
Twitter: Multi_Ling_Mat
Facebook: https://www.facebook.com/multilingualmatters
Blog: www.channelviewpublications.wordpress.com

The policy of Multilingual Matters/Channel View Publications is to use papers that are natural, renewable and recyclable products, made from wood grown in sustainable forests. In the manufacturing process of our books, and to further support our policy, preference is given to printers that have FSC and PEFC Chain of Custody certification. The FSC and/or PEFC logos will appear on those books where full certification has been granted to the printer concerned.

Typeset by Deanta Global Publishing Services, Chennai, India.

To my parents, Elizabeth and Gil Mendoza

Contents

Acknowledgments

First, I am grateful to the teachers and students who participated in my study. It is an institutional and societal privilege to be a linguistic ethnographer documenting the daily interactions and challenges of the plurilingual English as a lingua franca classroom, and I learned many things from my participants, for example, how fostering learners' genuine self-efficacy and building a cohesive, mutually supportive classroom community are the bedrock of all good teaching. I learned that we all share responsibility for how we position one another linguistically, culturally, academically and socially, and that teachers are crucial actors in shaping this responsibility. The pedagogical and extracurricular dedication of teachers at the school where this research took place, and the initiatives they shared at national conferences, show how Hawai'i and the US need to value what excellent public school teachers do for society under the most challenging circumstances.

Second, I wish to express my gratitude and love to my PhD supervisor, Christina Higgins. The education scholar Dan C. Lortie coined the term 'apprenticeship of observation' to describe how people tend to teach anything in the same ways that they themselves were taught that thing. I am sometimes at a loss for words to describe what exactly it is you taught me about scholarship – perhaps the term Hawaiians use, *kuleana*, to describe our social responsibility in context, with regard to the places we inhabit and the lives that exist there, comes close. Not to see these as merely furthering our goals, but to realize we have to make ourselves useful, to care and to learn alongside others. Sociolinguistically speaking, we also have a responsibility with regard to how we draw on institutional and societal discourses, frame identities and position ourselves in daily interactions, taking into account that what we say and do to achieve positive identity positionings and work toward our goals impacts the lived experiences of others.

I would also like to thank other scholars who helped me understand the context of Hawai'i and the sociolinguistic forces that shape education: Betsy Gilliland, Graham Crookes, Georganne Nordstrom, Sarah

Allen and Kent Sakoda. I am grateful to my Ilokano translator, Mario Doropan, who made this study possible.

I recognize friends and colleagues who contributed to the atmosphere of *kuleana*, responsibility to one another and to the communities and networks we are part of, that characterizes the Department of Second Language Studies and affiliated departments at the University of Hawai'i at Mānoa. Even if they did not comment on drafts of this book, they shaped the writer's worldview: Jayson Parba, Jiamin Ruan, Jiaxin Ruan, Huy Phung, Ha Nguyen, Yuka Matsutani, Yuhan Lin and others.

In a different way, the book's ideas were also shaped by my parents and in-laws in Canada – Gil and Elizabeth Mendoza, Donna and David Olsen – who are not applied linguists but point to the quiet love that characterizes everyday life, suggesting that scholarship must exist in a symbiotic relationship with the day-to-day issues with which people are faced. My love reaches out to my brother Miguel 'Miggy' Mendoza for always helping me to become a better person. And even though I need to work on showing it, my deepest gratitude goes to my husband, Kent Olsen, who can be credited for many of the influences already described and much more.

Figures and Tables

Figures

Tables

Excerpts

Transcription Conventions

(2.0) pause length in seconds
(.) micropause of <0.2 seconds
falling intonation ↓
rising intonation ↑
[overlapping speech
… omitted speech
>fast speech<
<slow speech>
°soft speech°
::: elongated speech
emphasis
:-) laughing while talking / smiley voice
XXX indistinct speech
= latching, or quickly adding to the last speaker's utterance
(actions accompanying speech)

Foreword

Anna Mendoza's new book, *Translanguaging and English as a Lingua Franca in the Plurilingual Classroom*, concerns the lives and experiences of high school students living in Honolulu, whose first or heritage languages include Cantonese, Cebuano, Chuukese, Ilokano, Ilonggo, Mandarin, Marshallese, Samoan, Tagalog and Vietnamese. The teachers in the classrooms Mendoza observes encourage students to use their 'whole language repertoires', which presents the author with an opportunity to analyze the complexities of multilingual classroom interactions, drawing on rich sociolinguistic theory to inform and extend ongoing scholarly conversations about teaching and learning in multilingual settings.

Mendoza's book explores the theoretical contrasts between *translanguaging*, *plurilingualism*, *code-switching* and *stylization*, among other important constructs. She reminds us that *plurilingualism*, which has been more remote from the US context, offers a compelling conceptualization of the nature of bilingualism that is in some respects complementary to *translanguaging*, but also contrasts in important respects. Mendoza views plurilingualism as 'an integrated competence with resources from different named languages – yet interaction-wise, people can orient to language(s) as distinct or as an undifferentiated whole' (this book, p. 14).

Plurilingualism has much more in common with early translanguaging theory, but contrasts with late translanguaging theory. As Mendoza notes, Cen Williams (1994) originally conceptualized translanguaging as a pedagogical technique for bilingual teaching in the Welsh context. 'Translanguaging concerns effective communication, function rather than form, cognitive activity, as well as language production', as Lewis *et al.* (2012: 641) explain. When the term was re-introduced in Ofelia García's 2009 book *Bilingual Education in the 21st Century: A Global Perspective*, which made *translanguaging* a household word in language education scholarship, its meaning had departed little from Williams' original intent: 'For us, translanguagings are *multiple discursive practices* in which bilinguals engage in order to *make sense of their bilingual worlds*' (García, 2009: 45, emphases in original). Importantly, García's

original use of translanguaging was in no way critical of similar constructs in sociolinguistics like code-switching. Indeed, García hastened
to add: 'Translanguaging therefore goes beyond what has been termed
code-switching ... although it includes it, as well as other kinds of bilingual language use and bilingual contact' (2009: 45). García's original
presentation not only fully accepts code-switching and other important
sociolinguistic constructs, but even engages in detailed discussions of
code-switching in both its theoretical and pedagogical domains (García,
2009: 48–50, 298–301).

However, García's treatment of translanguaging theory morphed
under the influence of Pennycook's postmodernist proposals in the language planning and policy literature. 'A postmodern (or postcolonial)
approach to language policy ... suggests we no longer need to maintain
the pernicious myth that languages exist', conjectured Pennycook (2006:
67). This idea, sometimes called *deconstructivism* for Derrida's (1967)
theory of deconstruction, implies that 'many of the treasured icons of
liberal-linguistic thought ... such as language rights, mother tongues,
multilingualism or code-switching' similarly do not exist (Makoni &
Pennycook, 2007: 22). Where there are no languages, there can be no
multilingualism. Thus, taking on a skeptical disposition toward the 'the
ontological status of language' (García *et al.*, 2017: 5), García similarly
questioned 'the very idea of multilingualism' (García *et al.*, 2017: 8),
and therefore viewed code-switching critically as well: 'But no matter
how broadly and positively conceived, the notion of code switching still
constitutes a theoretical endorsement of the idea that what the bilingual
manipulates, however masterfully, are two separate linguistic systems'
(Otheguy *et al.*, 2015: 282).

A number of scholars, including Mendoza, have rejected the decon-
structivist turn in translanguaging in favor of a *multilingual perspective*, which, like early translanguaging theory, views multilingualism
as socially significant and psychologically real (MacSwan, 2017). (For
examples of critical discussions, see Block, 2018; Cummins, 2017,
2021; Edwards, 2012; Grin, 2018; Jaspers, 2018; King & Bigelow, 2020;
Kubota, 2014; Mackenzie, 2014; Shi & Rolstad, 2022; and chapters in
MacSwan & Faltis, 2020 and MacSwan, 2022.) As Mendoza notes and
illustrates, 'there is much evidence that distinct languages *are* real for
people even if they are social constructions, and must be examined to
explain domains of language acquisition and processes of identity negotiation' (this book, p. 14).

The contribution of early translanguaging scholarship to bilingual
pedagogy remains an important dimension of language education
research, which Mendoza extends and develops in her book. While
translanguaging and *plurilingualism* have different origins and tend to
be used in different policy contexts, as Mendoza elucidates, the principal
theoretical contrast relates to *deconstructivism*; late translanguaging and

plurilingualism contrast in this regard, but early translanguaging and plurilingualism are approximate synonyms. Both accept the social and psychological reality of linguistic diversity, and allow 'students' multilingual and multimodal practices to be seen from an *asset-based* rather than a deficit-oriented perspective' (Mendoza, this book, p. 13).

Rejecting deconstructivism allows Mendoza to draw on a broad range of sociolinguistic concepts to engage in an analysis of her data. In a lucid presentation of the history, linguistic diversity and sociopolitical context of Hawai'i, Mendoza describes dynamic waves of language contact affecting the Hawaiian language, plantation Creole, Hawai'i Creole English, the languages brought to the Hawaiian islands by Cantonese, Portuguese, Japanese, Korean, Filipino and Micronesian immigrants, and the association of dialects and language diversity with racism and linguicism toward and across communities of color. Mendoza's analysis captures heritage language, first language, second language and language contact phenomena vividly, drawing on constructs now anathema to deconstructivists.

Code-switching, too, is an important component of Mendoza's analytical toolkit. As she aptly notes, the repudiation of code-switching among deconstructivists is 'sometimes fueled by a lack of understanding of what code-switching is' (this book, p. 18). Mendoza relies on Peter Auer's (1998) interactional theory, a sociolinguistic model of code-switching concerned not with the underlying grammatical structure of language alternation, but with the conversational contribution of the switch itself, from one language to another. (Also see Auer, 2022 for a discussion specifically focused on code-switching as it relates to deconstructivism.) *Stylization* is another important construct for Mendoza; she defines it based on the work of sociolinguists like Nikolas Coupland, Christina Higgins and Priti Sandhu as a knowing and somewhat exaggerated use of linguistic resources which deviate from what would normally be expected in a specific social context.

An important theme of Mendoza's work throughout is the need to create environments which validate the home language resources of children to create more inclusive teaching and learning for all. 'Teachers and students must not only celebrate linguistic diversity, but also raise awareness about systemic inequalities that privilege some language and literacy practices over others which are *equally* skilled and adept ...' Mendoza reminds us (this book, p. 161). Language powerfully expresses identity, and serves as an instrument of racial (or *raciolinguistic*) oppression (Alim *et al.*, 2016). Language ideology may thus serve as a strategy to 'indoctrinate the people in a mythified version of reality', as Freire (1985: 86) put it. Critical language awareness involves students directly in the task of 'denouncing the mythos created by the right' (Freire, 1985: 86), a mythos that equates national unity with linguistic homogeneity. Mendoza not only rejects this mythos, but forcefully argues that practically implementing a translanguaging classroom – in which people are not only *told* they can translanguage but are *convinced* to translanguage – requires more than promoting linguistic diversity and hybridity. She uses interactional sociolinguistic analyses to demonstrate that teachers must create pragmatically appropriate bi/multilingual norms for the linguistic landscape of their classrooms, which reframe and position every student's language repertoire in an asset-oriented light.

On the other hand, another important theme of Mendoza's book is that it is not enough for the teacher to validate students' language repertoires. Students must do the same for one another, in a class that is not only linguistically diverse but where students from the same ethnolinguistic group may have dissimilar plurilingual repertoires. She critically discusses linguistic and cultural hegemonies at the neighborhood and school level, the interactional dominance of classroom language majorities, the researcher's impact when they promote their specific forms of bi/multilingualism with academic authority, and the power of individual students with formidable amounts of cultural capital in the dominant societal language, the classroom majority home language and peer group codes. Drawing on the pedagogical principles of *joinfostering* (Faltis, 2001), Mendoza highlights the need for teachers to socialize students into a culture of 'reciprocity and accountability' to positively shape one another's learning environment. 'When all the languages in one's repertoire are legitimized, and one's ways of speaking those languages are legitimized, and one's ways of translanguaging are legitimized, only then would one be comfortable drawing on one's whole language repertoire (i.e. translanguaging) in any situation, including a classroom situation' (this book, p. 177). It is Mendoza's rejection of deconstructivism that allows her to argue that social justice in classrooms and schools can only be achieved through a recognition of named languages in the emic perspectives of participants on the ground.

References

Alim, H.S., Rickford, J.R. and Ball, A.F. (eds) (2016) *Raciolinguistics: How Language Shapes Our Ideas About Race*. Oxford: Oxford University Press.

Auer, P. (ed.) (1998) *Code-switching in Conversation: Language, Interaction, and Identity*. London: Routledge.

Auer, P. (2022) 'Translanguaging' or 'doing languages'? Multilingual practices and the notion of 'codes'. In J. MacSwan (ed.) *Multilingual Perspectives on Translanguaging* (pp. 126–153). Bristol: Multilingual Matters.

Block, D. (2018) The political economy of language education research (or the lack thereof): Nancy Fraser and the case of translanguaging. *Critical Inquiry in Language Studies* 15 (4), 237–257. https://doi.org/10.1080/15427587.2018.1466300

Cummins, J. (2017) Teaching minoritized students: Are additive approaches legitimate? *Harvard Educational Review* 87 (3), 404–425. https://doi.org/10.17763/1943-5045-87.3.404

Cummins, J. (2021) Translanguaging: A critical analysis of theoretical claims. In P. Juvonen and M. Källkvist (eds) *Pedagogical Translanguaging: Theoretical, Methodological and Empirical Perspectives* (pp. 7–36). Bristol: Multilingual Matters.

Derrida, J. (1967) *De la grammatologie*. Paris: Minuit.

Edwards, J. (2012) *Multilingualism: Understanding Linguistic Diversity*. New York: Bloomsbury Publishing.

Faltis, C. (2001) *Joinfostering: Teaching and Learning in Multilingual Classrooms* (3rd edn). Upper Saddle River, NJ: Merrill Prentice Hall.

Freire, P. (1985) *The Politics of Education: Culture, Power and Liberation*. New York: Bergin and Garvey.

García, O. (2009) *Bilingual Education in the 21st Century: A Global Perspective*. Malden, MA: Basil/Blackwell.

García, O., Flores, N. and Spotti, M. (2017) Language and society: A critical poststructuralist perspective. In O. García, N. Flores and M. Spotti (eds) *The Oxford Handbook of Language and Society* (pp. 1–16). Oxford: Oxford University Press.

Grin, F. (2018) On some fashionable terms in multilingualism research: Critical assessment and implications for language policy. In P.A. Kraus and F. Grin (eds) *The Politics of Multilingualism: Europeanisation, Globalization and Linguistic Governance* (pp. 247–273). Amsterdam: John Benjamins.

Jaspers, J. (2018) The transformative limits of translanguaging. *Language and Communication* 58, 1–10. https://doi.org/10.1016/j.langcom.2017.12.001

King, K.A. and Bigelow, M. (2020) The hyper-local development of translanguaging pedagogies. In E. Moore, J. Bradley and J. Simpson (eds) *Translanguaging as Transformation: The Collaborative Construction of New Linguistic Realities* (pp. 199–215). Bristol: Multilingual Matters.

Kubota, R. (2014) The multi/plural turn, postcolonial theory, and neoliberal multiculturalism: Complicities and implications for Applied Linguistics. *Applied Linguistics* 37 (4), 474–494. https://doi.org/10.1093/applin/amu045

Lewis, G., Jones, B. and Baker, C. (2012) Translanguaging: Origins and development from school to street and beyond. *Educational Research and Evaluation: An International Journal on Theory and Practice* 18 (7), 641–654. https://doi.org/10.1080/13803611.2012.718488

Mackenzie, I. (2014) *English as a Lingua Franca: Theorizing and Teaching English*. Cambridge: Cambridge University Press.

MacSwan, J. (2017) A multilingual perspective on translanguaging. *American Educational Research Journal* 54 (1), 167–201. https://doi.org/10.3102/0002831216683935

MacSwan, J. (ed.) (2022) *Multilingual Perspectives on Translanguaging*. Bristol: Multilingual Matters.

MacSwan, J. and Faltis, C.J. (eds) (2020) *Codeswitching in the Classroom: Critical Perspectives on Teaching, Learning, Policy, and Ideology*. Language Education Tensions in Global and Local Contexts series. Washington: Center for Applied Linguistics; New York: Routledge.

Makoni, S. and Pennycook, A. (2007) Disinventing and reconstituting languages. In S. Makoni and A. Pennycook (eds) *Disinventing and Reconstituting Languages* (pp. 1–41). Clevedon: Multilingual Matters.

Otheguy, R., García, O. and Reid, W. (2015) Clarifying translanguaging and deconstructing named languages: A perspective from linguistics. *Applied Linguistics Review* 6 (3), 281–307. https://doi.org/10.1515/applirev-2015-0014

Pennycook, A. (2006) Postmodernism in language policy. In T. Ricento (ed.) *An Introduction to Language Policy: Theory and Method*. London: Blackwell.

Shi, L. and Rolstad, K. (2022) 'I don't let what I don't know stop what I can do' – How monolingual English teachers constructed a translanguaging English program in China. *TESOL Quarterly*. https://doi.org/10.1002/tesq.3204

Williams, C. (1994) Arfarniad o ddulliau dysgu ac addysgu yng nghyd-destun addysg uwchradd ddwyieithog [An evaluation of teaching and learning methods in the context of bilingual secondary education]. Unpublished PhD thesis. University of Wales, Bangor, UK.

1 Introduction

This study is about multilingual students in two high school English classes in the US, an Inner Circle English-speaking country (Kachru, 1986) where 'Standard US English' is institutionalized in schools. Even if this variety can never really be clearly defined, Lippi-Green (2012: 62) describes it as closest to the English 'of primarily white, middle- and upper-middle-class, and midwestern American communities' that tend to speak no other language than English to a great degree, which makes it unlikely for other languages to influence their variety of English.

In contrast, the students in this study live in Honolulu; many are from blue-collar families that have Cantonese, Cebuano, Chuukese, Ilokano, Ilonggo, Mandarin, Marshallese, Samoan, Tagalog or Vietnamese in their funds of knowledge. Whether or not English is their strongest language, they have spent parts of their lives in multiple countries, and their *individual language repertoires* (i.e. the sum of their language knowledge) consist of *asymmetrically distributed resources* from multiple languages (i.e. unequal across various domains such as everyday, academic and pop culture). The asymmetry of people's language repertoires and the influence of an individual's languages on one another are two phenomena that are often socially stigmatized, even though they are universal across anyone who is the slightest bit bi/multilingual. These phenomena are often noted in the two classes – not only by students from different ethnolinguistic backgrounds, but also by students from the same ethnolinguistic background with different life trajectories.

In the two English classes of 10–15 students, teachers encourage students to use their whole language repertoires in oral conversation and small-group discussions to help each other learn. This practice has been referred to as translanguaging, which García (2009) defined as the use of the entire language repertoire to learn, make meaning and navigate the social life of the class. Translanguaging is an exponentially growing field of inquiry in education (Poza, 2017) and the ways in which it supports linguistic equity has been well researched, particularly in bilingual and heritage language (HL) classrooms and increasingly in English as an additional language classrooms (e.g. García & Li, 2014; García &

Kleyn, 2016; Palmer *et al.*, 2014; Tian *et al.*, 2020). What is under-researched is the effect that the translanguaging of each individual has on others, how this impacts different individuals' opportunities to learn and how people understand each other in terms of both literal communication and identity negotiation when they translanguage.

Also important is the position of the students' languages in their geographic and sociohistorical context. For example, Hawai'i has a unique history, national identity, racial hierarchy, language demographics and immigration patterns unlike the continental US, where many translanguaging studies in education have taken place. In Hawai'i, Spanish speakers account for only 6%–7% of the population of students designated English language learners (ELLs) (Hawai'i P-20 Partnerships for Education, 2018). This is not the same as the continental US, where Spanish is a major diasporic language in California, Florida, the Midwest and the Northeastern corridor. Moreover, in Hawai'i, students speak what are often known as 'less commonly taught languages' (LCTLs) as first languages (L1s) or HLs.[1] For many of these languages (Ilokano, Chuukese, Marshallese, Tagalog, Samoan, Pohnpeian, Vietnamese, Tongan, Cantonese, Kosrean, Korean, Cebuano/Visayan), there is little to no formal schooling available until university, if even then. It does not take long for language loss to happen, in that some children and youths' proficiencies in LCTLs may be *receptive only*, in that they can understand but cannot speak the languages, because of the kind of exposure they had in their homes and communities: they hear other languages spoken around them but get into the habit of speaking back to others in English. In addition, the literacy skills of students who are heritage users of LCTLs are particularly likely to suffer attrition in reading, writing and academic literacies even more than those of heritage users of languages like Spanish, which means that it will be harder for LCTL users to draw on literacy practices in their home languages to help themselves learn, even in the early years.

Therefore, some of the common findings of translanguaging research, particularly with Latin@/Latinx students in the US, or transnational Chinese students in the UK (García & Li, 2014), can be questioned, such as the ease with which students readily translanguage between their languages in oral communication (Palmer *et al.*, 2014), or the extent to which students' literacy skills in their home language can scaffold their literacy skills in English (Cummins, 2005). Many students from LCTL backgrounds who mostly grew up in the US may be *both* less willing *and* less able to translanguage in classroom contexts, while those who have recently arrived from the same countries of origin tend to have stronger proficiency in the languages of their countries of origin and might very well have the need *and* ability to translanguage in ways their US-raised peers cannot, with implications for group dynamics and individual identity positioning. Thus, this study makes contributions to translanguaging research by examining how LCTLs are used alongside English as a lingua franca (ELF) in K–12 classes in English-dominant countries.

1.1 Aims of the Book

This book situates itself in the field of bi/multilingual education, analyzing multilingual practices (translanguaging, code-switching, stylization) and ELF use together, particularly with regard to interactional positioning. While it is possible to study one or another type of language use, all are important for knowing how students deal with classroom tasks and the social life of the class in linguistically diverse English-medium classrooms where people tend to share *some* linguistic resources with others but do not share other linguistic resources – and where translanguaging networks have central language brokers, such as bilingually fluent users of English and the class majority non-English language, and linguistic outliers, such as English-dominant students or those who speak a classroom minority language (Androutsopoulos, 2015; Malsbary, 2013). This has implications for balancing student needs in lesson planning and instruction, as well as for classroom management. From a less instrumental perspective, it also has implications for equitable, inclusive and reciprocal teaching and learning in the *plurilingual, English as a lingua franca* classroom.

To understand the impact of individuals' translanguaging on one another, or how some types of translanguaging by some students can encourage, support or inhibit other types of translanguaging by other students, or why translanguaging seems to occur more instinctively for some individuals than others, I draw on the method of linguistic ethnography (Copland & Creese, 2015; Rampton, 2006), a method for studying the social life of classrooms that has commonly been employed in translanguaging research in bilingual and HL education (e.g. Creese *et al.*, 2014, 2015; Hamman, 2018; Li, 2014). While translanguaging research often questions the existence of named languages and focuses on the use of the whole linguistic and multimodal repertoire to make meaning (García & Otheguy, 2020; Li, 2018; Otheguy *et al.*, 2015), I combine my analysis of this process with a study of the meanings of *named* or *distinct* languages from a socially constructed perspective (Bucholtz & Hall, 2005; Rymes, 2014). In other words, instead of starting with either the assumption that participants do (not) see distinct or separate languages when they use them, I try to find evidence of their orientation toward or away from distinct or separate codes in particular dialogues and interview data, and how they are defining those codes and drawing the borders between them – whether participants orient to an utterance as containing one language after another or as an undifferentiated whole, and how so. These evaluations may or may not exist at other moments.

In addition, when classroom participants orient to distinct codes, I analyze what this means for peer-to-peer scaffolding of language learning, for example as students use multilingual resources to problem-solve and mull over target forms (Swain & Watanabe, 2012). I also explore how bi/multilingual practices in English learning lead to the construction of classroom identities (Wortham, 2006), as some students take on identities as frequent translanguagers and academically competent students who help others bi/multilingually, other students present themselves as non-translanguagers in both self-description and actual language use and others translanguage only in certain situations. By triangulating questionnaire, interactional and interview data, I examine how language practices are related to group identities and how learner identities are constructed through translanguaging over time. These social processes can be related to which group has valued models of bi/multilingualism (members with high proficiency in *both* the L1/HL and academic English used in monolingual ways), or which group can define normative English because their accents are most common in the class and/or 'standard' in the home country. In other words, it is important to arrive at an emic[2] understanding of who is a valued model of bi/multilingualism and what counts as a legitimate instantiation of a code, and the social processes through which this understanding is mutually constructed, to see the extent to which translanguaging practices contest dominant language hierarchies in a class.

Like Creese *et al*. (2014, 2015), I also take into account teachers' language backgrounds and how this affects their identity positions in class, as well as my own identity as a classroom ethnographer, in promoting certain languages or language practices over others. I am quite certain, for example, that my identity as a Filipino speaker in a Filipino-majority high school led to the challenging of certain hegemonies (e.g. the linguistic hegemony of English, the primacy of Spanish in US translanguaging research) and the reinforcement of *other* hegemonies (e.g. Filipino dominance in the school, and in Pacific Islander studies in Hawai'i). This positionality is examined in more detail in Chapter 3, and I return to it in the concluding chapter when I discuss implications for studies in which the researcher shares language resources with some participants but not others.

In all, this book has two main aims. The first has already been mentioned: to do translanguaging research with an eye to distinct codes as well as the integrated use of linguistic and multimodal resources (Canagarajah, 2011; Creese & Blackledge, 2015; Li, 2018; Otheguy *et al*., 2015) and the educational benefits of allowing students to learn with their entire language repertoires (García & Kleyn, 2016; García & Li, 2014; Menken & García, 2010; Tian *et al*., 2020). From an emic perspective, that of our classroom participants, we need to examine how distinct codes are defined and used in interaction, learning and classroom language policy (Bonacina-Pugh, 2012; Saxena & Martin-Jones, 2013) and how this might differentially affect individuals (Allard *et al.*, 2019; Malsbary, 2013).

The book's second aim is more practical. All classrooms, even ostensibly 'monolingual' ones (e.g. a class of Spanish L1 speakers in a content and language integrated learning [CLIL] class in Spain; a class of white L1 English speakers in upstate New York), are linguistically diverse in ways seen and unseen, and the same student will have multiple identity positions available as they make identity bids at different inter-actional moments through their language use (Bucholtz & Hall, 2005).[3] Whatever they choose as an identity bid – for example, as a competent speaker of a named or peer-group language[4] – they have a right to have this bid recognized, and also a responsibility to ensure that the bid does not negatively impact the potential bids of others. For teachers to man-age these social relations and build *critical language awareness* (that is, awareness of everyone's right to their ways of speaking, and awareness of how language competence is not always an objective reality but based in subjective and collectively agreed upon perceptions) among students that is so key to linguistic inclusion and equity, teachers must assess how students use language in the absence of explicit bi/multilingual pedagogy, for example, in a class that is officially English medium with bi/multilingual class members. Linguistic ethnographies like this one can help shed light on these social processes: what happens and in what ways to shape it further.

1.2 Background of the Study

English language instruction and English-medium instruction for academic subjects is a worldwide phenomenon given the global domi-nance of English (Lin, 2016). In Inner Circle English-speaking countries, which Kachru (1986) defines as Australia, Canada, New Zealand, the UK and the US, an interesting dynamic occurs between translanguaging and English use. Despite the differences between these countries and the lin-guistic heterogeneity within them, they are seen as places where English is 'native' and set the norms for English in other parts of the world. Even if many other countries, for example, India and Malaysia, have many fluent speakers of English, in these countries, students primarily acquire English in formal educational settings by drawing on another dominant, hegemonic regional or national language, such as Hindi or Malay, as a lingua franca to teach and learn English. In contrast, students in plu-rilingual, English-medium classrooms in Inner Circle English-speaking countries more often orchestrate English learning and navigate the class' social life by speaking languages that some, but *not all* peers, understand or have a 'heritage' connection to (though heritage is, of course, a sub-jective perception as well as a social construct). *This means that, when a language other than English is used, some classroom participants may have no understanding of the language, no heritage claim to it and no intention or need to learn it; in other words, translanguaging has as much potential to exclude as well as include.* This would not be the case if all participants shared the same two or three languages to varying degrees, as in bilingual/HL classrooms, where maximizing translanguaging with shared resources facilitates inclusion.

In the two high school English classes in this study, all students must eventually pass a national exam to demonstrate sufficient command of English to 'exit' English as a second language (ESL). This exam is administered by the World-Class Instructional Design and Assessment (WIDA) Consortium across 40 US states and the District of Columbia. WIDA exams are used to identify ESL students and assess their levels of English proficiency from Kindergarten to Grade 12; in Hawai'i, there is a period in January and February in which students' current levels are assessed. Six levels of English proficiency are assessed through a grade-appropriate examination: 1 – Entering, 2 – Beginning, 3 – Developing, 4 – Expanding, 5 – Bridging and 6 – Reaching. Students' performance on WIDA is accordingly linked to their coursework. One class in this study is a 'sheltered' English 9 class, which means students who still have the ESL designation but a WIDA score of 2.5 or above take the national curriculum in that grade and subject with a teacher who is trained in teaching English language learners (ELLs) and can integrate language and content instruction (for more on 'sheltered' classes in the US, see Short *et al.*, 2011). Students get credit for sheltered courses on their transcripts; they count the same as 'regular' courses in those subject areas. In the other class in this study, in which ninth- and tenth-grade students had WIDA scores between 1.8 and 2.5, instruction was focused on the English language itself; hence, I call the class ESL 9/10. Students in this class will transition into grade-level sheltered subject classes, typically within a semester or a few semesters. If they are older, ESL courses may delay their high school graduation, or they can later take adult education classes or the General Education Diploma (GED) exam[5] to obtain a high school diploma. Course type is relevant because ESL classes enroll only newcomers from different countries, whereas 'sheltered' classes contain a mix of newcomers and students who have mostly grown up in the US and speak another language or languages apart from English at home.

Another important contextual factor apart from course type is the nature of the diaspora. Allard (2017) contrasts Latin@/Latinx diasporas in New York with those in the mid-Atlantic US in terms of how established they are, and her research shows that this has implications for translanguaging in classroom language policy, program design and pedagogy. In New York, where translanguaging has been widely researched by Ofelia García and colleagues through the City University of New York–New York State Initiative on Emergent Bilinguals (CUNY-NYSIEB) Project

(Hesson *et al.*, 2014; Sánchez & Menken, 2019), there is more entrenched school and state support for Spanish–English bilingualism and, as a result, bi/multilingualism more broadly. In places like the mid-Atlantic US, which have been historically English dominant rather than multilingual, and have recently experienced an influx of blue-collar Spanish-speaking immigrants, translanguaging policy and pedagogy do not carry the same positive social and political associations surrounding diversity. Allard (2017) argues that we need to look at translanguaging in its ecology – the linguistic landscape of the community and the relationships between speakers of different languages – operating on multiple timescales. In the mid-Atlantic town she studied, the Latin@/Latinx population rose from 3% to 28% between 1990 and 2010, and the school went from having no special classes for ESL students (i.e. sink or swim) to ESL and sheltered classes. Unfortunately, it was sometimes hard to make teachers, parents and students see the benefit of the ESL and sheltered classes because people observed that students' everyday spoken English developed much faster in the 'sink or swim' mainstreaming approach. That is, conversational proficiency can be attained through natural immersion, but this is not so with academic literacy, which requires deliberate pedagogical scaffolds (L1 use and accessing prior knowledge in L1 being very important).

In the 'sheltered' classes Allard studied that enrolled only ESL-designated students taught by qualified teachers, students developed spoken English slower, and had less room for electives, but received better instruction in academic subjects with bilingual support and teachers trained in language pedagogy. However, these benefits were not immediately apparent to some community members, who desired 'total English immersion', an ideology that was further supported by the monolingual English linguistic landscape and lack of bilingual school personnel. Allard (2017) argues that translanguaging pedagogy is empowering if broader structures give high status and visibility to bilingualism; without these, students and their families can internalize views hostile to translanguaging even if it is helpful to them.

In Hawai'i, the question of diaspora is complicated given the presence of multiple waves of immigration from many different countries. The 'old' diaspora consists of Pidgin (Hawai'i Creole) speakers from a range and mix of Hawaiian, Japanese, Chinese, and non-Hawaiian Asian and Pacific Islander ethnic backgrounds (this is one group united by their language, Pidgin, and familiarity with local culture), while the 'new' diaspora consists of immigrants from different countries who arrived following the 1965 Immigration Act, which prioritized family unification and led to the development of immigration chains (Fujikane & Okamura, 2008). Some students from the new diaspora may have spent all or most of their life in Hawai'i, being English dominant with some knowledge of Pidgin, which despite its negative stigma has local currency (Higgins, 2010), but others have recently arrived and have limited knowledge of both English and Pidgin. All students in English 9 and ESL 9/10 are, in fact, from the new diaspora, but I found a wide range of cultural affiliations depending not only on country but also on age at immigration and individual preferences.

Generally speaking, Hawai'i has a great deal of tolerance and even active support for ethnolinguistic and cultural diversity because of its multicultural history, but socioeconomic stratification between different groups such as Japanese, Filipinos and Micronesians still leads to a great deal of linguistic and cultural tension (Fujikane & Okamura, 2008; Ratliffe, 2011; Teodoro, 2019), which will be explored further in Chapter 3, on research context and methods.

A third contextual factor, apart from program design and diaspora conditions, is the presence of focal and non-focal immigrant groups. From longitudinal case studies of high schoolers in California over 14 months, Malsbary (2012) proposed the construct of 'focal immigrant group' for the majority immigrant group most often portrayed in discourses about immigrants in the region (in her case, Mexicans), and compared the experiences of students who were and were not in this group. One Mexican student found friends quickly, but also experienced prejudice from Latin@/Latinx students who had been in the US longer. Three students who had few people to talk to from their own group had somewhat less predictable experiences: to become isolated, to join a pan-ethnic group or to be 'adopted' by a different ethnic group (as in the case of a Pakistani and Saudi Arabian student who found a group of friends from Brazil). While Malsbary's (2013) classroom ethnography showed that the focal immigrant group experiences most of the benefits of oral translanguaging due to more speakers of their language, her case studies (Malsbary, 2012) show that students with more unusual linguistic and cultural profiles vis-à-vis the ecology of their school have the advantage of the widest range of options for group belonging and identity construction since their identities are not pre-emptively constructed by media discourses and social stereotypes; see similar findings from Enright (2011), who studied an outlier in the focal immigrant group.

In the sheltered English 9 class in this study, the class majority consisted of Filipino students whose L1 was Ilokano. The school was one of four schools in Hawai'i with the largest population of ESL-designated students (20%–22%), and about 60% of students with the ESL designation were Filipino, most of them Ilokano L1 speakers.[6] The class majority shared Ilokano, Filipino (Tagalog) and English trilingualism with Juan, the teacher, and his regular substitute, Ed, even though Juan was more proficient in academic English, which had a significant impact on students' translanguaging practices when Juan was teaching versus Ed. There were also three boys who spoke the Micronesian language Chuukese as their L1, three singletons[7] who spoke Cantonese, Marshallese and Samoan, three students of Ilokano heritage who were English dominant, and one student of Ilokano heritage who appeared Filipino dominant.

In ESL 9/10, the focal immigrant group consisted of Filipino students who often translanguaged across English and Filipino and were of Cebuano, Ilonggo, Ilokano and Tagalog heritage. There were also singletons who spoke Mandarin, Marshallese and Vietnamese as their L1s/HLs, and no English-dominant students since it was a class of newcomers. Although the teachers in ESL 9/10 were bi/multilingual, they were not bi/multilingual in the same languages as the students. Like Juan, Kaori (who spoke Japanese and was married to an Italian) had immigrated to the US as an adult. Rayna, the student teacher completing her teacher certification practicum in both classes and doing most of her teaching in Kaori's class, immigrated to the US from Korea as a teenager.

To summarize the background of the study, I draw on the framework of US bi/multilingual education scholar Guadalupe Valdés (2020: 117), who explains that classroom context can mean anything from *framing mechanisms*, such as ideologies of language, class and identity, to *mediating elements*, such as educational climate, policies and program design, to *teacher and learner characteristics*. All of these must be explored when interpreting whether any language practice is standard or deviant from the expected choice, and what linguistic hegemonies it contributes to or challenges.

1.3 Chapter Outline

In Chapter 2, on theoretical constructs, I provide an overview of the types of language practices I studied in the classes by defining plurilingualism; translanguaging, code-switching and stylization; English as a lingua franca (ELF); and positionality.

In Chapter 3, on research context and methods, I discuss the sociolinguistic context of Hawai'i in terms of immigration, language policy in public education, the school setting and methods of data collection and analysis using linguistic ethnography (Copland & Creese, 2015; Rampton *et al.*, 2015). I also discuss my researcher positionality in light of my own bi/multilingualism and identity bids, analyzed for the effects they had on participants and data collection and analysis.

Chapters 4 and 5 deal with the findings in each class as a community of practice with its 'small culture' (Holliday, 1999) evolving over the academic year. Chapter 4 examines the differences in the translanguaging of multilingual majorities, minorities, singletons, newcomers and old-timers in sheltered English 9. This chapter argues that *an essential aspect of getting any student to translanguage is an activity that is pragmatically appropriate given the language demographics of the class, and puts that student's repertoire in an asset-oriented rather than a deficit-oriented light.* I explain what such practices mean for students with different language backgrounds: majority, minority or singleton, newcomer or old-timer. Chapter 5 investigates the relationship between translanguaging and ELF awareness (Friedrich & Matsuda, 2010; Seltzer & García, 2020) in the ESL 9/10 class dominated by a majority of vocal Filipino boys. Using sociolinguistic tools and participant interviews to analyze interactions in this class, I suggest that the key to fostering linguistic equity for quieter Filipino boys, Filipino girls and language minority students was not so much to promote translanguaging over 'English only', as it was to *address the underlying insecurity of the interactionally dominant group of students across various aspects of their language repertoires.* Addressing such insecurity would address these students' need to make self-preserving interactional moves that negatively positioned their classmates and the teacher, and would have resulted in more learning rather than purely socially oriented translanguaging practices and dispositions.[8]

In Chapter 6, I analyze the language identities of two students over the course of the study. One was an English-dominant student and heritage speaker of Ilokano in English 9; the other was a speaker of a stigmatized dialect of Filipino who struggled with reading and writing in ESL 9/10. I use their cases to argue that translanguaging cannot be a critical educational practice challenging linguistic hierarchization and standardization, as it has been portrayed in the current research literature with few qualifications, unless *expanded notions of academic literacies and the legitimacy of multidialectal translanguaging in academic work, including in students' heritage languages,* are adequately addressed (Hornberger & Link, 2012; MacSwan, 2000; Valdés, 2001).

Chapter 7 is about the study's pedagogical implications. It outlines a distinct translanguaging pedagogy for the plurilingual, ELF classroom, which is needed for a situation in which class participants do not always share the same languages when they translanguage and are not part of a single bi/multilingual imagined community. When teachers' language repertoires may not resemble students', students are not all from the same ethnolinguistic group, those from the same ethnolinguistic group speak English and the languages of the home country to different degrees of proficiency and according to more or less 'standard' varieties, language minorities and singletons are present and everyone has their own identity bids at stake, this book explores what is needed to support each class participant to realize their responsibility to create not just a translanguaging space, which they would probably naturally do anyway, but one that is equitable (Allard *et al.*, 2019), critical (Hamman, 2018) and safe (Charalambous *et al.*, 2016).

Chapter 8, the conclusion, comments on the study's theoretical contributions, limitations and directions for future research.

Notes

(1) I define first languages (L1s) as languages spoken by students who have immigrated relatively recently, and heritage languages (HLs) as languages spoken by students at home even though they have largely grown up in the 'host' country. While I acknowledge that the line between these terms can be blurry, it is important to recognize from a pedagogical and interactional view that relatively new arrivals are L1 dominant, while HL speakers are dominant in the host country's language.

(2) The social construction of reality from participants' point of view.

(3) Bucholtz and Hall (2005) argue that language forms index, or point to, certain identities. However, these identities are not a 'given' but a negotiated and shared understanding between conversation participants. For example, is a Korean high school student using African American English indexing a hip-hop artist identity, a K-pop fan identity, a rebellious student identity or a (fake) Black identity? As can be seen in this example, without attention to context we do not know if this is cultural appropriation or legitimate self-expression, and whom, if anyone, the verbal act may harm. Sometimes participants cannot reach a shared understanding of the indexicality (what the form points to), and multiple conflicting identity positions ensue (Hall, 2014).

(4) A named language is a language recognized as such, like Sami or African American English. A peer-group language is a code that a group of peers speak, such as the Ilokano + English + Korean + Filipino social language of some students in the English 9 class in this study.

(5) The GED exam is a set of four tests in math, language arts, social studies and science, which when passed provides certification that the test taker has US or Canadian high school-level academic skills.

(6) There is no linguistic majority among students designated English language learners (ELLs) in Hawai'i, the largest group (Ilokano speakers) comprising only about 20% of the ELL population. The next seven largest groups, in order, are speakers of Chuukese, Marshallese, Tagalog, Spanish, Japanese, Samoan and Mandarin. Speakers of each of the last three languages comprise about 4% or 5% of the ELL population. In fact, the top five languages make up 56% of home languages and another 65 languages make up the other 44% (Hawai'i Department of Education, n.d.).

(7) The term 'singleton' is from Allard *et al.* (2019) and refers to a student who is the only speaker of their L1/HL in a class.

(8) The word 'disposition' has two meanings in the Oxford English dictionary: 'inherent mind or character' or 'the way in which something is placed or arranged, especially in relation to other things'. In this book, I use the word to describe how people in a classroom community are disposed to relate to one another, which not only becomes routine but also evolves unexpectedly over a school year (Wortham & Reyes, 2017).

2 Theoretical Constructs and Multilingual Practices in K–12 Education

In this chapter, I first address contemporary understandings of bi/multilingual language use by describing five key constructs and how they relate to communication in a class: *plurilingualism* and *translanguaging* with an integrated language repertoire, *code-switching* and *stylization* involving named languages and *English as a lingua franca* (ELF). This is because, no matter what the linguistic composition of the class in an English-dominant country, class members will use both an integrated language repertoire, as well as distinct named languages, and ELF. I conclude with the argument that no matter the focus of language analysis when researching bi/multilingualism in K–12 education, researchers must always take into account a sixth construct, *positionality*, to develop a critical and practical lens on how the teacher and all students in the class can create valuable learning experiences for one another regardless of what exists in their language repertoires.

2.1 Plurilingualism and Translanguaging

While multilingualism is a term used to describe societal contact as well as individuals' acquisition of particular languages, plurilingualism (Coste *et al.*, 2009; Piccardo, 2013) describes a person's agency to use resources from their whole language repertoire in concert to get things done. 'Getting something done', like opening a bank account, can involve the integration of languages, modalities (e.g. gestures and images) and even technological devices. The theory of plurilingualism also suggests that individual language repertoires evolve over time based on people's biographies, migration experiences and entrance/exit from different communities, and thus there is value in taking individuals rather than languages as the unit of analysis in explaining language learning and use. In other words, the question is not 'How good is Andrew's French for opening a bank account?' but 'What multilingual and multimodal resources can Andrew draw on to open a bank account in Quebec?'. This focus on the individual does not mean that social forces can be ignored in that individual's experiences (Marshall

& Moore, 2018), but what it does suggest is that a person's linguistic repertoire reflects perhaps not so much a lineup of socially constructed named languages arranged in parallel acquisition according to a linear yardstick, but a dynamic set of resources

> gathered, developed, shed, and replaced in a continuous process of repertoire change [with no end goal or state of perfection]. … To put it simply, mobile people take along just the amount of linguistic resources they require, and during their journeys, these resources are complemented by a continuous feed of new ones. (Blommaert & Horner, 2017: 9)

Similar to the term *plurilingualism*, the term *translanguaging* (García, 2009; García & Li, 2014; Otheguy *et al.*, 2015) does not conceptualize multilingual development as full and balanced competence in all of a person's languages. Since it is not a matter of speaking all of one's languages fluently and in a native-like way, but using the whole language repertoire, and sometimes a mix of languages and multimodal resources to get things done according to the situation, both plurilingualism and translanguaging allow students' multilingual and multimodal practices to be seen from an *asset-based* rather than a deficit-oriented perspective. One difference between plurilingualism and translanguaging, however, is in their origins. As a theory, plurilingualism originated in the European Union (EU) to describe the linguistic competencies of EU citizens for work or study purposes. This has implications for how immigrants versus the 'cultural mainstream' are evaluated on their linguistic competencies:

> Plurilingual Europeans continue to be conceived of as 'native' speakers of a national language…. The national and linguistic identity of Europeans is not moved, even if their language repertoire expands to consist of what are considered bits of other national languages, creating speakers with broader horizons, and encompassing a more European persona. … In contrast, plurilingualism for black and brown refugees acts differently. A plurilingual education, in the limited cases where it exists, gives these students access to what is considered their 'first language' in order to integrate them linguistically to a 'new' and more valuable European national language. (García & Otheguy, 2020: 23)

In contrast, translanguaging (as a way of describing language use rather than a specific pedagogy) originally referred to how Latin@/Latinx students in the US make meaning without regard for the boundaries between two named languages (García, 2009; García & Otheguy, 2020). As such, translanguaging theory has more 'grassroots' origins, though it has since undergone a conceptual shift and exponential scholastic uptake that have obfuscated its original social justice intent and led to theoretical hegemony (see Block, 2018; Jaspers, 2018; Lewis *et al.*, 2012; Poza, 2017).

Another difference between plurilingualism and translanguaging is that academic research on plurilingualism does not tend to question the idea of distinct languages. For example, plurilingual studies can analyze how named languages such as Mandarin, Arabic and Farsi are orchestrated in action in class (Marshall & Moore, 2018). In contrast, translanguaging theory goes so far as to question the psycholinguistic reality of different 'named' languages (Otheguy *et al.*, 2015), since languages are, at least to some extent, social inventions. On this point, translanguaging scholars draw from Makoni and Pennycook's (2007) book *Disinventing and Reconstituting Languages* to suggest that there is a connection between the dismantling of language distinctions and the disruption of a monolingual status quo predominant in formal education. For example, Li (2011: 1234) describes translanguaging spaces as involving 'creative and critical use of multilingual resources by individual speakers'.

Since this study takes into account named languages as social realities from the viewpoint of participants, I see plurilingualism as what exists in the individual repertoire – an integrated competence with resources from different named languages – yet interaction-wise, people can orient to language(s) as distinct or as an undifferentiated whole. As I illustrate in this chapter, there is much evidence that distinct languages *are* real for people even if they are social constructions, and must be examined to explain domains of language acquisition and processes of identity negotiation. However, the fact that people's individual repertoires are integrated and holistic, showing their 'multicompetence' (Cook, 1992), as observed in psycholinguistics (Grosjean, 1989) as well as sociolinguistics (Pennycook & Otsuji, 2014), is unquestionable (see essays in MacSwan, 2022). In classroom interactions, I see translanguaging as one potential use of language, '*without regard for watchful adherence to the socially and politically defined boundaries of named (and usually national and state) languages*' (Otheguy *et al.*, 2015: 283). There are other social practices, however, that involve distinct codes, for example, in task management (code-switching) and identity positioning (stylization). In the following sections, I discuss classroom research on these practices relative to classroom research on translanguaging, beginning with that term.

2.2 Translanguaging in the Classroom

Even though translanguaging has always been something human beings do, widely promoting it as *warranted* and *beneficial* in a classroom setting where monolingual language ideologies prevail is no mean feat. This is the legacy of Ofelia García, the Latina American scholar who is the main figure behind translanguaging theory. Guadalupe Valdés (2020: 137), another well-known US scholar of bi/multilingual education, explains that García *et al.*'s translanguaging construct goes beyond pedagogical strategies, taking into account language ideologies and 'making teachers aware of the importance of their own philosophical stance in a context in which children's ways of speaking are often devalued'.

The definition of translanguaging was originally much narrower: it was first used by a Welsh heritage language (HL) educator (Williams, 1994) to refer to a specific pedagogical technique in which a teacher switched input and output in two languages (in this case, English and Welsh) to build students' proficiency in their weaker language (in this case, Welsh). An academic colleague of that teacher, Colin Baker, drew attention to this teaching practice in a collection of studies of bilingualism in education called *Foundations of Bilingual Education and Bilingualism* (Baker & Wright, 2017), whose first edition was in the 1990s, Ofelia García being one of the contributors. Baker was aware of the benefits of translanguaging, originally called *trawsieithu*, which promoted deeper understanding of the lesson content, developed the weaker language, facilitated home–school links and integrated early learners with fluent speakers (Lewis *et al*., 2012). Today, such teacher-led translanguaging practices are known by the term 'pedagogical translanguaging' (Cenoz & Gorter, 2020), to contrast them from dynamic, spontaneous student interactions.

These interactions became the research focus of Ofelia García, who saw the potential in language teaching beyond the alternation of named languages. In her seminal book *Bilingual Education in the 21st Century* (García, 2009), which introduced dynamic bilingualism and dynamic translanguaging, she noted that the process of multilingual communication involved much more than input in one language and output in the other, as children switch rapidly back and forth between languages in the same utterance to achieve a single communicative end. A bi/multilingual mind, she stressed, is not a bicycle with two or more identical wheels but an all-terrain vehicle in which each part serves its own function and not all languages need to be fully acquired with the monolingual native speaker as the target. The wheels 'turn, extend and contract, [and] make up for each other' (García, 2009: 143). García continued to develop dynamic bilingualism with her London-based colleague Li Wei, in another seminal book, *Translanguaging: Language, Bilingualism and Education* (García & Li, 2014). This book dealt with educational contexts in which recognizing this kind of bi/multilingualism (i.e. dynamic) went hand in hand with social justice.

Sociolinguist Li Wei has done research on dynamic bi/multilingualism within and beyond the classroom among ethnically Chinese youth in HL 'complementary schools' in the UK. In an ethnography of Mandarin and Cantonese HL classes for 10-12 year olds, Li (2014) found that students were cosmopolitan in their linguistic and cultural funds of knowledge – even if the school curriculum, which privileged the more traditional aspects of Chinese culture and Mandarin over other Chinese languages, did not always recognize this, promoting speaking (standard)

Chinese only in class and discouraging dynamic translanguaging. Dynamic bilingualism reveals the weakness of institutionalized HL education: it essentializes and compartmentalizes languages and cannot account for the bi/multilingual communication of 21st-century youth. Such education may also inadvertently, and with the best of intentions, construct essentialist representations of particular language communities (Ganassin, 2020), or boundaries between Chinese transnationals and other residents of the English-speaking countries where they study, live and work.

The effects of a lack of dynamic bilingual education among Latin@/Latinx students in the US are even more grave, as this impacts their mainstream schooling and further educational opportunities. Another colleague of García's, Kate Menken, demonstrated the need for a dynamic orientation to bilingualism in New York public schools (Menken & García, 2010; Menken & Kleyn, 2010). Menken's research was on students who had been in US schools for 7+ years and had not tested out of the English language learner (ELL) designation, and were given the condescending label LTELLs ('long-term English language learners') (see Menken *et al.*, 2012). Many of the LTELLs Menken studied in New York were Spanish-speaking youth who had grown up in the US and whose schooling had not allowed for academic Spanish development, even though they spoke Spanish at home. Nor had this schooling ever helped them catch up to grade-level academic English, because they had always been in a 'sink-or-swim' English-only learning environment since they first started school. In a three-year study of three New York high schools (Menken & Kleyn, 2010), Menken, Kleyn and four research assistants interviewed 5 administrators, 4 teachers and 29 students in Grades 9–12 who had been in the US for an average of 10 years. They found that although schools provided instruction in both Spanish and English, the lack of *dynamic* bilingual programs was not responding to these students' needs. The students' English-only English as a second language (ESL) classes, which were designed for newcomers to the US, were too easy, and they felt disengaged. Spanish foreign language classes with a Spanish-only language policy, designed for their fellow Americans who did not speak Spanish at home, were too easy for the same reasons. However, grade-level academic subject instruction in either Spanish or English, also monolingual, was too hard, and the same trend was found for the 29 students as a group – though they lacked grade-level literacy skills in English, their literacy skills were worse in Spanish. Standardized tests, administered monolingually (in English or Spanish only), found that they read and wrote 3 years below grade level in English and 3.5 years below grade level in Spanish.

A clue as to what might best be done for these students lies in how to teach academic texts to monolingual English speakers who struggle with academic literacy, and who need to discuss academic texts in everyday

English with their teacher and peers to make the material accessible. What these bilingual students need is for the teacher to let them discuss texts' meaning in a mix of Spanish and English, and again work in a mix of Spanish and English to plan their academic writing about the same texts in academic English or Spanish. The teacher can optimally help students if the teacher can speak both languages; if not, allowing dynamic translanguaging in 'unpacking' difficult texts and 'repacking' the information in students' own words and then scaffolding to express the same ideas in academic language, is a powerful process in itself. In a class with a target-language-only policy, whether English or Spanish, there are only two options: for students to follow the policy with content that is too easy, or to struggle with grade-level content since they are not able to draw on their entire language repertoires to master it. Either way, they learn very little.[1]

To concretely outline dynamic translanguaging pedagogy and extend it beyond English–Spanish bilingualism, García *et al.* (2017) identified three features of a translanguaging approach to education: translanguaging *stance*, translanguaging *design* and translanguaging *shifts*. In layperson's terms, these correspond roughly to teacher attitudes toward multilingualism, lesson planning to involve multilingualism and spontaneous interactions while teaching that invite multilingualism. Seltzer and García (2020) illustrated what this looked like in the classroom of high school English teacher Ms Winter, who was not very proficient in any language other than 'standard' American English and taught a class of mainly Latinx and African American students. From the beginning of the semester, Ms Winter told and continued to remind students that they could communicate their understanding in whatever style of language or multimodal practices they saw fit during the process of learning: her translanguaging *stance*. When it came to languages, she used authors, artists and public figures, as well as examples of multilingual student work, to draw her class' attention to the fact that it is possible to have intellectual discussions in any register of English, or write exemplary works of literature through multilingual, multidialectal and multimodal translanguaging, and that subject experts, artists and successful students did so all the time.

For translanguaging *design*, Ms Winter included different varieties of English – Euro American, African American and postcolonial literature – in her syllabus, and taught a variety of forms of literature that were all of a high standard. She pointed out how the authors used their integrated language repertoires to make meaning, drawing on resources from different languages to achieve the rhetorical whole. Ms Winter also put students in groups and assigned each group an author whose work they would study over the course of five weeks for the author's influences, voice, linguistic choices, engagement with audience, censorship and critique. Students read and shared excerpts of their authors' works, biographical readings, articles, criticisms and interviews: 'the combination of the authors' writing and writing *about* their writing provided models of both translingual text production and critical metacommentary about language' (Seltzer & García, 2020: 34).

As for translanguaging *shifts*, these are spontaneous teacher actions that 'respond to students' language, questions, and critique, none of which can be predicted' (García *et al.*, 2017: 36; see also García & Kleifgen, 2020). In class, Ms Winter built on student observations, drawing connections between the literature and the high-quality works of students to continually convey the message that one did not have to speak monolingual, middle-class 'standard' American English to be taken as intelligent or knowledgeable. The work at the City University of New York–New York State Initiative on Emergent Bilinguals (CUNY-NYSIEB) has provided numerous resources for teachers like Ms Winter to continue to develop professionally and access materials and assessments that fully capture students' creativity and critical thinking using their whole language repertoires, even in officially English-medium K–12 classrooms.[2] The same can be said for the ROMtels Project, a partnership between a primary school district in Newcastle, UK, and several European universities that has published primers on translanguaging for teachers, teacher educators and schools in English, Finnish, French, Romanian and Spanish.[3]

In sum, translanguaging in classrooms can be defined as (1) a centering of the linguistic practices of multilingual and multidialectal speech communities; (2) an asset-based stance on multilingualism that focuses on what language users have rather than on what they lack; (3) a teaching approach that encourages meaning-making across the entire repertoire of linguistic and semiotic resources; and (4) critical practices that challenge linguistic hierarchization and standardization.

2.3 Code-Switching

The rise of the term 'translanguaging' in educational scholarship and the increasing validation of multilingual practices to learn in K–12 settings, particularly in the US following the work of Ofelia García, has led to a repudiation of an older-term, code-switching, in scholarly circles – sometimes fueled by a lack of understanding of what code-switching is. To be clear, code-switching is not *diglossia*, which Fishman (1967) defined as the separation of languages, dialects or registers for high/low, formal/informal or standard/non-standard purposes (e.g. the ideology in the US that it is best to speak 'standard' English in academic settings or while doing a white-collar job). Other misconceptions are that code-switching is an outdated theory of language, that code-switching researchers believe individuals have separate compartments for separate languages in the brain (in fact, they were among the first to study how this was not the case) and that code-switching imposes a top-down, researcher's perspective on language use by assigning language labels to utterances since people experience language use more fluidly (in fact, people experience language borders as fluid as well as distinct since people both code-switch and translanguage all the time).

What, then, is code-switching? Decades ago, François Grosjean (1989), a scholar of bilingualism at Université de Neuchâtel in Switzerland, published a paper in the academic journal *Brain and Language* with the catchy title 'Neurolinguists, Beware! The Bilingual is Not Two Monolinguals in One Person'. Similar to Ofelia García, he argued:

> The bilingual is NOT the sum of two complete or incomplete monolinguals; rather, he or she has a unique and specific linguistic configuration. The coexistence and constant interaction of the two languages in the bilingual has produced a different but complete linguistic entity. An analogy comes from the domain of track and field. The high hurdler blends two types of competencies, that of high jumping and that of sprinting. When compared individually with the sprinter or the high jumper, the hurdler meets neither level of competence, and yet when taken as a whole the hurdler is an athlete in his or her own right. … A high hurdler is an integrated whole, a unique and specific athlete; he or she can attain the highest levels of world competition in the same way that the sprinter and the high jumper can.
>
> In many ways, the bilingual is like the high hurdler: an integrated whole, a unique and specific speaker-hearer, and not the sum of two monolinguals. He or she has developed competencies (in the two languages and possibly in a third system that is a combination of the first two) to the extent required by his or her needs and those of the environment. The bilingual uses the two languages—separately or together—for different purposes, in different domains of life, with different people. Because the needs and uses of the two languages are usually quite different, the bilingual is rarely equally or completely fluent in the two languages. Levels of fluency in a language will depend on the need for that language and will be domain specific… (Grosjean, 1989: 6)

Grosjean's work is reviewed by MacSwan (2017) in a 'A Multilingual Perspective on Translanguaging', published in *American Educational Research Journal*. In that article, MacSwan discussed the misconception that Grosjean and his colleagues (who tended to use the term 'code-switching' in those days) assumed that people had different processing compartments for different languages. As the above excerpt from Grosjean shows, the early psycholinguists did no such thing – quite the opposite. However, the limitation of their studies is that they were mostly interested in studying children picking up two first languages (L1s) simultaneously at home, often up until the point when the languages start to become unbalanced in terms of subject-specific and professional communication, leading to age-level proficiency in only one L1 by adulthood.[4]

Such studies of bilingualism conceptualized bilinguals as those who had early childhood immersion in two languages, and who could form a mixed language utterance without breaking the grammatical rules of either language, with intuitive rather than explicit grammar knowledge. Early code-switching researchers gave little account of late bi/multilingualism, involving L2, L3, etc., speakers who do not translanguage/code-switch in grammatically perfect ways, and those who only have emergent proficiency in their additional languages. In other words, early psycholinguistic work on bilingualism had strong nativist orientations. It argued that the individual language repertoire was an integrated whole, but at the same time such research focused on grammatical flawlessness of a sort, asking how children managed to reconcile the two codes (their two L1s, or maybe an L1 and a HL) grammatically in an integrated utterance. However, this is not to say that this work did not also have a social justice aim. It proved that bilingual children who mixed two languages, such as ethnic minority children, were not deficient in either language; in fact, there was something phenomenal in their systematic two-grammar juggling act (MacSwan, 2017).

There is another type of code-switching – *interactional*, not psycholinguistic – which is the definition of code-switching used in this study. In the 1990s, sociolinguist Peter Auer argued that code-switching was too muddy a term, as it was being used to describe two phenomena that required different names: (1) the bilingual child's ability to mix languages without breaking the grammatical rules of either, which Auer called speaking a mixed code (because it is *one* code that anyone who grows up immersed in, say, English and Spanish will generally follow), and (2) code-switching as Auer thought it should be defined. Auer noted that when people switch gears in interaction by changing the language/dialect – or in the case of monolinguals, through changing the speech register or using a paralinguistic cue like clearing the throat or making a gesture – this indicates that they are shifting topic, task, phase of the conversation or addressee. A linguistic or multimodal cue shows others in the conversation that 'shifting gears' is taking place (Auer, 1998).

The codes in this kind of code-switching exist from an emic perspective: it is not what counts as a distinct language in grammar books, but what is *perceived by participants* as a language distinction. That is, if a switch between two languages is perceived as meaning something in conversation, it is code-switching; if not, people may simply be speaking a mixed code. Likewise, a monolingual may or may not think someone clearing their throat in the middle of a monolingual conversation implies a conversational gear shift. Thus, a switch in language or dialect, or a gesture, may be a code-switch; seconds after that, the same switch in language or dialect, or the same gesture, has no interactional meaning and individuals are simply using their entire language repertoires to communicate (translanguaging).

To illustrate classroom code-switching, here is an example that involves a switch between languages:

> Teacher: (in English) Close all your textbook and class workbook. (in Cantonese) There are some classmates not back yet. Be quick! (in English) Now, any problem about the class work? (R. Johnson, as cited in Lin, 2013: 200; original Cantonese not provided)

The aside about hurrying up, Lin (2013) observes, could have been achieved without a linguistic code-switch into Cantonese, such as a change in volume or tone of voice. Why then use Cantonese? Lin argues that only a switch into students' L1 would have relayed the message's urgency and the teacher's annoyance, tempered by the informal tone carried by the code in this context. That is, only Cantonese would have achieved all the social meanings (understood in context) that the teacher wanted to achieve.

Classroom code-switching research has shown how bi/multilingual teachers manage the class and scaffold the learning of bi/multilingual students, for example, reading a passage of academic English text and then code-switching into a non-academic register of English or another language to deconstruct and explain it (Jacobson & Faltis, 1990; Lin, 2013; Martin-Jones, 1995). When students code-switch themselves, for example in small-group work (Bonacina-Pugh, 2012; Filipi & Markee, 2018), reasons may include shifting in and out of different tasks, directing attention to a specific addressee, signaling alignment or non-alignment with others or negotiating the medium of communication. When teachers code-switch for pedagogical purposes, they typically use another code that classroom participants orient to as such, to give important background or contextualizing information about the text, or to explain key language features in the text, thus developing students' metalinguistic awareness (Jacobson & Faltis, 1990); if a distinct code were not perceived, this instruction would be less clear. Students may also code-switch by reading out their group essay text or presentation text in 'academic' English, and negotiating how to improve it in their L1 or a mix of languages, which Swain and Watanabe (2012) call 'languaging' without the 'trans'. This does not mean that people devalue non-English codes, or that people even expect each code to be spoken in a particular way. *A close analysis of interaction and data triangulation* is needed to know whether participants perceive distinct codes, and if so, what they are trying to achieve when they use them – and further, what identities emerge for people as they mobilize their linguistic and multimodal resources, whether these identities are equitable, whether the codes are equal in the interaction and how all this affects opportunities to learn (Hamman, 2018; Rajendram, 2021).

In other words, when distinct codes are drawn on to get things done (Auer, 1998), it does not always mean that they carry the higher/lower value that they do in the wider society in that particular situation. This has implications for how the classroom culture can be designed by the teacher to counter the more common-sense indexicalities or social meanings of mixed language use (see Bucholtz & Hall, 2005; Hall, 2014). In other words, teachers can help students to see translanguaging and code-switching as a normative way of being, especially among bi/multilinguals, and including among the most verbally adept and English-proficient students. This view goes against the prevailing view of such bi/multilingual practices as only ever arising due to lack of English knowledge, when in fact this is not the case. Bi/multilingual students who can function monolingually in English still continue to use other languages for a myriad of purposes, ranging from a managerial gear shift when organizing group roles, to a juxtaposition of 'read-aloud text' and 'explanation' when tutoring a peer, to a choice laden with sociopolitical meaning.

Of course, sometimes code-switching *does* indicate some form of diglossia among teachers and students; for example, in Asker and Martin-Jones' (2013) study of a secondary school English as a foreign language (EFL) class in Libya, teachers code-switched between Arabic and English (reading aloud and giving directions in English and elaborating in Arabic), though they avoided Berber, the local language, while teaching. In contrast, students used Berber in 'off-stage' interactions (e.g. small-group tasks) and rarely in whole-class interactions, in which Arabic and English were the languages of display. Thus, societal diglossia can affect micro-level code-switching. However, just because this is one function of code-switching does not mean it is all there is to code-switching. Moreover, there are still multiple orders of linguistic authority rather than a single center of linguistic authority in a classroom: students' use of a minoritized language with peers occurred because using only Arabic and English for social interaction might be construed as snobbish; thus, a student less proficient in Berber could be marginalized, even if they were more proficient in academic registers of Arabic and English. That is why local hegemonies and different types of linguistic capital (Blommaert, 2007) must be considered in the linguistic analysis of classroom interaction through methods like linguistic ethnography.

When use of a code has inherent recognizable meaning, it can be used to make identity bids even when the speaker is not all that proficient in it. This brings us to stylization.

2.4 Stylization

Stylization is defined as a somewhat exaggerated, knowing deployment of linguistic resources that are recognizable as being Language X or the speech of Group Y, but which deviate from the language resources typically expected in that social context (Coupland, 2003). In a study on self-stylization, Canagarajah (2012) investigated how youth in the Sri Lankan Tamil diaspora in Canada, the UK and the US constructed their ethnic identities even when their proficiency in their HL was limited, drawing on the use of certain Tamil words. As Vishi, a teenage girl from California, explained:

> When most of my Tamil friends, I'll call them paNTi [pig], but that's actually their name, a term of endearment almost, you know. Like 'paNTi come here and show me this please,' like that. With them it is always Tamil things here and there, especially for inside jokes and stuff. … It's funny because even with my White friends, if I get mad at them or something, I'll say, 'You paNTi, are you that bad?' And they go, 'What?' (Canagarajah, 2012: 128)

Even if Vishi and other ethnically Tamil youth could not converse in their HL, uttering certain Tamil words in the presence of non-Tamil acquaintances built in-group solidarity, which Vishi referred to as 'inside jokes' that served to distinguish these youth as Tamil users. In addition to language knowledge, these youth displayed cultural knowledge, as shown by one boy, Raju, saying to his grandmother, 'Hi, caniyan. Where's my cooRu [rice]?' (Canagarajah, 2012: 124). His nickname for his grandmother comes from the name for Saturn (Cani), which means misfortune in Hindu astrology – an insult typically used for those who are unlucky or evil. However, the grandmother did not treat the nickname as an insult, accepting her grandson's attempts at bonding. Canagarajah (2012: 125) suggested: 'Perhaps she is mildly amused, and even appreciative, that her grandson is using Tamil words to establish rapport with her'. Stylization revealed the youths' deep emotional investment in a Tamil identity, as they needed to establish their place in their families and communities, with solidarity, esteem, power and status at stake. Behind all the playfulness, there were serious functions of legitimation and distinction (from non-members of their group) in their use of Tamil.

In contrast to self-stylization, there is other-stylization. In an ethnographic study of a white middle school teacher in Hawai'i from the continental US, Lamb (2015) showed that the teacher, Mr Cal, used Hawai'i Creole (Pidgin) to build rapport with students when it was interactionally appropriate to do so. During such moments of play, Mr Cal's students welcomed his inauthentic use of Pidgin, recognizing it as an attempt at Pidgin even though it was not accurate. Mr Cal did not (and probably could not) converse in Pidgin, nor did he claim to speak this language. However, he could, on certain occasions, legitimately use it without being seen as a cultural appropriator, to create a positive dynamic within the class.

On the other hand, there are also acts of negative other-stylization, which often occur in people's absence rather than their presence.

From this position of relatively unchallenged discursive power, Sandhu (2015: 215) notes that 'the stylizer has the freedom to high-light certain aspects of the other's language, ignore others and also to add elements which might not be present in the "real" speech being emulated'. In a study that spanned several trips to India over seven years (2005–2012), she conducted interviews with 34 women from diverse socioeconomic backgrounds to examine how they constructed the impact of English- or Hindi-medium education on their lives. Often, she noticed that women who were educated in English nega-tively stylized the English accents of Hindi-medium educated people. Thus, while self-stylization is a way to claim group membership with limited resources in the group's language, other-stylization is a dis-cursive strategy in which linguistic commentary is used to construct group boundaries. Nevertheless, Chun (2009: 35–36) argues that the line between the two terms can be blurry, as people also, sometimes subconsciously, modify their speech to more closely match the speech of linguistically different others in conversation, and since this action suggests accommodation or rapport building, it results in 'ambigu-ity between linguistic acts that ostensibly create social sameness and those that inherently suggest social difference'.

Another, more durable kind of stylization that blends elements of self- and other-stylization is *language crossing*, which involves use of non-HLs that one affiliates with (Leung *et al.*, 1997) for one's own iden-tity claims. This construct is commonly associated with Ben Rampton (1995, 2011a, 2011b), who conducted groundbreaking studies on mul-tilingualism in British schools in the 1980s and 1990s to show that stu-dents were using many more languages than those from their own ethnic backgrounds with major social import – even if their proficiency did not extend beyond a few words or phrases. Being of different and sometimes mixed ethnicities, the blue-collar teenage boys who participated in his research all used Cockney English and posh English, Jamaican Creole and South Asian English, to stylize their speech. Cockney and Jamaican Creole were drawn on to play tough, posh to express sexual interest and South Asian English to feign social incompetence and crass bourgeois values. These are only examples; each of these codes had a wide range of possible meanings that were context specific (but generally, South Asian English was the least positively associated code, and this could have been the result of old-timers positioning newcomers negatively).

If there was one code that deeply signified who the boys were, Rampton argued that it was a multilingual adolescent mixed code which included features of all the languages and dialects above that united them as one pan-ethnic social class. Poignantly, they carried this code into adulthood, when it conveyed nostalgia (Rampton, 2011a). Its social meaning, or indexicality, changed over time as the teenage boys grew into adult community members; what was once a code for affronting teachers was later used to touch base with an old friend or warmly welcome someone in a pub.

According to Rampton (2011a: 291), in ethnically mixed urban neighborhoods, linguistic forms emerge and are assigned context-specific meanings that are *both* connected to *and* distinct from their places of origin, 'represented in media and popular culture as well as in the informal speech of people outside'. Furthermore, language crossing not only happens between immigrant languages but also with different, recognizable varieties of English whose varying social meanings people understand and also negotiate. In the next section, I discuss the use of ELF in K–12 classrooms in Inner Circle English-speaking countries.

2.5 English as a Lingua Franca

English as a lingua franca goes with other terms used to identify English as a global language, such as World Englishes (WEs), which are nativized, systematic and codifiable varieties of English spoken in countries where English is one of the languages used in government and official domains, e.g. what Kachru (1986) identified as Outer Circle English-speaking countries like Hong Kong, India, Kenya, the Philippines, Singapore and Tanzania.[5] In contrast to WEs, ELF refers to the dynamic, non-codifiable, norm-fluid English spoken by people with *different* L1 backgrounds, in both intra- and international communication, e.g. communication between Indo-, Chinese- and French-Canadians or communication between Swedes, Chileans and Japanese (Friedrich & Matsuda, 2010). Additionally, ELF competencies encompass the communication and accommodation skills involved in such exchanges (Jenkins *et al.*, 2011).

What WEs and ELF have in common is that they decenter 'native' and 'standard' English users, mainly British and Americans of European ancestry, as models for all the world's other English users. This is not to say that students should cease to be exposed to 'standard' British or American English in learning materials, but that they should just as importantly be exposed to the varied ways people use different forms of English in daily life, including in high-stakes and professional contexts (e.g. academic, business and government transactions). In ELF pedagogy, what are traditionally seen as errors in pronunciation and grammar due to influence from other languages may not be assessed as such if utterances are comprehensible and, in fact, the form used suits the situation (Chan, 2014).

Thus, Friedrich and Matsuda (2010) explain that ELF is not a variety of English but a *function* that English performs in multilingual contexts. While lingua francas are not a modern phenomenon, 'there has never before been a single language which spread for such purposes over *most* of the world, as English has done' (Ferguson, as cited in Friedrich &

Matsuda, 2010: 21). When people with different language repertoires use ELF, each person uses the English variety/ies and resources they know and combines these with multimodal communicative strategies. Although the nature of the English that emerges in conversation varies from context to context depending on the individuals involved and the dynamic unfolding of their interaction – hence ELF is local rather than universal in nature – what is common to all contexts of ELF is negotiation of meaning and de-emphasis of surface forms that largely do not affect meaning.

Friedrich and Matsuda further argue that ELF is a sociolinguistic construct, not a term that can be used to describe language acquisition, as language acquisition implies learning target forms (e.g. a variety of English). Although teachers may aim to teach ESL according to the norms of the English-dominant country in which they are located, they must remember that English use in that country is by no means uniform (indeed, there is plenty of variation among 'white native speakers'); hence, the term EIntraL (English as an *intranational* language) may be preferable to ESL, as EIntraL recognizes that English is owned by all who speak it in the country (Friedrich & Matsuda, 2010: 25). ELF is therefore an umbrella term that includes EIntraL, English in international communication and World Englishes.

Ways to teach ELF have been investigated by Vettorel (2016) in the context of Italy. Vettorel describes the following ways to teach it at the middle-school level, designed by teachers in a pre-service and in-service professional development program at the University of Verona: (1) curricula that foster awareness of the spread of English around the world, its diversification and contact with other languages; (2) critical discourse analysis of texts that present English as monolithic (e.g. in an ELT curriculum that mentions Australia as an English-speaking country, there are no examples of Australian English); (3) research into World Englishes examining pronunciation, spelling, grammar, vocabulary and idioms, showing the legitimacy and grammatical systematicity of different varieties; (4) guest speakers (e.g. community leaders) who speak different varieties of English; (5) videos of famous people (e.g. actors, athletes, politicians) from foreign countries addressing international audiences in different varieties of English; (6) films and documentaries in different varieties of English; and (7) linguistic landscape activities in which students have to interview multilingual people in their neighborhood using ELF. The project at the University of Verona aimed:

> to involve students in realizing how, in real communication contexts, even not far from the place where they live, English works as a lingua franca, with people coming from different parts of the world and using the language with different accents and lexicogrammatical features. (Vettorel, 2016: 121)

Vettorel observed that when teachers and students are aware of ELF in their own natural contexts of communication, it increases their linguistic and cultural tolerance. Without consciousness-raising professional development, she thinks it unlikely that teachers will notice 'it is people, not language codes, that understand one another' (Bamgbose, as cited in Vettorel, 2016: 127).

Given the shared critical language awareness orientations that characterize scholarship on translanguaging and scholarship on ELF, there is surprisingly little educational research combining these two agendas, while some might even hold the belief that translanguaging compromises ELF and vice versa. Translanguaging studies investigate how students dynamically use their whole language repertoires to learn even if a class has officially one language of instruction or teaches one language at a time (García & Li, 2014), while ELF research focuses on students' use of ELF according to 'post-norm' approaches and flexible communicative practices (Dewey, 2012). While some may attach greater importance to ELF in an English class, or assume that a focus on ELF threatens the diversity of languages, there is no competition between ELF and translanguaging, as both constructs are based in a pedagogy that recognizes the dynamic and complex use of language in real life (García, 2009; Matsuda, 2018).

In the past decade, researchers of both translanguaging and ELF have published plenty about their constructs' practical implementation in classrooms, and what both these bodies of research have in common is an emphasis on teaching language awareness (Borg, 1994) – open-minded language attitudes, flexible communicative practices and investigation of how people actually use language(s). Responding to those who may call the ELF orientation 'ideological' or see it as token political correctness, Matsuda (2018) argues that it has less to do with politics and more to do with a practical approach to teaching that considers how authentic English interactions play out. This is where the third-generation scholarship on ELF (Sifakis, 2019) meets contemporary scholarship on translanguaging (even though both constructs have undergone significant evolution; for translanguaging's, see Lewis *et al.*, 2012). Making virtually the same argument as ELF scholars, translanguaging researchers Canagarajah and Wurr (2011) explain:

> What enables people to communicate is not a shared grammar, but communicative practices and strategies that are used to negotiate their language differences. Furthermore, these strategies are not a form of knowledge or cognitive competence, but a form of resourcefulness that speakers employ in the unpredictable communicative situations they encounter. ... The norms that are thus operational in a multilingual interaction are hybrid, and accommodate the languages the different persons bring to the interaction. (Canagarajah & Wurr, 2011: 2–3)

At times, there is a mismatch between the 'monolingual utopias' students are exposed to in classroom materials and their actual intercultural encounters (Mori & Sanuth, 2018). This is similar to the mismatch between 'standard' English instruction and context-specific WEs and ELF interactions (Chan, 2014; Matsuda, 2018). Due to common critical and pragmatic orientations, translanguaging and ELF are undoubtedly linked. A translingual or lingua franca stance legitimates the linguistic repertoires of all language users and their actual communicative practices, rather than textbook models that are not only 'native' speakers but also *monolingual* 'native' speakers (Ortega, 2014) whose utterances show no influence from any other languages.

Over the past decade, the language pedagogy recommendations from translanguaging and ELF scholarship have been resoundingly similar:

- Students must be exposed to a variety of linguistically adept models to show them what they can skillfully accomplish with language (Seltzer & García, 2020).
- Students must examine how languages are actually used in daily life, in a multitude of translingual, WEs and ELF encounters (Sayer, 2010; Vettorel, 2016).
- Students must explore their individual repertoires, so that each student develops their voice and exercises creativity in their ways of using language(s) (Kohn, 2018; Seltzer, 2020).
- Students must critically analyze 'standard' forms of language so as to be able to use them in contexts that require them, but not in the belief that they are inherently superior for these purposes (García *et al.*, 2017; Janks, 2004).
- Teachers need considerable agency and autonomy to implement critical pedagogy in the specific contexts in which they work (Dewey, 2012).

All this literature suggests that there has been considerable research on teachers' uptake of translanguaging and ELF in the classroom, even if it is all relatively recent. What remains under-researched is the way *students* understand and enact translanguaging and ELF. To understand these from the perspectives of different students in a class, as this study aimed to do, it is necessary to consider positionality.

2.6 Positionality

Ample research suggests that different individuals can have vastly different experiences in the same classroom setting depending on their positionality, or identities that are evoked through use of certain linguistic resources (Rymes, 2014) or (non-)display of funds of cultural knowledge in class (González *et al.*, 2006). Positionality is affected by contextual factors, including the class linguistic or cultural majority, the status of people's languages in the wider society (which in some places can amount to open hostility toward particular languages seen as those of the 'enemy'; see Charalambous *et al.*, 2016), the ways in which the teacher's teaching style and cultural references can privilege some forms of knowledge and norms of interaction over others (Duff, 2002) and the ways in which multilingual students who have more socially valued cultural and linguistic capital – such as a strong command of academic English *plus* 'standard' academic proficiency in their L1 – can marginalize other forms of multilingualism. I now explore each of these factors that affect the positionality of groups or individuals.

Allard *et al.* (2019) studied the impact of the classroom language majority on teachers' use of bi/multilingual strategies in a multi-grade ESL classroom in Philadelphia. Since most, but not all, students shared Spanish as an L1, some of those who were non-Spanish speakers or singletons (the only speakers of their L1 in the class) felt that the teacher spoke too much Spanish, and viewed this as inequitable. However, Spanish-speaking students, many of whom were refugees with post-traumatic stress disorder, benefited academically and socioemotionally from the Spanish–English bilingual teacher's pedagogy, and composed bi/multilingual identity texts (essays, poetry and drawings) about difficult life experiences. In a study of a high school ESL class in California in which Spanish was also the most commonly spoken home language, Malsbary (2013: 12) identified two students who were the most proficient in both Spanish and English, Maritza and Alejandro, as 'the classroom's synaptic connections' since they did most of the language brokering and understood nearly all of what was said in class, in contrast to Spanish-dominant classmates, the teacher who only knew English or classmates who spoke other languages at home. Likewise, the high school student Vee in Androutsopoulos' (2015) study was the most bilingually fluent of seven friends in a small Greek-medium secondary school in Germany, and her social media account was the most active in the group's; multilingual posts were almost always linked to her, while more peripheral group members remained monolingual in their communication in the network. Thus, two factors in determining individual and group positionality in an English as a lingua franca classroom are the majority non-English language and an individual's proficiency in this language *and* English.

Another important factor is the status of students' languages in the wider society. In a linguistic ethnography of 'majoritized' and 'minoritized' translanguaging at a Norwegian high school, Beiler (2021) compared a regular Grade 11 English class, an accelerated class for Grade 10 students undertaking the Grade 11 English curriculum and a sheltered class for Grade 11 English repeaters, many of whom spoke other languages at home apart from English or Norwegian. She analyzed translanguaging between English, Norwegian and other languages with regard to markedness, which she defined as the extent to which translanguaging was taken as unremarkable or noticeable, and if noticeable, how it was evaluated. Beiler (2021) found that English–Norwegian translanguaging was well noted and evaluated negatively in the accelerated and mainstream classes, but it was unmarked and permitted in the sheltered class, where the teacher wanted immigrant students to learn Norwegian and there were somewhat lowered expectations for English use; the teacher even encouraged such translanguaging on one occasion, whereas he explicitly discouraged students from speaking Norwegian in the advanced class. In addition, across all three classes, translanguaging using non-Norwegian languages was far rarer than translanguaging between English and Norwegian, suggesting that the former was even more marked and seen as less socially acceptable, and when it happened, it was evaluated negatively as a sign that certain groups of students were gossiping behind others' backs.

Another example of the negative indexicalities of translanguaging was examined in Charalambous *et al.*'s (2016) ethnography of a school in Cyprus, a country with a bloody history of ethnolinguistic conflict between the Greek side and the Turkish side. In the Greek Cypriot school they studied, children as young as seven or eight years old knew the consequences of speaking their home language, Turkish. Even though Turkish-speaking students came from a variety of national backgrounds, and all students in the school were highly multilingual 'with diverse and complex migration trajectories' (Charalambous *et al.*, 2016: 336), the labelling of Turkish as the language of the enemy led students who spoke it for any reason to fear showcasing this language knowledge, even if the situation was relatively safe – for example, when their teacher, Thalia, asked them what they would say to comfort a storybook character, a girl named Meltem, in Turkish. In another study, this one focusing on elementary teachers' attitudes toward translanguaging, Al-Bataineh and Gallagher (2021) found that Emirati teachers were appalled by the suggestion that they should encourage children to translanguage between Arabic and English, which in their society pointed to cosmopolitan arrogance if youngsters tried out such translanguaging with family members and older relatives. All of these studies point to the necessity of considering the wider social meanings of the different languages used in translanguaging.

A third factor that affects individual/group positionalities, apart from classroom majorities and wider societal ideologies, relates to the ways in which the teacher's teaching style and cultural references can privilege some forms of knowledge and norms of interaction over others. In an ethnography of two high school social studies classes in Vancouver, Canada, Duff (2002) found that Canadian-born students spoke more extensively about various topics, including Chinese culture, than their recently arrived Chinese classmates. She found that the teachers favored a teaching style largely based on class discussions, and used everyday talk and pop cultural references to explain abstract academic concepts – which made the lessons very engaging and accessible for Canadian-born students, and extra difficult for newcomers who had to deal not only with the difficult language in course texts but also the fast-paced oral conversations in English, which sometimes included cultural references they did not know. Although these practices were meant to be pedagogically supportive to students who struggled with text-based academic literacy, they revealed that the Anglo-Canadian teachers were used to only one way of making social studies content 'accessible', which did not help learners whose L1 was not English. (The teachers were encountering such learners for the first time in their careers, around the year 2000, due to the 1997 exodus of immigrants from the former British Hong Kong.)

A fourth factor to consider encompasses the socioeconomic backgrounds of individual students and their individual cultural biographies, which also affect their positionality in the translanguaging classroom. In a fifth-grade elementary class in Malaysia, Rajendram (2021) found that students from white-collar families typically used more English due to neoliberal language ideologies and pressure from parents who believed that proficiency in English offered the best pathways to higher education and reputable careers. On the other hand, students from blue-collar families used more Tamil and Malay in addition to English across an array of tasks and language domains, as they lived in linguistically diverse neighborhoods and translanguaging was a regular part of their lives. (This is not to say that white-collar students are always the most English dominant in any place; in the study reported in this book, the most English-dominant students, at least when it came to English in everyday conversation, were blue-collar old-timers in Hawai'i.) Moreover, similar to Charalambous et al.'s (2016) findings about ethnolinguistic conflict, one finding in Rajendram's study was that ethnically Tamil students who had knowledge of Tamil, English and Malay sometimes resisted using Malay as a result of political conflict between Tamil and Malay ethnic groups and inequitable relations between the national language and Tamil, which positioned them as deficient speakers of Malay regardless of social class.

All these studies involving positionality in multilingual classrooms suggest that translanguaging to allow students to use their whole language repertoires to learn is just *one* of the necessary ingredients for linguistic equity. This becomes apparent when we look at individual and group positioning using distinct languages, the identities they play up or play down through language use and the boundaries they put up or ignore due to subjective and socially constructed evaluations of others as linguistically similar or different (Bucholtz & Hall, 2005; Davies & Harré, 1990).

2.7 Summary

Constructs like translanguaging are indicative of the conditions of late modernity (Appadurai, 1996; Vertovec, 2007), which have challenged the 'one nation, one country, one language' discourse of many countries that have experienced not only increased levels of immigration but also more transnationalism, in which people, including K–12 students, routinely shuttle back and forth between different countries for study, work or visiting relatives, in addition to maintaining transnational networks over the internet (Lam & Warriner, 2012). In sociolinguistic scholarship, there have been moves away from conceptualizing culture as membership in ethnic and national communities to seeing people with hybrid identities on- and offline (Blommaert, 2010; Dovchin *et al.*, 2017). However, it is important to note that:

> as a descriptive catch-all term, 'hybridity' per se fails to discriminate between the diverse modalities of hybridity, for example, forced assimilation, internalized self-rejection, political cooptation, social conformism, cultural mimicry, and creative transcendence. (Shohat, as cited in Kubota, 2016: 482)

Rymes and Smail (2021) have critiqued the construct of translanguaging by arguing that much translanguaging research collapses the distinctions between these kinds of hybridity. They note that both the early Welsh translanguaging scholarship and García and Menken's scholarship in New York evoke their specific contexts deliberately and link translanguaging pedagogy to social justice: 'they contextualize cross-linguistic acts within broader (though specific) histories of marginalization and argue that validating or cultivating those acts can lead to better lives for bilingual people' (Rymes & Smail, 2021: 5). Currently, however, Rymes and Smail observe:

> a proliferation of descriptions of translanguaging (often going beyond multilingualism to include, e.g., multimodality, multimedia literacy, gesture, gaze) and to identify, more precisely, the 'good' accomplished by these practices. ... At these larger scale levels, the individuals and their unique communicative situations get left behind. (Rymes & Smail, 2021: 8)

Even when translanguaging pedagogy does not simply encourage students to express themselves with their full language repertoires, but is accompanied by an explicit intention to challenge linguistic and cultural hierarchies, that intention may be critical in some ways but not in others, or support the interests of some groups more than others. In a chapter titled 'Translanguaging as Resistance Against What and for Whom?', Lee (2019) argues that locus of enunciation (Mignolo, 2003) is crucial: 'the locus of enunciation, or place of speaking, involves a recognition of how one's personal histories, cultural backgrounds and ideological commitments shape one's behaviors or perspectives' (Lee, 2019: 114). He gives the example of Korean popular media, which is celebrated for translanguaging and for going against traditional, monolingual, 'standard' Korean and 'standard' English language ideologies. At the same time, he critiques the multimillion-dollar industry of translingual K-pop, in which shareholders and profiteers from families that have the most access to an elite Korean and English education 'readily appropriate the sentiment of a populace enthralled by the symbolic upheaval of the very norms and values that the elite embody and will continue to profit from' (Lee, 2019: 114–115). In another example regarding locus of enunciation when it comes to *transglossia*, the mixture of codes and modalities in Web 2.0, Sultana (2021) points out that people can translanguage in playful, ludic ways to abuse Others in bigoted, racist, sexist, homophobic, jingoistic or religiously intolerant discourse, wittily combining texts and images to offensively portray individuals or groups. Transglossia, she argues, can be creative, democratic, ingenious, collaborative and distributed across many participants – yet also vile. In addition to translingual practices not being critical in themselves but only given a well-informed and ethical locus of enunciation, these practices co-exist with those that align with more traditional national language ideologies, leading to paradoxes and contradictions in people's everyday interactions.

Bi/multilingualism can still be constructed as separate, parallel monolingualisms in the emic discourse and perspectives of our research participants; languages can still be attributed hierarchical value, even subconsciously in situations where a minoritized language is explicitly promoted (Hamman, 2018); social inequality is ever present, particularly class differences (Block, 2018). There are still language education policies about which languages to teach and learn, by whom and how (Kubota & Lin, 2009; Skutnabb-Kangas *et al.*, 2009). Language will always be symbolic capital (Bourdieu, 1991), and different groups of people have different degrees of control over the reception of linguistic and cultural resources in particular social environments and in the wider society at large. Perhaps most disturbingly, (auto)ethnographies have shown that raciolinguistic ideology reproduces itself on different scales, even in educational settings that serve or are run by people from minoritized, immigrant or indigenous backgrounds (hooks, 1989; Jaspers, 2011; Talmy, 2008; Zavala, 2015).

For these reasons, it is necessary to call individuals to account, even minors who are very demonstrably oppressed by societal discrimination, government policy and inequitable school systems, for their actions in classrooms and toward each other, along with their teachers and classroom researchers – such as the author of this study – who go into social spaces promoting multilingualism and translanguaging but do not come with a neutral or value-free set of cultural alignments. By seeing the local contexts in which we teach, learn and do educational research in terms of their politics and histories, and interrogating ourselves over our assumptions and practices, we can come to more honest understandings of how linguistic equity is achieved in plurilingual classrooms where a national language is the lingua franca.

Notes

(1) This is not to say that the only purpose of translanguaging is to scaffold acquisition of the target language, or that people should not be allowed to use their entire language repertoires to do academic and professional work, even after monolingual competencies in a dominant language have been acquired.
(2) https://www.cuny-nysieb.org.
(3) https://research.ncl.ac.uk/romtels/resources/guidancehandbooks.
(4) Nevertheless, these bilinguals maintain an intuitive sense of permissible and impermissible grammar constructions in both languages.
(5) However, the term 'codifiable' is both true and untrue, as the norms of any variety of English, including WEs, are re-negotiated in real time (Higgins, 2009).

3 Research Context, Methods and Data Collection and Analysis

Every K–12 classroom has its language policies and practices influenced by theories of language acquisition and bi/multilingualism, educational and language policies at wider societal levels and a host of sociolinguistic factors (Valdés, 2020). In this chapter, I describe the sociolinguistic context of Hawai'i and the school where the study took place. I discuss why the method of linguistic ethnography is useful for researching the impact of institutional and societal ideologies on classroom interaction. I also describe data collection and analysis, and explain how my own bi/multilingual practices and identity bids affected the research process. I conclude with a critical examination of researcher positionality in bi/multilingual K–12 research settings.

3.1 The Historical Context

A discourse that describes Hawai'i as a multicultural melting pot can be seen in the following newspaper editorial, which explains that racism exists, but goes on to downplay its effects:

> To be honest, Hawaii's egalitarian atmosphere is not utopia; some racial issues occasionally (but rarely) rise to the surface. It was in this nonviolent and benign atmosphere that a 'hapa-haole' teenager (half white, half something else) could come closer to terms with all cultures that formed his intelligent, introspective person, and laid a foundation for his future.[1]

I used to present this quote to students in a first-year seminar at the University of Hawai'i while still a PhD student. This seminar was called *SLS 150: Learning Languages and Communicating in a Globalized World*. I would put the quote as the teaser, or first slide, in a lecture titled 'Sociolinguistic Timeline of Languages in Hawai'i'. This lecture is a synthesis of readings (e.g. Reinecke, 1969; Sato, 1985, 1994) in the undergraduate course *SLS 430: Pidgin and Creole English in Hawai'i*, taught by Kumu Kent Sakoda, and my own secondary research (Appleseed Center for Law and Economic Justice, 2011; Fujikane & Okamura, 2008; Liu *et al.*, 1991;

Talmy, 2008; Trask, 2000, 2004; Van Dyke, 2007). One of the problems with analyzing racism and linguicism in Hawai'i is that the histories of different groups are often presented one at a time and held up against whiteness, whether those groups are Kanaka Maoli (indigenous Hawaiians), kama'āina (speakers of Pidgin descended from plantation workers) or post-1965 Immigration Act residents from various countries. It is only by synthesizing these histories that we can come to understand how the state's history of racism and linguicism compares to that of the continental US – particularly the role that people of all racial backgrounds have played in colonizing Native Hawaiians, limiting each other's socioeconomic mobility and creating discourses of racial superiority and class distinction within and across ethnicities. Nevertheless, compared to other parts of the US, Hawai'i is relatively tolerant of diversity. The 'melting pot' in the public imagination began with the mass immigration of contracted laborers in the 1870s, a cross-cultural contact that has led to the birth, decline, rise and revitalization of various languages over more than a century (Figure 3.1).

Figure 3.1 shows (1) the decline and revitalization of Hawaiian; (2) the origins (pidginization) of a contact language, its development into a fully fledged language (Hawai'i Creole) and its decreolization into a dialect of English (Hawai'i Creole English or Hawai'i English); (3) the history of locals of Japanese ancestry from immigration to persecution to socioeconomic hegemony; and (4) the aftermath of the 1965 Immigration Act and the arrival of additional waves of immigrants in a state already rife with socioeconomic inequalities and environmentally unsustainable development.

Of course, the story begins much earlier than this timeline shows. Haunani Kay Trask, a Hawaiian historian and activist, explains:

> The economy of pre-haole [foreigner] Hawai'i depended primarily on a balanced use of the products of the land and sea. Each of the eight habitable islands was divided into 'okana (separate districts) running from the mountains to the sea. Each 'okana was then subdivided into ahupua'a, which ran in wedge-shaped pieces from the mountains to the sea; each ahupua'a was then fashioned into 'ili

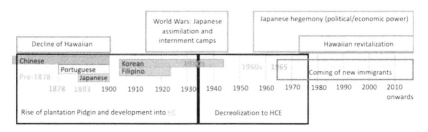

Figure 3.1   Sociolinguistic timeline of Hawai'i (from the author's lecture slides)

(subdistricts) where the 'ohana (extended families) who cultivated the land resided. ... As in most indigenous societies, there was no money, no idea or practice of surplus appropriation, and no value storing or payment deferral because there was no idea of financial profit from exchange. ... Exchange between 'ohana who lived near the sea with 'ohana who lived inland constituted the economic life of the communities which densely populated the Hawaiian islands. The exchange system allowed each ahupua'a to be economically indepen-dent. (Trask, 1991: 1198)

Captain Cook's arrival in the 1770s brought disastrous consequences to this society. In just over a century, 95% of the Hawaiian popula-tion died of foreign diseases such as syphilis, gonorrhea, tuberculosis, smallpox, leprosy and measles – declining from 1 million to 40,000 from the 1770s to the 1890s (Fujikane, 2005; Trask, 1991). The Hawaiian way of life also changed fundamentally due to colonial contact. One ali'i (chief) succeeded in establishing a European-style kingdom: ruling from the 1780s to the 1810s, Kamehameha I uni-fied the islands through conquest using modern Western weaponry. The Hawaiian kingdom was internationally recognized as its own nation and engaged in diplomacy and trade with other nations until US annexation in the 1890s. It had two dynasties: the Kamehameha dynasty and the Kalākaua dynasty. The last two monarchs, from the 1870s to the 1890s, were King David Kalākaua and his younger sister, Queen Lili'uokalani.

King Kalākaua's reign (1874–1891) was beset by an economic crisis as well as a sovereignty crisis, which were linked. Since the economic structure of Hawaiian society changed from a self-sustaining society of *ahupua'a* to a kingdom that had to deal with other countries, the Hawaiian economy relied on whaling as its primary export industry. In the early 1800s, Hawaiian waters were frequented by whaling ships with international crews, like those in the 1851 novel *Moby Dick*.[2] By the 1870s, the whaling industry was depleted. Hence, the white haole elite who had settled permanently in Hawai'i decided that from then on, the Hawaiian economy had to be 'self-sustaining' – that is, to revolve around their plantations. In 1875, they pressured King Kālakaua to pass the Reciprocity Treaty between the United States and Hawai'i, which was anything but reciprocal. This agreement resulted in tariff-free trade with the US to the detriment of Hawaiian society, and allowed for the importation of massive cheap immigrant labor for the plantations. From the 1870s to the 1890s, the Hawaiian population was dwarfed by these waves of immigrants – Chinese, Micronesian, Japanese, Portuguese, Filipino and Korean – with indigenous peoples comprising 79.2% of the population in 1880 and 3.8% in 1932 (Reinecke, 1969). The Portuguese-speaking population rose from 436 to 8600 from 1876 to 1890, while the Japanese-speaking population rose from 12,300 to 56,000 from 1890 to 1900 (Roberts, 2019). Although plantations run by whites existed before 1878, it was not until that time that the pineapple and sugarcane industries boomed and the ethnic composition of the islands changed. At the same time, railroads were being built across the US and naval trade routes established between Hawai'i and California.

More trouble came in 1887, with the Bayonet Constitution and the Pearl Harbor Treaty, which gave the US exclusive rights to Pearl Harbor, a key military base from which it could continue colonizing missions eastward (e.g. Guam, the Philippines). The Bayonet Constitution of 1887 decoupled voting and citizenship in a way that severely undermined Hawaiian sovereignty. Under these bizarre laws, a non-naturalized resident of Hawai'i could vote in the kingdom's elections, as long as that individual had a certain net worth ($3000 in property or $600 in annual income) and was literate in Hawaiian or a European language. This granted voting rights and the ability to shape the kingdom's legislation to white landowners and upwardly mobile white plantation workers from Portugal who were used to balance out the Hawaiian voter population, but did not grant voting rights to the masses of Asian plantation workers. As Van Dyke (2007: 146) put it, 'the constitution removed every paradox that had previously confounded [white] haole citizens... by making the nation belong to them without requiring that they belong to the nation'.

After this, enough Hawaiians and part-Hawaiians remained in the legislature to put up some struggle (see Van Dyke, 2007: 148). In 1890, constitutional amendments reduced the amount of property a voter had to own from $3000 to $1000 and allowed only 'subjects' instead of mere 'residents' to vote, although female suffrage did not yet exist. When the king died in 1891, his sister, Queen Lili'uokalani, exercised even more resistance to the white landowners. The constitution she prepared to present to her subjects in January 1893 would have reiterated the reforms of 1890, changed the House of Nobles to a body of 24 individuals appointed by the monarch for life rather than a group elected for 3-year terms by those with property and increased the House of Representatives from 24 to 48 seats up for election. In other words, the queen, who remains a respected historical figure in Hawai'i today, fought both for Hawaiian sovereignty and for more equal political representation. Unfortunately, her attempted reforms were the catalyst for annexation. In 1893, haole landowners, in collusion with US ambassador John L. Stevens, called in the US navy to protect American interests in Hawai'i. They occupied the islands, arrested the queen and forced her to sign her abdication, which she did to spare her close supporters from being executed and her subjects from the outbreak of war. Hawai'i became a US territory, and in the 1950s, a state. In the 1990s, the US government officially recognized this illegal overthrow, though the state Hawai'i remains.

What of the kama'āina, the (mostly) Asian descendents of the plantation workers? By the 1893 overthrow, 99% of schools were English medium to cater to the islands' linguistic diversity. Thus, from the 1890s until the 1930s, children growing up in Hawai'i were taught through English-medium instruction, but what many were actually speaking outside of class was Hawai'i Creole, commonly called 'Pidgin' – a language that dates back to a Hawaiian-, Japanese- and English-lexified pidgin on the plantations but could also have existed as an earlier pidgin during the whaling industry. Because of the settlement of Pidgin speakers on plantations, the use of a pidgin beyond an *ad hoc* contact language caused it to evolve into a grammatically systematic and fully developed language, a creole (see Pinker, 1994: chapter 2). In schooling contexts, Pidgin was mistaken as 'broken English' rather than a language with a grammar as complex as that of any other language, and children were often punished for speaking it. Despite this, it remained widely spoken, while Hawaiian was in decline (Bickerton & Wilson, 1987; Sato, 1985).

As the 20th century progressed, another economic shift – from the plantation industry to the tourism industry – caused Pidgin itself to decline. Over time, the language increasingly began to resemble English through numerous word borrowings; today, it is a mutually intelligible dialect of English unlike the original creole (which was not intelligible to English speakers), yet maintains its own rules of grammar. What caused this language shift, called decreolization,[3] was the end of the plantation era and the rise of the tourist industry, which remains Hawai'i's primary industry today. As former plantation workers moved to the cities from the 1930s on, there emerged an upwardly mobile group of Pidgin speakers who entered white-collar professions, while some of their counterparts remained in relative poverty, working in the service sector (Sato, 1985). This led to a situation in which Pidgin developed different varieties ranging from the acrolect (white-collar Hawai'i English) to the basilect (lower-class Pidgin). While the basilect is stigmatized, Pidgin and Hawai'i English are used to claim a 'local' identity superior to new immigrants, and hence this language has both negative and positive indexicalities, or social meanings (Higgins, 2015). Some see decreolization as language loss and the inability of younger generations to speak Pidgin, while others see the process as language maintenance through evolution. Sato (1994) explains that the push for standard English has always been in tension with the pride locals feel about the variety of English spoken in Hawai'i. This tension came to a head when the board of education (BOE), a committee of the Hawai'i Department of Education, published a memorandum stating:

> Standard English will be the mode of oral communication for students and staff in the classroom setting and all other school related settings except when the objectives cover native Hawaiian or foreign language instruction and practice. (Sato, 1994: 133)

The act was met with widespread backlash from parents, teachers, academics, activists and some parts of the mass media, such that the BOE amended the statement to one that simply 'encouraged' teachers to model 'standard' English.

It is worth noting the role of locals of Japanese origin in the socioeconomic shift, as they comprised a large portion of upwardly mobile Pidgin speakers. After the oppression and discrimination Japanese people in Hawai'i experienced during WWII, the most appalling example being the Japanese internment, in the 1960s locals of Japanese ancestry gained political ascendancy as the Japanese-led Democratic Party defeated the white-led Republican Party in the state legislature. Indeed, the Wikipedia page of Hawai'i's Democratic Party claims that it has 'held onto a solid majority since 1962, with near-complete control over the state's congressional delegation and its legislative and executive branch'. This is corroborated by Okamura (2008), who notes that ethnic Japanese are dominant in government, education (principals and teachers) and white-collar jobs in Hawai'i. In other words, Hawai'i is the only US state where whites are not predominant in white-collar professions; instead, educated Asians are. Importantly, Japanese, Chinese and Filipinos in Hawai'i do not like to be called 'haole' because of prejudice suffered from whites. Ultimately, however, these Asian Americans too are settlers. The California-based Asian American studies scholar Candice Fujikane (2005) explores such 'Asian settler colonialism' in the United States in her critique of a 1979 novel, *Homebase* by Sam Wong. In that novel, the protagonist, Rainsford Chan, struggles to negotiate racist ideologies that insist he can never be fully 'American' even though his great-grandfather was a builder on the Central Pacific Railroad through the Sierra Nevada. Memories of his grandfather evoke legislative acts that restricted Chinese immigration and denied Asian immigrants full participation in American 'democracy'. On Christmas Eve 1969, Rainsford finds himself on Alcatraz Island, where he meets a sympathetic American Indian who says: 'My ancestors came from China thirty thousand years ago and settled in Acoma Pueblo… This is your country. Go out and make yourself at home'. Questioning an Asian American's right to make this claim, Fujikane writes:

> When Rainsford tells us, 'My grandfather's island is Angel Island. It was there that he almost died, and that makes it his island' (S. Wong, 1979: 80),

his account resonates with so many other Asian American texts that narrativize the blood, sweat, and semen poured onto American soil by Asian immigrants... their right to claim America. Ultimately, however, the presence of Native peoples is a reminder of that which Asian Americanists would prefer to forget: that Asian Americans can never claim America, not because of white racism, but because it is Native land. (Fujikane, 2005: 84)

Returning to Hawai'i, that state saw further demographic changes following the US Immigration Act of 1965. Through this act, immigration policy across the United States became focused on family unification, resulting in immigration chains built up of blood or marriage ties. In a study of US census data and Immigration and Naturalization Service annual reports (1972–1985), Liu *et al.* (1991) proposed a 'dual chain' theory of post-1965 immigration from the Philippines to the US ('dual' referring to white-collar and blue-collar families). Comparing Filipino immigration flows in New Jersey with those in California and Hawai'i, they found that white-collar immigration was predominant in New Jersey and blue-collar immigration in Hawai'i, while both chains (blue- and white-collar) were active in California. Thus, Filipino American communities reproduced social stratifications in the Philippines. In Hawai'i, new waves of Asian immigrants from the same countries that once populated the plantations tend to have limited knowledge of Pidgin and to speak their own languages in their own communities, separate from the kama'āina who are unified by this language.[4] A fairly recent census showed that people who self-identified as Filipino had surpassed those who self-identified as Japanese, the latter declining from 16.7% in 2000 to 13.6% in 2010, while Filipinos in 2010 comprised 14.5% of the population.[5]

Post-1965 immigrants also include Pacific Islanders such as Samoans and 'Micronesians', an umbrella term for people from the Marshall Islands and the Federated States of Micronesia (Chuukese, Kosraeans, Pohnpeians and Yapese).[6] Micronesians formed one of the first groups to work on the Hawaiian plantations, and unlike the others, they tended to return to their home islands when their contracts were done. However, they have been immigrating to Hawai'i more permanently since the 1970s because of devastation to their islands wrought by US atomic bomb testing. Known as COFA or Compact of Free Association immigrants, they are legally allowed to work in the US as compensation for this environmental devastation, but often cannot get more than minimum wage jobs and are excluded from many social benefits that other immigrants have, such as food stamps and Medicaid.[7] COFA immigrants suffer poor health outcomes, poverty and homelessness from this lack of federal support, which, combined with language barriers and discrimination from other groups,[8] impact their access to housing and employment. In one community report, a Micronesian woman testified that she covered her child's ears when she heard a joke on a radio station that Micronesians and cockroaches were the same – 'they both multiply' (Appleseed Center for Law and Economic Justice, 2011: 15).

Through all this, Native Hawaiians, who define themselves as the first human inhabitants and the only ones who have an indigenous claim to the Hawaiian islands, remain colonized by everybody. Saranillo (2008) notes that immigrants' desires for citizenship and equality, and their competition for socioeconomic mobility, are part of the colonial structure. For example, when Filipino Americans went on strike in Hawai'i in 1924, they brandished a US flag and a portrait of Lincoln, aligning themselves with US discourses of equal opportunity, but at the same time legitimizing US colonization of the islands. In another case, ethnically Filipino Governor Benjamin Cayetano (in office from 1994 to 2002) pressured members of the Office of Hawaiian Affairs (OHA) to resign after a lawsuit that successfully allowed non-natives with interests in economic development to run for election to this office whose purpose was to protect indigenous land. Cayetano also attempted to stop regular state payments to the OHA, offering instead a one-time compensation of $251 million and 360,000 acres of land, which the board members refused as they resigned. According to Saranillo (2008), Cayetano's actions were influenced by Senator Daniel K. Inouye, the state's Japanese American representative in Washington at the time. (Both Inouye and Cayetano styled themselves as former working-class boys who became successful through hard work.)

Hawai'i's multicultural melting pot myth, which portrays immigrants, particularly Asians such as Japanese, Chinese, Koreans and Filipinos, as working hard to achieve the American dream, disregards Hawaiians' poor health outcomes, overrepresentation in prisons and confinement to service sector jobs. Trask (2004) notes that blame for this system rests more on white rather than immigrant settlers who call themselves 'local', yet have no land base or traditional culture native to Hawai'i. Although the Hawaiian language revitalization movement, which began in the 1970s, is a successful one seen as a model for other language revitalization movements (Brenzinger & Heinrich, 2013; Galla, 2009; Kapono, 1995), Hawaiians not only want cultural and socioeconomic advancement, but they also want their lands back, to have control over the resources on those lands and to exercise self-governance, rather than simply being granted cultural recognition or socioeconomic mobility in a colonial order. Before her death, Trask (2004) expressed sympathy and solidarity with Micronesians:

> Allow me to shock you with a profile of our health statistics. Below one year of age, the Hawaiian death rate is more than double the overall state average. … In every age category up to age 30, the Hawaiian death rate

is never less than double and is often triple the equivalent mortality rate in our islands. With just under 20% of the state's population, Hawaiians account for nearly 75% of the state's deaths for persons less than 18 years of age. (Trask, 2004: 10)

We must all remember that the world's first hydrogen bomb was tested on Bikini Island. The force of this weapon was 1,000 times stronger than the Hiroshima Bomb. Marshall Islanders were used as guinea pigs to test the effects of contamination. They were never told of the bomb's effects, and were not removed before testing (Keju-Johnson, 1998: 16). Predictably, cancer is now widespread among the Marshallese. They have one of the highest rates of severely deformed children, including 'jellyfish babies' who have no heads, arms, legs, or human shape. ... Such babies are born not only on islands declared radioactive by the Americans, but on all attols and five major islands in the Marshalls archipelago (Ibid.: 17). Before such tests, Marshallese people enjoyed incredible longevity, with many of their people living over 100 years. Today, they have young women with a life expectancy of 40 years of age. The United States tested 23 bombs on Bikini Island and 43 on Enewetak. (Trask, 2004: 12–13)

It is important to note, in the words of Marshallese poet Kathy Jetnil-Kijiner (2011),[9] that Micronesians are not American Dream immigrants, but indigenous people with ties to their land, poisoned by atomic bomb testing and threatened by climate change:

tell them about the water
how we have seen it rising
flooding across our cemeteries
gushing over the sea walls
and crashing against our homes
tell them what it's like
to see the entire ocean__level__with the land
tell them
we are afraid
tell them we don't know
of the politics
or the science
but tell them we see
what is in our own backyard
...
but most importantly tell them
we don't want to leave
we've never wanted to leave
and that we
are nothing without our islands.

In Hawai'i, one must consider not only hegemony as embodied by white people – I saw no students who appeared to be white at the school, although it is possible that a handful may have been there in the sea of 2400 students. Other conflicts and hegemonies exist on a more local scale: of acrolect over basilect Hawai'i English speakers; of 'white-sounding' Asians over others; of settlers over indigenous peoples; between different groups of settlers (historically Portuguese over others; now, Japanese dominance in Hawai'i). One group of immigrants (Filipinos) was dominant in the school and neighborhood where this study took place. This brings me to the sociocultural dynamics of the institution itself.

3.2 The School Context

I have given the school the pseudonym 'Traffic Light High' because it is not near a beach, but in a hot, urban area of Honolulu with visible poverty and homelessness. While gun violence is rare, the streets of this neighborhood are overrun with children and youth during after-school hours – children and youth who live in overcrowded, multi-family homes, making the best use of the roaming spaces available to them outdoors, which include small businesses (convenience stores, gas stations, hole-in-the-wall restaurants, pawn shops, grocers), a few chain stores and some residential areas. Waiting at bus stops, on every other block, are people who need medical attention and cannot afford it: they are elderly, have disabilities or are experiencing homelessness. New kids, always a steady stream of new kids due to family chain migration (escaping environmental devastation in Micronesia, earning US dollars to afford education and healthcare for relatives back in the Philippines), are shown the ropes by still fairly recent arrivals.

When I volunteered in the school's Filipino American club with my advisor and several other graduate students in 2017–2018, the school was one of the four most ethnolinguistically diverse secondary schools in Hawai'i, with 20%–22% of students designated English language learners (ELLs). In the year of this study and the year prior, 59%–60% of students were Filipino, mostly Ilokano, 11%–14% were Micronesian or Marshallese, 8%–9% were Samoan, 9%–10% were Native Hawaiian and 7%–9% of students came from other backgrounds. Hawai'i's ELLs show incredible linguistic diversity – five languages make up roughly 56% of home languages of students with the ELL designation (Ilokano, Chuukese, Marshallese, Tagalog and Spanish, the last represented by only 6% of ELL-designated students), while another 65 languages make up the other 44% of home languages (Hawai'i Department of Education, n.d.).

Ethnic tensions at the school occasionally surfaced, for example at an end-of-school-year assembly called Mayday, which I attended in spring

2018. A stage (the 'court') was set up in the gymnasium with a collection of thrones belonging to the king and queen of Hawai'i, a prince and princess from each island and kings and queens from the 'visiting' islands of Samoa, the Philippines, Japan, Greece and the Marshall Islands. Hula dances were performed by the Hawaiian court, interspersed with dances led by each visiting couple. The Marshallese dance was the only dance in which audience members joined in, displaying wild conviviality and solidarity, students waving a large flag of the Marshall Islands. However, during the Filipino dance, which was scheduled last, the volume of applause reached such thunderous levels that it seemed the auditorium's roof would come off, and so many flowers and decorations were thrown onto the stage that performers were virtually buried in them. This display of Filipino pride suggested the message '*This is OUR turf*' despite the centrality of Hawaiian culture in the program, the Micronesian pride displayed earlier and the relatively low socioeconomic and cultural status of Filipinos in Hawai'i.

On a positive note, the teachers at the school – who welcomed me into their classrooms, listened to my study's findings[10] and journeyed to the National Council of Teachers of English (NCTE) conference in 2019 – were extremely professional and dedicated. As documented in this book, teachers of multiple English as a second language (ESL) classes worked hard to publish a multilingual creative writing anthology that had a successful launch at a public library in spring 2019 and had sold 654 copies by the time the project was presented at the NCTE conference in Baltimore, Maryland, that fall. The ESL department's session at the NCTE conference featured multiple presentations about the multilingual, multimodal literacies taught in different levels of ESL classes at the school: studying place-based literature from Asian and Pacific Islander nations, textual and oral; exploring social issues such as poverty and homelessness (which students may have experienced firsthand) through community ethnography and storytelling, while critiquing developments such as high-end malls and luxury condos, and asking questions like, 'What makes a community? What different communities are we part of? What is in our community? How can we make our community better?'; exploring museums to learn about Hawai'i and people's shared history and various experiences of it; and doing inquiry-based service projects. These teachers ground their pedagogy in the HĀ (Breath) philosophy of education adopted by the Hawai'i BOE, which has six components: Belonging, Responsibility, Excellence, Aloha, Total well-being and a sense of Hawai'i (Hawai'i Board of Education, 2015; Lupenui *et al.*, 2015).[11] It is my view that HĀ is different from most other education policies outlining desired student competencies that one might find in any part of the world. Even though the HĀ framework does not explicitly articulate a decolonial intent or solidarity with the Hawaiian sovereignty movement (given what many immigrant groups have to lose if they did so; see Trask, 2000), the HĀ educational framework is much more concerned with *local community relations* than with globalization, and is unique in this regard.

Another positive fact that is worth highlighting is that linguistic and cultural diversity have for a long time been ingrained in Hawai'i as a normal part of everyday life, and educational policy at the state level embodies widespread institutionalized support of multilingualism, such as the Multilingualism for Equitable Education Policy 105-14 (Hawai'i State Department of Education, 2016). The legitimization of multilingualism as a right *and* a resource (Ruiz, 1984) is seen in the number of students who graduate with a Seal of Biliteracy, an award given to students in most US states in recognition of proficiency in at least two languages by high school graduation,[12] and conferences related to Hawaiian, Pidgin and immigrant languages occur regularly in the education system. At the school, outside the office for ELL counseling was a colorful sign saying 'Welcome' in many languages, with the language label underneath: Chuukese, Hawaiian, Ilokano, Marshallese, Samoan, Tagalog and Vietnamese.

Given that the two biggest ethnic groups of ELLs in Hawai'i are Filipinos followed by Micronesians, it is significant how they are positioned in the school's ELL program upon arrival. Generally, students from the Philippines arrive with higher World-Class Instructional Design and Assessment (WIDA) test scores because the Philippines is an Outer Circle English-speaking country and a former colony of the US. They typically test into Foundation 2, which I call ESL 9/10 in this study, rather than a class for beginners in English, called Foundation 1 (Figure 3.2). This results in Foundation 2 having a large Filipino-speaking majority.

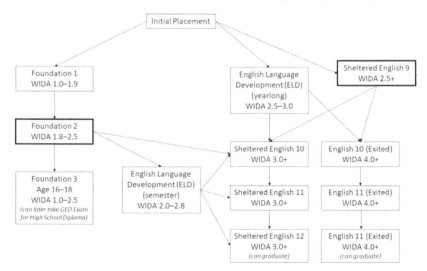

Figure 3.2   ELL program benchmarks (courtesy of ESL Department Head 'Kaori')

Moreover, Filipino students' greater experience with US educational norms (textual literacy, standardized testing and a society that evaluates high school students by their college/university acceptance outcome) leads to a greater degree of familiarity with the US public school system and statistically better educational outcomes within this system compared to those of Micronesian students. Ilokano and Chuukese are the two most common languages for ELL-designated students statewide, yet according to a survey commissioned by the Department of Education (Hawai'i P-20 Partnerships for Education, 2018), high school graduation rates for students who had exited ESL were 95% for Ilokano first language (L1) students, compared to 66% for Chuukese L1 students. As for postsecondary education, 45% of Ilokano L1 students who had exited ESL by high school graduation went on to complete a college degree or certificate in six years, compared to 13% of Chuukese L1 students who had exited ESL by high school graduation. That is, even when cultural priorities are accounted for (e.g. caring for community members experiencing illness or death in the family and missing weeks of school to do this, which is a very important part of Micronesian culture and leads to high levels of absenteeism among the most dedicated students), there is still systemic discrimination in the primacy of *print literacy* in access to higher education, which disadvantages students from cultures whose literacy practices are mainly oral (Perez Hattori, 2020). While college and university attendance rates for both Filipinos and Micronesians are still far below those of middle-class white and Japanese students, they are higher for Filipinos.

Although most of the Filipino students in the school were of Ilokano heritage, there were also Filipino students of mixed heritage or those who spoke other home languages such as Tagalog, Ilonggo and Cebuano. In both English 9 and ESL 9/10, the class majority was ethnically Filipino, but the linguistic majority in each class (Ilokano or pan-Filipino) determined the main language used in translanguaging alongside English as a lingua franca (ELF). I also noticed that the phonology of Philippine languages influenced what was considered 'normal' English pronunciation, and that Korean, which some Filipino youth affiliate with because of K-pop culture in the Philippines, was important to certain students in English 9 (see 'language crossing' in Chapter 2). Thus, what actually went on at the level of each classroom in terms of language standards and the value assigned to different languages is illuminated through linguistic ethnography.

3.3 Linguistic Ethnography

Linguistic ethnography is the study of social life through analysis of language, primarily in spontaneous oral interaction, which makes it an apt method for studying how high school students use language(s) to learn and navigate the social life of classrooms. When explaining linguistic ethnography to students, I define it as 'the study of language in society with a dual focus on *context* and *contextualiza-tion*'. An overview of the development of this methodology makes this definition clear.

In the 1970s, Dell Hymes (1974) proposed using the tools of anthropology to examine smaller cultures than had previously been researched – groups of individuals rather than imagined communities such as 'speakers of Language X'. To do such research, Hymes coined constructs such as the speech community (e.g. the English 9 class), the speech situation (e.g. a workshop by a visiting poet), the speech event (e.g. a conversation between students during the workshop) and the speech act (e.g. each maneuver a student makes in that conversation). By studying communication at these levels, Hymes developed tools for analyzing what Holliday (1999) called 'small cultures', such as a family, a workplace or a classroom. This approach to studying *context* became known as the ethnography of communication (EoC), and its goal is to map out the organization of communication in a community of practice through participant observation and detailed descriptions of daily lives, as well as how actions at particular moments and in particular spaces are connected and constrained by other actions across space and time.

Early research that applied EoC in classrooms found that the social practices and speech patterns in a classroom could be linked to wider societal ideologies. Heath (1983) showed how the literacy and storytelling practices of working-class Black and white children in the US differed from each other's and from those of middle-class white children, while school practices mirrored those of the last group, contributing to inequalities in educational outcomes. Duff (1995) documented how oral practices in a classroom in Hungary changed from *felelés* (recitations) after the fall of the Soviet Union to more Western-style, open-ended discussions. Watson-Gegeo (1988: 576–578) argued that the promise of ethnography in language classrooms was that it provided a new lens for examining learning: how students negotiate the social life of the small culture, without which effective language acquisition cannot take place. At the same time, Watson-Gegeo explained that individual action does not exist in a vacuum but is embedded in a series of concentric rings representing wider and wider ways of being within the school, neighborhood and society. Similarly, Duff (2002: 293) states that EoC studies make connections between classroom interaction and 'the larger socio-educational and socio-political contexts and issues surrounding language education and use and academic achievement'.

Despite the rich potential of EoC, it only forms half of linguistic ethnography since EoC focuses on a speech community's language practices in relation to wider societal ideologies, rather than on how individuals interpret and shape the context of particular interactions as they unfold. This is the difference between *context* and *contextualization* discussed by Auer (1996). While it is a truism that social context is important in any interaction, Auer points out at least five definitions of context, noting that others may also exist: (1) linguistic context, or what previous utterances an utterance links back to (Bakhtin, 1981); (2) non-linguistic sense data, such as physical surroundings; (3) features of the social situation; (4) participants' common background knowledge; and (5) channel of communication (the medium), such as face-to-face talk and text chat. Auer (1996: 20) argues that describing 'context', no matter how richly, is not enough to explain verbal interaction because 'basically everything can become a *context* for a linguistic *focal event*. The more interesting question surely is **how** this *becoming-a-context-for-something* is accomplished'.

Interactional choices, verbal and non-verbal, *must* make relevant or invoke contextual factors: in some cases, the physical surroundings are important while in others they are not; in some moments in conversation, age, gender, race, class or linguistic differences between participants matter and in others they do not. Auer points to John Gumperz' (1982, 1992) work on contextualization, as key to understanding how conversational participants not only fit their utterances into contexts but also make those contexts jointly recognized through contextualization cues. In other words, it is not a collection of material or social facts but a collectively negotiated schema about what identities and roles are relevant for the interaction that determines context. The task of the ethnographer is to recognize which material or social facts are salient for participants and which are not by examining their interactions.

Another way to see context versus contextualization is in the difference between brought along identities that pre-exist the conversation and brought about identities negotiated in the conversation (Zimmerman, 1998). Even if participants have shared knowledge of brought about identities (e.g. mother, gay rights activist, navy veteran), they must still be evoked, no matter how implicitly: 'turned from invisible (and interactionally irrelevant) dispositions (potentialities) into commonly available grounds on which to conduct the interaction' (Auer, 1996: 20). The study of this process, called contextualization, is called interactional sociolinguistics (IS; Goffman, 1981; Gumperz, 1982), and it forms the other half of linguistic ethnography (Figure 3.3). IS is concerned with the meaning-making practices through which participants build and negotiate shared frames of interpretation.

The study of context and contextualization requires researchers to combine the tools of linguistics *and* ethnography (Copland & Creese, 2015; Tusting & Maybin, 2007). Linguistic ethnographers typically

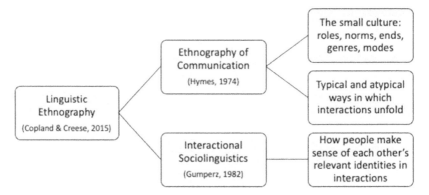

Figure 3.3   Use of linguistic ethnography in the study

do not do research among participants for many years, nor do they necessarily need to follow participants into every sphere of their lives – however, they do need to collect enough data to know the 'small culture'.[13] In the case of a class at school, the linguistic ethnographer needs to get to know the *context*, such as who the classroom partici-pants are; what kinds of events are ritual, routine or commonplace versus unusual or aberrant; and what institutional or ideological systems and structures exist at various levels (EoC) to understand the frames of reference that participants draw on when they 'bring about' identities through *contextualization cues* (IS), many of which are lin-guistic in nature. This requires an interdisciplinary approach. 'Open linguistics up' and 'tie ethnography down' are truisms for linguistic ethnographers (Copland & Creese, 2015; Rampton *et al.*, 2015). Through ethnography, talk in classrooms can be linked to its wider social, historical or political context, and through linguistic analysis of contextualization cues, the aspects of context relevant to the inter-action can be tied to empirical data suggesting the participants find them relevant (Tusting & Maybin, 2007).

   As other linguistic ethnographers, linguistic anthropologists of edu-cation and sociocultural linguists who study educational institutions have done (e.g. Bucholtz, 1999; Martin-Jones & Saxena, 2003; Pérez-Milans, 2013; Rampton, 2006; Wortham, 2006), I examine people's trajectories of identification and forms of social positioning through language use in the two classrooms. Instances of 'positioning' occur when people identify themselves in ways that relate to one another and to wider societal discourses (Bamberg, 1997; Davies & Harré, 1990). Who in each class presents themselves and is recognized as a valued model of bi/multilingualism? What counts as a legitimate instantiation of a code? What are the social processes through which these understandings are mutually constructed? What are the consequences for people? And what are the implications for teaching and learning in plurilingual, English as a lingua franca classrooms?

3.4 Data Collection

I gained access to the school through my PhD supervisor, Christina Higgins, who was organizing a conference on Pidgin (Hawai'i Creole) during the second year of my PhD. During the spring semester that she spent organizing the conference, she, I and our colleague Kevin Baetscher also ran a semester-long weekly after-school course on critical language awareness (Hélot & Young, 2002) in the school's Filipino American club – in collaboration with their club teacher, Juan, who taught English 9 in this study. Christina drove Kevin and me from the lush, affluent suburbs surrounding the university to Traffic Light High, and back again, for almost an hour each way, in the thick of Honolulu traffic. This, I believe, was intended to help me build connections with the school community, and it was through the volunteer work that Juan allowed me to conduct ethnography in his class the following academic year. When he suggested I observe other ESL classes to get a sense of where his course was in the broader context of the ESL program, I happened to observe Kaori's class. During that experience, I thought it would be beneficial to study translanguaging in a language I spoke (Filipino) as well as a language that necessitated working with a translator (Ilokano), and Kaori thankfully agreed to let me study her class as well.

During preliminary fieldwork (August–November 2018), I visited the school biweekly to observe Juan's English 9 and occasionally Kaori's ESL 9/10. During the official data collection period (13–14 weeks from January to May 2019), I collected nearly 70 hours of audio-recorded data from both classes, amounting to 250 pages of single-spaced transcripts of moments involving mixed language use as well as other events when language use was relevant, such as students making claims or commenting on their own or each other's proficiencies in various languages. I also sought to understand whether and how individuals took up opportunities to think aloud and communicate using English as a lingua franca or bi/multilingually. However, other forms of data were needed to contextualize these interactions, which I describe below.

(1) *Observation and field notes.* During my weekly visits to the classes, which were typically 75 minutes long, I audio-recorded the whole period with two audio recorders and took notes on what occurred every few minutes, transcribing speech as best I could and detailing the wider context of the recordings. These field notes allowed me to

pinpoint moments of interest to examine more closely in the interactional analysis of the audio-recorded data.

(2) *Language questionnaire.* I gave a brief questionnaire (Appendix 1) to students about their use of languages other than English (LOTEs) in class. The first of three questions asked them to rate how often they used a LOTE in class: never, rarely, sometimes, often or always. These five subjective terms were not meant to measure the actual amount of LOTE use – two students may have different ideas of what 'sometimes' entails. Instead, what the questionnaire aimed to capture was the degree to which students positioned themselves as frequent or infrequent translanguagers. I also examined how they positioned themselves as frequent or infrequent translanguagers in interviews, during which I followed up on what they put on the questionnaires. In the case of some students, there were discrepancies between what they put on the questionnaire and said in the interview, or between these and their audio-recorded language use.[14]

The second item on the questionnaire asked students to check all the ways in which they used a LOTE if the answer to the first question was 'always', 'often' or 'sometimes' – such as speaking the LOTE, thinking to oneself in the LOTE, taking notes in the LOTE or using a bilingual dictionary. I also included an 'Other' option with a blank space. The third question was an open-ended one that asked them to explain their response to the first: if they never or rarely used a LOTE, why did they avoid using it? If they used a LOTE sometimes, often or always, what did it do for them? The questionnaire thus served as a springboard for individualizing the interview questions about students' use of LOTEs in class.

(3) *Semi-structured interviews.* I carried out semi-structured, audio-recorded interviews with four students in English 9 and five students in ESL 9/10 who agreed to be interviewed, which was a quarter of each class of 14 or 17 students. These interviews happened throughout the study with one student each week who agreed to be interviewed during lunch break. Thus, in some interviews I had known the student for longer than in others. I was flexible in selecting the next interviewee based on who I hadn't spoken to yet and what interesting data had presented itself recently, but this was mitigated by individuals' willingness and availability during that day (Table 3.1). Two active students in English 9, He and Kix, agreed to be interviewed twice. Kok and Skusta, two students in ESL 9/10 from the Visayas (a cultural background that becomes significant in Chapter 6), were interviewed together.

Table 3.1   Language use events discussed in individual interviews

Student(s)	Date(s) of interview	Events discussed
English 9		
He	Jan. 17 and Mar. 28	Jan. 17: Rizze and her friends' regular use of 'Filipino' (He calls it this instead of Ilokano); his and his other friend's use of bits of Mandarin in Japanese class; Juan helping a student by explaining in Ilokano.
		Mar. 28: He complains that his Chuukese-speaking classmates 'don't have the book' and 'don't come to class most of the time'; he says, 'I don't care who I work with. Just that they gotta help with the work'. We talk about how Eufia and Rizze once spoke mock Chinese to He (this topic makes him uncomfortable).[15] He expresses the opinion that even though it's better for weaker students to have assistance in Ilokano, students who are more fluent in English would benefit from trying to speak English.
Kix	Jan. 15 and Apr. 4	Jan. 15: Kix estimates that he and his friends speak Ilokano and English in class in a 50-50 ratio, and that in total 20% of all class talk is in Ilokano; he says he observes that Bob and his friends talk in 'their language' sometimes, but that it is rare. He tells me that Ilokano is useful for vocabulary clarification (see Excerpt 2), but says his strongest academic language is English due to his English-medium schooling in the Philippines. He also notes that Ilokano may be interpreted as 'talking about others' and so he only uses it with his friends to do the class work, mentioning that sometimes Juan joins in.
		Apr. 4: Kix calls English a 'universal language' but that Ilokano is important for him and others to be more comfortable talking to each other. We discuss how Jhon doesn't use Ilokano, even though Kix states that he can: 'He can understand and he cannot—he can speak but he chooses not to'. Next, we discuss why Kix speaks Ilokano with Juan but not the substitute, Ed. We move on to his affinity for Korean (K-pop and K-dramas), and how he, Eufia and Konan go to Ms Rayna, the student teacher, to learn more after school. He says he and his friends Fetu, He, Eufia and Rizze socialize by joking around to show their friendship, including harsh-sounding words like 'shut up!' A special way of intoning 'shut u::↑p↓' shows they're just joking.
Kleo	Jan. 24	Kleo shares a poem she wrote for the multi-class anthology about her dad's departure, with the words 'Life for me is an abandoned neighborhood' (building on Juan's metaphor activity, asking students to write the journal entry: 'My life is a…'). She agrees with Kix that English and 'Filipino' are spoken in a 50-50 ratio during class (like He, she mistakes Ilokano for the national language). She talks about learning Ilokano words from her friends Kix and Eufia, and guesses why her Chuukese-speaking classmates don't use Chuukese in class: 'Maybe because like (2.0) they don't (.) they don't wanna be rude, 'cuz maybe they think like, oh, maybe they're like—people will think like they're swearing or talking'.[16] She says she holds back talking to Bob and Raoul in Chuukese with the few words she knows (she had one Chuukese grandparent) because she can't pronounce the Chuukese 'R'.[17] We discuss her heritage language limitations and English dominance, and her career aspirations: 'I wanna make my family proud, and not only that, I wanna be the first—there are Marshallese actresses in the Marshall Islands… but I wanna go to like California and like (.) be in a real movie that everyone could actually see. … I'm always like (.) act in front of my friends (.) to like make them laugh. And it does work. I always make my friends and family laugh'.
Jhon	Apr. 11	Jhon expresses that he hears LOTEs in class 'every time' and that He teaches him Chinese words. We discuss why he prefers an English-only classroom language policy (see Chapter 6). He mentions sometimes that he observes He doesn't understand the Ilokano used by Ilokano-speaking students. He also says he only uses Ilokano with friends and family. When I ask 'Why only friends?' he says, 'Cuz (.) I trust them more. (laughs)'[18]

ESL 9/10

Cookie	Jan. 31	We talk about how he can read and write in both Ilokano and Filipino, but he calls Ilokano spelling a bit different. He says Filipino is spoken in ESL 9/10 so he and his friends can understand one another: Flow-G, Skusta, Kok, Ricky, etc. They are like 'brothers' and they swim at Waikīkī Beach on the weekend. We discuss why they get a bit rowdy in their Filipino use (Excerpt 10). I ask him if the girls might want a chance to speak, and he says, 'pagka nataon' (when the moment comes), and adds 'di ko alam miss' (I don't know miss). When I call it 'kalokohan' (mischief), he contends: 'para masaya naman miss' (so we can be jolly/have a laugh miss).
Kok and Skusta	Feb. 7	We discuss the Visayan accent, which Skusta calls 'matigas' (hard), with Kok agreeing 'Oo' (yes). I ask them how Hawai'i is for them. They find it rather boring – limited places to ramble, they say. They explain that in the Philippines, young men like them like going to the computer café and basketball court. Kok says he isn't among those who go to Waikīkī Beach because his parents don't allow him to go out; they say he's too young. Skusta says, 'Totoo naman' (it's true), and Kok laughs. They tell me they go to Kalākaua to play basketball. Then we discuss their education back in the Philippines, which involved mixed language teaching (e.g. Ilonggo and English). The conversation circles back to how they are a minority in Hawai'i among their mostly Ilokano peers. I ask about their language knowledge and find both of them know four or five languages with varying degrees of proficiency and in varying domains. Then we discuss their loud use of Filipino in ESL 9/10 with the Ilokano majority (Excerpt 11), and like Cookie they both say it's 'patawa lang' (just for laughs). Finally, we discuss challenges for them studying in an English-medium school, and they express a need for the teacher to speak clearly and slowly.
Flow-G	Feb. 21	We start by talking about how Filipino languages can help with class work, but he says only the educational assistant uses them. 'Sila lang po yung nagsasabi kung ano yun – kung hindo ko po maintindihan' (Only she tells me what it is – if I don't understand). I confirm, then, that his friends don't do it? He snickers and replies, 'Hindi po.[19] Puro kalokohan po yung mga yon' (No. They're just full of mischief.) He points out that Skusta speaks loudly; Cookie drums.[20] He and his buddies play basketball in Kalākaua Park on weekends and go to the beach. He likes to write lyrics, especially in Filipino, and he corrects my pronunciation of 'pagbasa' (reading). He says he understands about half of the words in the story they're reading, Mildred D. Taylor's *The Gold Cadillac*. We discuss why they don't use English to help each other out with the class work, only Filipino, and he says they can get teased on their English (Excerpt 12). He speaks English with cousins and nieces/nephews who are local, presumably because this is the language they understand, and with friends in the cafeteria.[21]
Juliana	Mar. 7	Juliana observes that her male classmates tease the teacher – 'pinagtritripan' (bullying, playing tricks on).[22] I ask if it happens in other classes, and she says only this one. Then, I ask what LOTEs she hears in class, and to my surprise, she mentions Korean and Chuukese, which I have not recorded. I ask if she has heard any Filipino, and she says 'Ilokano lang po. (indistinguishable mumbling) Ilonggo (indistinguishable mumbling)'. I then ask, 'Wala kang naririnig na Tagalog sa klase?' (You don't hear any Tagalog in class?), which my recorders have picked up a great deal of. She says, 'Meron po. Pero knoti lang'. (There is. But just a bit.) I believe this non-factual answer was Juliana's attempt to save face – she may have felt that I would judge her for Filipino use, especially since a lot of it is off-task, as Flow-G admitted. When I ask why people use LOTEs in class, she says 'Para maabot po yung mga pangarap nila' (so they can fully reach their desires, i.e. fully express themselves). Of her own language and literacy skills, she says she writes better in Filipino than in Ilokano, and enjoys writing Disney fanfiction. The conversation returns to Rayna, the student teacher, of whom Juliana says: 'Hindi po niya maintindihan kung ano po pinaguusapan. Alam po ni Ms Rayna kung binabastos na siya'. (She can't understand what's being said. Ms Rayna knows when she's already being disrespected.) On the other hand, Juliana notes that Filipino is good for explaining 'figurative language'.

In addition to interviewing students, I interviewed both teachers to get a sense of their cultural and educational backgrounds and migration histories, and to develop a deeper sense of their bi/multilingual repertoires (see Appendix 2 for student and teacher interview questions). I interviewed Juan and Kaori twice: to collect biographical information in February and at the end of my data collection in May to do participant checking of overall patterns of classroom language use.[23] Rayna, the student teacher in both classes, came into the study later on, and I obtained her consent to record and transcribe classroom interactions when she was teaching, but did not interview her.

I tailored interview questions based on recent interesting bi/multilingual interactions in the data, sometimes choosing the next interviewee based on them, or creating a 'data handout' for the participant to look over prior to the interview (Appendix 3). The choice to do so led the data gathering to grow in directions that I felt were good leads. At the same time, I was able to focus several students' attention on the same phenomenon, for example, by asking Kix and Jhon about whether Ilokano was useful for learning in English 9, or by getting several Filipino boys' perspectives on why they used Filipino to 'goof off' in ESL 9/10.

(4) *Audio-recordings of classroom interaction.* I recorded all of the lessons I observed from January to May to better capture moments of bi/multilingual language use that I would transcribe and analyze in detail. There were two recordings per lesson, as there were two audio-recorders that I put near the students around whom much oral translanguaging activity happened – Kix and Eufia in English 9 and Flow-G and Skusta in ESL 9/10.[24] This data was central to the study; it allowed me to see what translanguaging, code-switching, self- and other-stylization and language crossing meant in two classroom ecologies. I used conventions of transcription informed by Gumperz (1982) and Hepburn and Bolden (2013), eliciting pseudonyms for the teachers and students who agreed to participate in the study. Following the work of scholars such as Rampton (1995), Talmy (2008) and Lamb (2015), I not only focused on participants' performance of their ethnolinguistic identities through the use of LOTEs but also on how they constructed other identities (e.g. academic, cosmopolitan) by drawing on resources in their language repertoires and contextualizing these in the moment. I was also interested in how different classroom participants negotiated asymmetries in linguistic and cultural knowledge.

Moreover, by following Rampton's (1995) methods in inviting participants to examine cases of language use that I had recorded and transcribed, I could ask them about the meanings produced in these cases and check my interpretations of the interactions with them. The participants' reports were not privileged over my own analysis; however, based on the principles of IS (Gumperz, 1982), participant perspectives were important in helping me achieve emic understandings of the data. Asking students to give metalinguistic commentary helped me clarify how they understood each other's language use, for example, whether the language labels students used (e.g. English, Filipino/Tagalog, Ilokano) matched what I would call the languages they used, as well as whether they were translanguaging or code-switching in line with my perceptions.

To develop analytical themes, I drew on types of *metalinguistic commentary* proposed by Rymes (2014), such as code labelling, pronunciation evaluation and forms of address, which could be studied through audio data alone. As these code labellings, pronunciation evaluations and forms of address (e.g. vocatives like 'oppa'/big brother from Korean dramas) emerged in conversation during class, I noted that the interviews did *not* yield the only examples of linguistic metacommentary, as participants regularly assessed their own and others' language use and performance as part of their social lives and not only when asked to do so by the researcher.

(5)   *Secondary research*. I collected documents such as reports commissioned by the Hawai'i Department of Education (Hawai'i P-20 Partnerships for Education, 2018) on Hawai'i's English language learners, data from the website of the WIDA Consortium, which administers the ESL exit test across 40 US states and the District of Columbia, handouts from staff meetings (demographic information, three-year plans, course catalogs) and artifacts from the classes (worksheets, activities, tests/quizzes). While I never intended to carry out fine-grained analysis of these documents, they helped to contextualize the audio-recorded activities and connect the course curricula to state and nationwide curricula. I also read about the history of language policy and education in Hawai'i by taking an undergraduate course on Hawai'i Creole and reading about Asian settler colonialism (e.g. Fujikane & Okamura, 2008).

3.5 Data Analysis

My first analysis of field notes and audio-recordings involved deductive and inductive coding[25] of the practices of each classroom's small culture. The deductive and inductive codes fell into four broad themes that helped me understand who in each class presented themselves and was recognized as a valued model of bi/multilingualism, what counted as a legitimate instantiation of a code and the social processes through which these understandings were mutually constructed. Analysis of dialogues and participants' reflections on them showed that some students experienced visible changes in their linguistic identity positioning over

Table 3.2 Thematic analysis of classroom data

	English 9	ESL 9/10
Theme 1: Episodes evoking linguistic competencies	• Academic competence in English • General English proficiency • Proficiency in a first or heritage language • Academic competence in a first or heritage language • Display of knowledge of a non-heritage LOTE (e.g. Korean)	
Theme 2: Other linguistic episodes	• Teacher (Juan or his regular substitute Ed) speaks Ilokano • Recognizing shared linguistic resources	• Language use with Kaori, the student teacher Rayna and the Filipino-speaking educational assistant
	• Teachers explicitly encourage translanguaging • Translanguaging, code-switching, stylization, language crossing • Scaffolding and echoing • Clearing up language misunderstandings • Metalanguage: code-labelling, pronunciation evaluation, forms of address	
Theme 3: Individual student data	• Diana, He, Jhon, Kix, Kleo	• Flow-G, Juliana, Skusta
Theme 4: Characteristics of the small culture	• Ilokano as a regular learning resource • Affiliation with Korean	• Machismo, being loud, goofing off • Classroom norms, counterculture and subculture
	• Multilingualism normalized and frequent in oral classroom interaction	

several months. Some of these students' names appear under 'Theme 3: Individual student data', and two students are discussed in Chapter 6, in which I explore how these two students' identities were shaped by language practices over different timescales (Mortimer & Wortham, 2015).

Since the social construction of linguistic and academic competence was a focus of the study, I first analyzed deductive themes about linguistic competencies (Theme 1). For these, I coded data related to the display of knowledge of various languages (whether stylized or generative/proficient) and explicit assertions of language proficiency and challenges to it – such as this conversation in Filipino: 'Ilokano ako gago' [*I'm Ilokano bastard*]; 'Pero sakin ka nagtatanong pag Ilokano gago' [*But you're asking me how to say things in Ilokano bastard*]. I also coded assertions of, and challenges to, students' academic competence across languages.

The second set of themes involved other language episodes. Some of these were inductive, in that I examined the data to see what other themes were recurring and how they related to each other (Strauss & Corbin, 1997). These included, for both classes, (1) echoing, repeating what someone else has said, e.g. when students did collaborative writing or worked out a passage of text, with more proficient students scaffolding their peers; (2) explicit encouragement of heritage (HL) or L1 use by the teacher; and (3) clearing up misunderstandings due to pronunciation, grammar, word choice, etc. I also coded deductively, with pre-established labels, for (1) metalanguage, or explicit talk about language forms; and (2) (trans)languaging,[26] code-switching, stylization and language crossing.

Other language episodes were about who typically used which languages with whom, or unusual language choices such as the cheeky use of Filipino to the student teacher, Rayna, which she could not understand. Conversely, Juan's students did not use Filipino with him, even though he could understand it, as they could use their more intimate shared language, Ilokano, for rapport-building and English for class purposes most of the time.

The third type of theme involved interesting data surrounding particular students. This data shows changes in positioning, identity and language use on different timescales (Mortimer & Wortham, 2015) – e.g. how Skusta was gradually ostracized by the 'loud' Filipino boys over a semester; how Juliana changed the way she participated in class due to a catalytic encounter with some boys; how the English-emergent newcomer Diana was supported by Ilokano-speaking peers to develop her English by leaps and bounds; how these Ilokano-speaking students became more respectful of the Cantonese HL singleton He; or why Jhon, a reluctant oral translanguager, was finally able to translanguage. There is no space to cover all of this individual data in this book, but Chapter 6 provides two illustrative cases.

The fourth type of theme was related to classroom norms, counterculture and subculture. For example, in ESL 9/10, the machismo of the vocal majority of Filipino boys undermined the teacher's authority and classroom norms. However, by the end of the semester, Rayna and the girls, not all of whom were Filipino, spoke up more often in English to get lessons back on track. In English 9, translanguaging involved not only Ilokano to do class work, but also Korean, the Ilokano L1 majority's language of affiliation, through which they displayed cosmopolitanism. For thematic analysis, I used NVivo, which allows for analysis of a large amount of data that is too unwieldy to examine using word processing software (Figure 3.4).

Figure 3.4 Working with NVivo 12

Following these thematic analyses, I constructed diagrams by hand of the social networks within each class reflecting (1) who was more or less vocal, in *any* language(s), and (2) who seemed close to whom, relationally speaking (see Chapters 4 and 5). Then, I brought up the data from relevant themes and focused on these in my interactional analysis of dialogues involving particular students, studying their dynamic identity trajectories across time (Chapter 6).

Before I discuss those findings, I first examine my own bi/multilingualism and identity bids, and the effects they had on participants, data collection and data analysis. One significant point is my identity as an ethnically Filipino university researcher who likely raised the status of Filipino languages even further in the school and contributed to their hegemony within the research site despite their marginalization in North American education.

3.6 Researcher Positionality: Sociohistorical

Since analysis of bi/multilingual repertoires and practices is derived from one's own bi/multilingual experiences, it is worth reflecting on my own background. I was born in the Philippines in 1986 and immigrated to Hong Kong at age five when my father's employer, the Hong Kong Shanghai Banking Corporation, posted him abroad. In 1996, when I was 10, the bank relocated our family to Vancouver, Canada, prior to the UK's return of Hong Kong to China in 1997. In British Hong Kong, I lived in an 'expatriate bubble' and learned no more than a few words of Cantonese, but attended the German Swiss International School, which offered English-medium education except for German class. I started learning French in elementary school after moving to Canada, and continued taking it in secondary school; even though it is rarely spoken outside of Quebec, it is a common academic subject nationwide. (I have since forgotten German, but have conversational proficiency in Tagalog and French.)

It must be noted that Filipino culture and languages do not have much cultural value in North America, despite the great many Filipinos there. The attempt to erase a Filipino ethnic identity was satirized in a *Honolulu Star Bulletin* cartoon (Figure 3.5) by Filipino American artist Corky Trinidad,[27] who explained:

> Filipinos born in Hawaii, as soon as they reached the age of reason, and the Filipinos migrating from the Philippines, as soon as they left the airport, became Chinese-Spanish or Spanish-Chinese-Singaporean or Spanish-Portuguese-Basque or Chinese-American-Irish or some such combination. (Trinidad, 2005)

According to Trinidad, they are not exactly lying, as Spaniards, Japanese, Americans, Indians, Chinese, Dutch, British and Russians all played some

Figure 3.5   Trinidad (2005) (courtesy of the *Honolulu Star-Advertiser*)

part in the Philippines' colonization – the primary colonizing countries being Spain (from the 16th century to 1898) and the US (from the turn of the 20th century until the end of WWII; Japan occupied the Philippines during the WWII period). While identity is a social construction, the extent to which Filipinos stretch their identity claims in certain situations such as those described by Trinidad has always struck me as both ridiculous and tragic. This has led to my fascination with the identity negotiations of students from less commonly taught language (LCTL) backgrounds whose L1s/HLs are not well represented in the public domain – especially those from populations with limited cultural, social and economic capital, whether they are from blue- or white-collar families.

One characteristic of this population is that their HL loss due to both social stigma and lack of learning resources tends to lead to receptive-only proficiency (i.e. 'I understand some of the language but can't produce it myself'), hence an inability to translanguage in oral communication, which in turn makes such multilingual students under-represented in studies of translanguaging and code-switching, as these largely involve written transcriptions of oral classroom conversation as their main data source. Of course, these HL speakers of LCTLs may perform other multilingual practices, such as stylization, because of the relatively stark separation of domains of language acquisition (i.e. little HL use beyond the home; see Mendoza & Parba, 2019).[28] That is another reason why I draw on different constructs for multilingual practices, rather than translanguaging alone, in this study.

It is now necessary to explain how I use the terms 'Filipino' and 'Tagalog', and this requires reference to some of the Philippines' colonial history. Unlike other countries colonized by Spain, the Philippines obviously did not acquire Spanish as a widely spoken language. BBC Mundo, the Spanish language section of the BBC, has a seven minute documentary on the question of why the Philippines is not a Spanish-speaking country, reproduced in a short article in the Filipino online magazine *Esquire*.[29] Briefly, there were few Spanish colonizers in the Philippines except for missionaries, and the missionaries were overwhelmed with the degree of linguistic diversity they faced (about a dozen major regional languages and hundreds of indigenous ones). These priests made do by learning the natives' lingua francas (just as they did with Nahuatl in Mexico and Quechua in Peru) and using those lingua francas to convert people to Catholicism. Thus, the missionaries learned the northern language Tagalog, which became the national language, called 'Filipino' in its official lingua franca form, and the central/southern language Cebuano, also called Bisaya/Visayan; it is the main language of the Visayas and Mindanao, the central and southern parts of the country. Only Philippine elites spoke Spanish in over 300 years of Spanish rule, and had the Philippine independence movement in the 1890s succeeded – ousting Spain and keeping out the US[30] – the Philippines might have been another Spanish-speaking country today. But instead, the succeeding colonizing power, the US, who had won a territory where only 2%–3% of the inhabitants spoke Spanish (Gonzalez, 1980),[31] transformed the Philippines into an Outer Circle English-speaking country (Kachru, 1986) through public education and mass media.

Today, the influence of Spanish is subtly pervasive: it is evident in lexical similarity between Filipino and Cebuano, the two most prominent Philippine languages besides English, arising from many borrowed Spanish words. A creole called Chavacano in the southwestern Philippines was born from a mix of Philippine, Castilian and Mexican Spanish after Spain granted the governance of the Philippines to the viceroy of Mexico in the 17th century, as Mexico was geographically closer. In addition, many Filipino names are from Spanish – including the country's name, after King Philip II of Spain.

When the US granted the Philippines political, if not economic, independence at the end of WWII, Manila elites moved to institute their primary language, Tagalog, as the national language, and in the 1950s, it was renamed 'Pilipino' in recognition of this status. In K–12 schools, students tend to be taught in this language,[32] though science and math may be in English and higher education is in English. According to Tupas and Lorente (2014), this leads to the intellectual and cultural marginalization of other linguistic groups, with formal education in the dominant ethnolinguistic group's national language plus English running alongside informal oral translanguaging including other languages – also the case with other incredibly linguistically diverse countries in Southeast Asia, South Asia and Africa (Skutnabb-Kangas *et al.*, 2009). Additionally, there can be strict ideological separation between 'official' languages in education, such as an English-only policy in English-medium classes (or, if Filipino is used, no 'Taglish', which is considered colloquial and inappropriate for school). Language ideologies that students were immersed in *prior* to their immigration to an English-dominant country will impact their views on translanguaging and ELF, and their evaluations of the language use of people from the same country in the US, as I explain in Chapter 5. These ideologies are often related to social class and regional inequalities transported from the home country, leading to differences in bi/multilingual language acquisition patterns within the same national or ethnic group (Valdés, 2001).

Politically, the Philippines is divided into three main regions: Luzon, the Visayas and Mindanao. In the middle and south (the Visayas and Mindanao), Bisaya/Visayan is the lingua franca, though it is more commonly called Cebuano (which is also an ethnic identity, i.e. Cebuanos). In Luzon, the more economically developed northern part of the country, two languages, Tagalog and Ilokano, dominate. Roughly 85% of Filipinos speak one of eight languages as their L1: Tagalog, Cebuano, Ilokano, Hiligaynon, Bikol, Samar-Leyte (Waray), Kapampangan and Pangasinan (McFarland, 2009). In addition, there are over 100 indigenous languages.

Recent developments have offered hope for mother tongues, or at least the 8–12 main regional languages. This has come in the form of Mother Tongue Based Modern Language Education (MTB–MLE) in the elementary years (Wa-Mbaleka, 2014), even though a student may *still* experience being taught in a second language under MTB–MLE if they do not speak the regional language at home. Layers of subtractive bilingualism may ensue: attrition of mother tongue upon starting school, hurdle transitioning from MTB–MLE to Filipino in later grades and struggles dealing with English higher education.

However, another positive development is the promotion of the term 'Filipino' to describe the national language in ways similar to Li and Zhu's (2013) term 'global Chinese'. In 1973, the Philippine National Assembly began a movement to replace Pilipino with a hybrid national language that would serve as a vehicle for various Philippine ethnolinguistic knowledges and practices (Tupas & Lorente, 2014). Yet, the extent to which this language – 'Filipino' – truly exists, or whether it is simply Tagalog/Pilipino rebranded, is a controversial issue, and I do not think there is a single truth behind the matter. In this book, I use both terms, choosing 'Tagalog' to describe my HL, as the social justice orientation behind the term *Filipino* does not render the word used to describe an ethnolinguistic group, *Tagalogs*, obsolete. However, more important than this terminological debate is the need to recognize how the language functions as a hegemonic national language, a hybrid pan-ethnic language and a low-prestige diasporic language. When it comes to the empirical data (e.g. interviews), I use the language labels participants have used.

3.7 Researcher Positionality: At the Research Site

Although classroom linguistic ethnographers are rarely members of the communities on which they do research, they are not simply 'outsiders' coming in to study participants, as pointed out by Creese *et al.* (2015), who studied youths' translanguaging in extracurricular HL classes in the UK. For example, Jonsson, a member of their research team, wrote about four language-related social positions that multilingual researchers have with their research sites when they study translanguaging:

> First and foremost, it is practical to understand the languages in which most school events take place since it allows me to immediately (without interpretation/translation) understand a particular situation… Second, sharing the same linguistic capital as the students brings me closer to the 'in-group'… Third, the mere fact that I am a bilingual, even though I might not necessarily be bilingual in the same languages in which the students are bilingual (for instance, they may position themselves as bilingual in Swedish and Greek, whereas I position myself as bilingual in Swedish and Spanish) makes us share the feeling of being a bilingual… Fourth, as a teacher at the school suggested, I contribute to the legitimization of the minority language Spanish in a context where Swedish is the dominant majority language by being a Spanish-speaking researcher, thus raising the status of Spanish in the eyes of the students. (Creese *et al.*, 2015: 138)

Jonsson captures four aspects of bi/multilingualism pertinent to linguistic ethnography: first, bi/multilingual proficiency for practical data collection purposes; second, knowledge of a group's language as cultural capital for the researcher; third, a shared identity as a bi/multilingual as cultural capital for the researcher even if the languages they share are not the same as those of the research participants; and fourth, authority conferred upon the researcher's language(s) in the site, due to the researcher's presumed academic expertise, and consequently on the participants who share those languages.

I reflect on my own positionality in my research environment with regard to these issues. My conversational oral proficiency in Filipino and my access to an Ilokano translator (one of Juan's former students whom he introduced me to, who was a BEd student at my university) allowed me to understand classroom participants' interactions – the first *in situ*, the second retrospectively. Although I could understand most classroom Filipino talk on the fly, unless it was very soft or fast, cultural and academic references were lost on me, and for the most part I had to let them go, since meetings with my translator, who grew up in Ilocos and Hawai'i, had to prioritize Ilokano. When it came to Ilokano, my translator was not only a translator but a generational and ethnolinguistic culture broker, giving explanations of data I would otherwise ignore. For example, he explained that what I heard as 'Enzo' was 'friend zone' (i.e. your crush just wants to be your friend), and when students kept saying 'tree port' during a group activity, he recognized it as a negotiation to cut the paper into 3/4 – a standard size for classroom paper in the Philippines.

Moreover, since our data sessions took place in my graduate student office, which was shared with a Korean colleague, she overheard one of the dialogues and explained that 'tangjinjaem' was not a real Korean word but one coined by the band BTS. Data collection in linguistic ethnography is thus affected by the language repertoires and cultural knowledge of the researchers and their access to language brokers. At the same time, a researcher's linguistic and cultural positionality goes beyond proficiency in various languages, which I discuss next.

Despite the fact that I mainly grew up in Canada, I felt recognized as a Filipino by staff and students at the school, even though I do not speak Tagalog fluently and do not speak my other HLs (Ilonggo and Waray) at all. For example, Filipino staff at the school more than once asked me, 'Saan ka sa atin?' – literally: 'Where are you with us?', i.e. 'Which part of the Philippines are you from?' Occasionally, I was invited to have lunch with them, and share homemade pancit (noodles) brought by an educational assistant from Panay in the Visayas. When I told her my grandfather was also from Panay, a primarily Ilonggo-speaking region, she taught me my first few words of Ilonggo. While I do not think that this had a direct bearing on the data collection, it made me feel welcome and positively affected my other interactions and mental focus.

Kaori's students, too, also talked freely with me in Filipino, but I used English with Juan's students since I almost never heard them speak Filipino. It is possible that some friend groups who were all Ilokano spoke Ilokano, while mixed friend groups spoke Filipino – or English in the case of He's group, which consisted of him (a Cantonese HL speaker) and three ethnically Filipino students who were not in the English 9 class but used that classroom for smartphone gaming during recess. Friend group language choice is an issue that can be investigated in an ethnography that looks beyond the classroom rather than being focused on the small cultures of specific classes like this study.

The third issue that Jonsson mentions, that of 'bi/multilingual' as a shared identity position even when people do not share languages, is important to consider in light of the wider social context. The school celebrated its diversity in cultural events and in the linguistic landscape, and being a bi/multilingual was the norm in this school where many staff were also bi/multilingual. I, and my study on translanguaging, were bolstered by the normalization of bi/multilingualism in the state and school, and from my reception as a Filipino, a member of the majority group at the school.

This brings me to the fourth issue: how I must have contributed to the legitimization of *both* bi/multilingualism in general (which I embrace) *and* Filipino-ness in particular (which I have mixed feelings about, given that the school already had a Filipino majority). It is notable that most of the students who chose to participate in all aspects of my study were of Filipino ancestry. Since I explained the study in English and Filipino, partly to demonstrate my proficiency in Filipino in a positive identity bid, I may have given the impression that it was Filipino ELLs or heritage speakers of Filipino, rather than translanguaging, that I was studying. I also think that ethnocentricity found its way into my subconscious research decisions; for example, when there was a new Filipino girl in Juan's class, Diana, who was quickly incorporated into the Ilokano-speaking group's translanguaging practices, I gave her a pseudonym and invited her into the study even though I didn't understand any Ilokano – whereas a new Chinese girl who entered Kaori's class at the same time only appeared as 'new girl' in my field notes, even though I knew a few dozen words in her language, Mandarin. This girl, to whom I later assigned the pseudonym Ellen, seemed to be an English beginner and was largely silent, but Summer (a Mandarin L1 student who was a singleton for most of the study until Ellen arrived) was occasionally asked to explain things to Ellen, and I regret that I did not follow up with Summer how the conversation went (even if only in field notes rather than audio-recordings).

Moreover, even though I did not have a Marshallese or Chuukese translator, I could have asked Marshallese and Micronesian students whether they had used their languages during each class at the end of class (e.g. writing yes/no on a cue card and a few sentences how, if so). The Federated States of Micronesia has 18 languages, the most widely spoken being Chuukese, Kosraean, Yapese and Pohnpeian. About half of Micronesians speak Chuukese as their L1, and others may speak it as a lingua franca; due to colonization, English is also widely used and Japanese is spoken by older generations. Thus, there were lost opportunities to study the multilingualism of non-Filipino students who may not have consented to be audio-recorded and/or interviewed, but might have shared more about their translanguaging with me in less invasive ways, if I had been more active in inviting them to do so.

I conclude this chapter by acknowledging the self-centeredness of researcher positionality. At the same time, I make the discussion of this potential self-centeredness and individual positionality key themes in this book's examination of what it would take to create an equitable bi/multilingual classroom. In the following chapters, I explore what kinds of multilingual language use can be heard in high school English classes where non-English languages are permitted but not part of official pedagogical practices. I examine how students benefit or experience challenges from oral multilingual communication, how being in the classroom linguistic majority or minority plays a role, how being a relative newcomer or old-timer (i.e. L1 or English dominant) impacts individual experiences and how speaking 'standard' or academic forms of English and other languages or being well-versed in school-based print literacies matters in legitimizing one's translanguaging practices.

Again, I reiterate the research questions: who in each class presents themselves and is recognized as a valued model of bi/multilingualism? What counts as a legitimate instantiation of a code? What are the social processes through which these understandings are mutually constructed? What are the consequences for people? And what are the implications for teaching and learning in plurilingual, English as a lingua franca classrooms? In interpreting my findings, I draw on my expertise in types of multilingual language use, my life knowledge as a multilingual Filipino-Canadian and what I learned as a student in Hawai'i.

Notes

(1) The quote appeared in an opinion piece titled 'Obama is a Product of Hawaii's Melting Pot' in the online version of Hawai'i's *Mail Tribune*. However, the link is no longer available.

(2) I include the detail about *Moby Dick* to point out that linguistic superdiversity is not unique to the modern age, as some translanguaging researchers have claimed: it existed in the whaling industry, on Vasco de Gama's ship, on the Silk Road, in the Roman Empire, etc.

(3) Some linguists propose that African American English is similarly a decreolized creole.

(4) Interestingly, when I was part of a group of volunteers who gave a Pidgin knowledge quiz to the students in the Filipino American club at the school where I did my doctoral research, we found that the students (like myself) knew very little, leading my co-volunteer to marvel that this was not the case with another group of ethnically Filipino students at another school.

(5) https://www.civilbeat.org/2011/05/11156-filipinos-overtake-japanese-as-top-hawaii-group/

(6) The school in this study is a blue-collar school with a mix of kama'āina and relatively recent immigrants, mostly from the Philippines. It was difficult to spot any white students. Regardless of diaspora, a school census at the time of my study stated that out of 10 students roughly six were Filipino, one Samoan, one Micronesian, one Native Hawaiian and one of another background.

(7) Arguably, the agreement is a continuation of exploitation rather than compensation.

(8) Kathy Jetnil-Kijiner's poetry has explored how Kanaka Maoli, kamaʻāina and immigrants of varying ethnicities hold negative stereotypes of Micronesians: https://jkijiner.wordpress.com/2011/04/13/micronesia-i-lessons-from-hawaii/.

(9) https://jkijiner.wordpress.com/2011/04/13/tell-them/.

(10) In spring 2019, I presented the findings of the study in the school library during each block of a single day, to teachers who were free to attend during their spare period. I also presented the findings at local conferences such as the annual Hawaiʻi TESOL Conference and the Hawaiʻi Department of Education Multilingual Symposium 2020.

(11) See an accessible introduction to the policy at https://www.hawaiipublicschools.org/TeachingAndLearning/StudentLearning/HawaiianEducation/Pages/HA.aspx.

(12) The Hawaiʻi Department of Education (HI-DOE) allows students to earn the Seal of Biliteracy with Hawaiian-plus-another-language or English-plus-another-language, and HI-DOE language assessments broaden the range of world languages to include Filipino (Tagalog), Ilokano and Vietnamese. However, no assessments are offered in Chuukese, Kosraean, Marshallese, Pohnpeian, Samoan or Yapese. For many Pacific Islander languages, literacies can be more oral than textual (Hawaiian being an exception, as the language has a literary tradition using the Latin alphabet as well as oral traditions). This means that many Pacific Islander students cannot earn the Seal of Biliteracy with their languages because 'literacy' in this sense does not fit into a US standardized testing framework that prioritizes textual literacy.

(13) Linguistic ethnography in the UK and Europe bears a strong resemblance to the linguistic anthropology of education/educational linguistics in the US, which Wortham (2008) describes as being concerned with 'language form, use, ideology, and domain'.

(14) These discrepancies did not happen often and are not the focus of this study. However, they reveal aspects of students' identity positionings as well as language ideologies. For example, one Filipino student, Juliana, reported that nobody spoke Filipino in ESL 9/10 during a one-on-one interview, when in fact Filipino talk was pervasive in the class. When I asked her if anyone translanguaged, she named students with other L1s as those who spoke their languages, even though my recorders did not pick up these languages at all. Since L1 use in class is sometimes constructed by teachers as undesirable, not only in the US but also in the Philippines where Filipino and English are the official languages, Juliana, who was a part-Ilokano, part-Tagalog student and had recourse to Filipino quite often in ESL 9/10, might have simply denied what she thought the *interviewer* thought was 'misbehavior' through L1 use. However, reported attitudes toward L1 use and other forms of translanguaging usually matched what students actually did in class.

(15) Eufia and Rizze spoke mock Chinese to He around Lunar New Year, calling him 'Hexing' and teasing him with 'Kong Hey Hexing'. When I recorded this, I told Juan about it, which led him to have a talk with Eufia and Rizze. This later led to Rizze saying in class, 'I didn't mean to hurt you, He', and both young women treated him much better from then on.

(16) It is more likely for people to think something underhanded is happening when a language that only a *few* people speak is heard, rather than a language spoken by a good number of people (but not everyone). This pragmatic consideration can lead to privileging the class majority non-English language and minoritizing/stigmatizing others in oral meaning-making (Beiler, 2021).

(17) I did not probe further into this comment. It could indicate that Kleo orients to the dominant language order by being closer to the Filipino students than Micronesian students, but it could also mean that she really is teased for not speaking her HL in a native-like way, and so avoids it.

(18) This suggests the precarity of using a HL, especially one that is less commonly taught and has little sociocultural capital: you can be judged by L1 speakers whose only capital as speakers of this language is their native-like way of speaking it.

(19) While English 9 interviews took place in English, ESL 9/10 interviews took place in Filipino. Of the English 9 students, only Kix could have spoken Filipino with me, but we used English for reasons of distance. In ESL 9/10, I believe students used Filipino due to less English proficiency and because this was the most commonly spoken LOTE in the class. The inclusion of 'po' every few words in the transcripts of all the ESL 9/10 students I interviewed shows they addressed me with the polite register, which is what one would use with a teacher. As with article choice in English, where to put 'po' in a sentence is a native-like intuition that L1 speakers cannot really explain the rules of.

(20) Cookie was actually an amazing drummer, but lost his drums when he moved to the US. He tried to maintain his ability by drumming in class with whatever was available.

(21) I believe Flow-G uses English with these interlocutors because he is close to them. Kix and Jhon also mentioned using a language with someone because you are close, or *not* using a language because you are *not* close. That language can be English or a LOTE, but if there are face threats and people are not close, it will not be used.

(22) From this study, I learned that there is actually a Filipino word for bullying. In an earlier paper, I suggested an English borrowing was necessary (Mendoza & Parba, 2019).

(23) Interviews and participant checking were not the same event, in that interviews probed into participants' explanations for their language use (their understandings of raw data/transcripts or my field notes), whereas participant checking involved participants reading drafts of my dissertation and this book. While both students and teachers were involved in interviews about linguistic events, participant checking was only for teachers, as there is sensitive subject matter in the manuscript (about teasing/bullying, disrespecting the student teacher and so on). This book was published the school year after the student research participants graduated, and they can revisit events from an anonymous and less socially precarious position should they happen to pick up the book in a visit to their alma mater.

(24) There was no special reason for having two recorders. That was how many high-quality audio-recorders I could afford, and how much I could feasibly transcribe in the timeframe of the study. It was not difficult to identify who was speaking since I had already been observing students for some months. Occasionally, a statement would be so brief that the speaker was unclear, and in this case the reader will see that I have put a generic label such as 'Male student'. Such an issue could have been remedied by choosing video-recording instead of audio-recording, but it is harder to obtain research ethics approval for video-recording in a K–12 classroom setting, and De Costa (2014) advises researchers not to use data collection methods that are more intrusive than necessary for answering research questions. For linguistic ethnographies, audio-recordings generally suffice (Copland & Creese, 2015).

(25) That is, some codes were pre-determined by the research questions while others emerged from the data.

(26) Swain and Watanabe (2012) define 'languaging' as the process of discussing which target forms are correct, or should be used, in a final product. This discussion can involve use of the whole linguistic, multimodal repertoire to negotiate the forms. García (2009) and Li (2018) define 'translanguaging' as using the whole repertoire to communicate or make meaning, not necessarily target form-related.

(27) The Wikipedia pages related to Francisco Flores 'Corky' Trinidad Jr (1939–2009) explain that he was known for his editorial cartoons for the *Honolulu Star Bulletin* and the Vietnam War comic strip *Nguyen Charlie*.

(28) I suspect that oral translanguaging between Filipino languages and English, and *transglossia* (Dovchin *et al.*, 2017), or translanguaging in digital spaces, between Filipino languages, English and languages of affiliation such as Japanese and/or Korean in social media, are more common in the Philippines than in the diaspora because it is in the Philippines' pop culture where such translanguaging actually happens. However, empirical research is needed to confirm this intuition.

(29) https://www.esquiremag.ph/culture/lifestyle/why-philippines-spanish-colony-language-a00225-20210515.

(30) Although the Philippines was not theirs to give, the Spanish ceded its Pacific territories to the US when it lost the Spanish-American war.

(31) This small percentage can belie the cultural value attached to Spanish. For example, the BBC Mundo video explains that although Spanish is not widely spoken, the oldest and most revered classics in Philippine literature are in Spanish.

(32) This is supported by interviews with Filipino students who participated in the study, most of whom said they did not read/write as well in their home languages as in Filipino. The exception was Kix, who received an English-medium education in the Philippines except for Filipino class.

4 'Sheltered' English 9: Multilingual Majorities, Minorities, Singletons, Newcomers and Old-Timers

In this chapter, I examine Juan's English 9 class in terms of the translanguaging of students in the Ilokano first language (L1) newcomer majority, ethnolinguistic minorities and singletons, and English-dominant 'old-timers' with different heritage languages (HLs). While this chapter's findings may be seen as common sense, what I want to highlight is the fact that the translanguaging practices of the classroom bi/multilingual majority have different affordances and limitations compared to the translanguaging practices of the classroom linguistic minorities, singletons and English-dominant students. At the same time, what is key to getting *any* student to draw on language resources they would not typically see as belonging to academic work – heightening the critical, social justice potential of translanguaging – is an activity that is pragmatically appropriate in the linguistic ecology of the class, and one in which the student's language repertoire is seen in an asset-oriented rather than a deficit-oriented light.

4.1 English 9 Class Activities

All English 9 courses at the school (sheltered, regular and honors) delivered the same curriculum, even though sheltered courses enrolled only students with the English as a second language (ESL) designation to allow for more explicit focus on language points in addition to immersion in a variety of literary works. The Springboard English 9 textbook (College Board, 2017) used across the US, with its theme 'Coming of Age', was the main course text; however, Juan relied on the textbook less in the second half of the school year, continuing the theme with *To Kill a Mockingbird*, *Romeo and Juliet* and one of his favorites, Sherman Alexie's *Flight*. Table 4.1 gives an overview of what the class did on the days I visited, from mid-January to early May. Genres studied included poetry, literary criticism, novels and drama. This overview highlights

Table 4.1 Sampling of lessons[1] in English 9

Jan. 17*	Metaphors and similes: Students must come up with, draw, and write a paragraph about their life metaphor based on the prompt, 'My life is a…'.
Jan. 24	Article about causes of anxiety and stress in adolescents; discussion on sources of anxiety and stress in students' lives.
Jan. 31	Students do individual three-minute presentations in front of the class about different types of adverse childhood experiences (ACE). (Examples: physical abuse, emotional abuse, sexual abuse and substance abuse.) At the end of the class, students count how many types of ACE appear in the protagonist Zits' life in the first chapters of Sherman Alexie's *Flight*.
Feb. 7*	Groups analyze Sherman Alexie's essay on why he writes gritty novels about adverse childhood experiences for his young adult audience.
Feb. 14	Small-group and whole-class discussions of recurring themes, similes and metaphors in *Flight*.
Feb. 21	Analysis of Paul Laurence Dunbar's poem 'We Wear the Mask' (late 19th century); application of the metaphor 'wearing a mask' to characters in *Flight*, including Zits' absentee father.
Feb. 28	Small-group and whole-class discussions of metaphors and similes throughout *Flight*, including what the title means.
Mar. 7	Poetry-writing workshop by local poet Celeste Gallo (pseudonym), who immigrated to Hawai'i as a child from the Visayas in the Philippines.
Mar. 28*	Beginning *Romeo and Juliet*: students work on an activity involving 'Who's who' in the cast of characters.
Apr. 4*	In small groups, students analyze a poem using TWIST (tone, word choice, imagery, style and theme); in the last third (25 minutes) of class, they have a test involving seven multiple-choice questions and a paragraph-long analysis of another poem using TWIST.
Apr. 11	Lesson on defining tragedy as a genre; going back and forth between individual brainstorming, small-group discussion and whole-class discussion. Lots of intertextuality, linking *Flight* to *Romeo and Juliet* to a YouTube video on Greek tragedy.
Apr. 18*	In small groups, students track particular characters across scenes in *Romeo and Juliet* in order to document character traits and relationships between characters.
Apr. 25	Workshop by visiting actors Mr Nick and Ms Marie (pseudonyms). Begins with some fun warm-up exercises. Next, students rehearse in pairs how to deliver three- to five-line monologues from *Romeo and Juliet*. Individual presentations in a supportive atmosphere, then Mr Nick performs the nurse's monologue for the students.
May 2	Preparation for the launch of the class' poetry anthology; students vote on the book cover. Juan talks about book-signing and shows the class his collection of autographed books. Going on the internet, he shows students how many copies their poetry anthology has already sold (188 at the time, but nearly 700 by the NCTE conference that fall), and shares an inspiring congratulatory email he has received from an ESL teacher at another school. Students analyze, then act out, Romeo and Juliet's meeting scene.

Juan's experience teaching English 9: themes (e.g. young people's problems) and activities (e.g. analysis of simile and metaphor) are recurring and build upon each other across units, from *Flight* to *Romeo and Juliet* to the students' own poetry writing.

It is my impression that students had a great deal of respect for their teacher, as he set high goals for his English language learners (ELLs), assigning them extensive reading in the form of age-appropriate realistic fiction and giving them 19th-century poems, postcolonial literature and Shakespeare to analyze. He also ensured that the thematic content was relatable and scaffolded understanding meticulously with clear explanations and numerous collaborative activities.

On the whole, Juan's teaching incorporated more of a translanguaging stance than a translanguaging design (García *et al.*, 2017). He welcomed use of languages other than English in class and told students to feel free to use these to help each other in small-group work, and he did not scold students when he heard them use other languages. However, he did not create lessons, materials or activities that invited students to use these languages except in creative writing for the class poetry anthology. Still, he went much further than most US teachers in terms of making space for non-English languages in intellectual inquiry.

4.2 The English 9 Teacher

Juan describes his profession as 'an accident'; in his senior year of high school, he didn't know what to go into, and an aunt suggested majoring in education because tuition fees were reasonable. After applying to the state university of Ilocos Norte (northern Ilocos), he was happy to receive a scholarship and chose to specialize in English education because it was the first decade of the 21st century and the call center industry was booming in the Philippines. Juan described himself as a student leader during his undergraduate career, and as someone who did not shy away from exploring different social issues. In his sophomore year, he took a theater class with a liberal professor from Manila, who had her students create one-act plays:

> I guess she just pushed us to really go outside of our box so, the play we created, my group did, we called it 'Sex Positions' (chuckles)—you can put that off the record but—it has nothing to do with intercourse, or whatnot. It was like looking at the, um (3.0) familial roles from the sense of gender, or sex. ... And then some of the professors were like, 'You have to take that down! Cancel the show!' or whatnot, but my professor was like, 'You know what, I approved it, just remove your posters, advertise differently' and then—we did the project. So, I guess, that kind of shows how ambitious—or a risk-taker I am, in the things I do.

Back then, he still did not consider teaching in the US, because he never realized he would have a chance to immigrate there. Ever since he was in elementary school, he, his sister and his father had petitioned to come to the US under the family reunification plan, but the papers took 10–11 years to process. Suddenly, in his last year of university, they learned that the application was approved. School administrators were very accommodating, such that he was able to finish his exams, action research and practicum in February so that he could immigrate to the US before his temporary visa expired. Although he graduated as salutatorian (#2 in his class), he did not attend the graduation ceremony because he had to leave the Philippines in February. He describes missing out on this as bittersweet, as he had had a memorable time at university.

Still in his early twenties, he worked at Walmart for a year and a half, while also teaching part-time in a private pre-school: 'I was exploring. Do I wanna teach here or not? But—I had that fresh grad drive because—I had to? So I was working on my Praxis [US licensure exam], certification, everything'. At that time, a friend teaching at his current school recommended an educational assistant position in special education. He applied, and was hired after a five-month process. He was an educational assistant until spring 2013 and became a certified teacher that summer, just as a permanent position opened in late July to teach sheltered English 9. My study thus covers his sixth year of teaching (2018–2019) and his first year as English department head.

Since Juan was sometimes elsewhere in the school due to administrative duties as a department head, Ed (an Ilokano man who appeared to be in his fifties) was his regular substitute. While Ed was also trilingual in Ilokano, Filipino and English, and like Juan spoke English with a Filipino accent, he did not seem to have the English proficiency to understand course texts and lead students to deconstruct them. During the classes when he substituted, he often acted as a proctor as students did work in small groups. He then collected their notes, worksheets, paragraph reflections or quizzes for Juan to mark. Moreover, I noted that Ilokano students hardly spoke Ilokano with Ed, as they sometimes did with Juan. Later in this chapter, I discuss this observation in relation to the topic of positionality.

4.3 The English 9 Students

There were 14 students in English 9 in 2018–2019, with a few coming or going throughout the year. In Juan's class, two students who participated actively and with confidence in their academic abilities were Kix, an Ilokano–Filipino–English trilingual with emergent proficiency in Korean, who immigrated to Hawai'i from the Philippines the school year before, and He, an English-dominant singleton of Cantonese heritage who had grown up in Hawai'i since the age of five. I selected them to focus on in my study due to their prominence in classroom interactions. Kix had a circle of Ilokano-speaking friends (all female) who were mostly also relative newcomers, and with whom he regularly sat: Eufia, Rizze, Clara and Aliah. These young women were unique individuals: Eufia was an eager learner as outspoken as Kix; Rizze was talkative and cheeky in Ilokano and a committed, if somewhat shy, English student; Clara was likewise sociable (though she seemed more dominant in Filipino) and was somewhat lackadaisical in class; Aliah, who had been in the US longer, only spoke English but understood Ilokano and was fairly quiet. Toward the end of the study, they were joined by Diana, an initially quiet newcomer who gained confidence due to Kix and Eufia's support, quickly transforming into an active bilingual (Ilokano–English) classroom participant. With the exception of Clara, Kix and his friends all had good attendance.

He, the Cantonese HL singleton, also had good attendance, and often sat with Jhon, an Ilokano HL speaker who had largely grown up in the US and was English dominant. In fact, He's group of friends, who weren't in the class but often 'hung out' in Juan's classroom during lunchtime to play games on their smartphones, were also English-dominant ethnic Filipinos. The other Ilokano students seemed to exclude Jhon in subtle ways, though Kix reported in an interview that Jhon socialized with them outside of class. The last student who attended class regularly was Fetu, an academically proficient and sociable Samoan boy who sometimes sat with He and Jhon, and sometimes with his friend Eufia in Kix's group.

The remaining students had limited attendance. These included Mike, a quiet boy who understood Ilokano but spoke mostly English, and three Chuukese L1 boys (Bob, Charlie and Raoul). Charlie transferred schools mid-year, between my pre-recording visits and audio-recorded visits; Bob and Raoul stayed on and tended to sit with He's company when they came to class. Kleo, a heritage speaker of Marshallese who left midway through my audio-recorded visits, tended to sit with her friends Kix and Eufia. Figure 4.1 shows the English 9 social groups from my perspective; letters are shorthand for students' L1s/HLs. The labels 'Center' and 'Periphery' denote which students were more or less vocal in *any* language(s). The label 'Distributed' means some individuals in this category were active class participants (i.e. Fetu, He) while the third was more quiet (i.e. Kleo). The non-English languages that students spoke could be their L1s or HLs. In Figure 4.1, I use the labels 'I' for Ilokano, 'Ch' for Chuukese, 'Can' for Cantonese, 'Mar' for Marshallese and 'S' for Samoan.

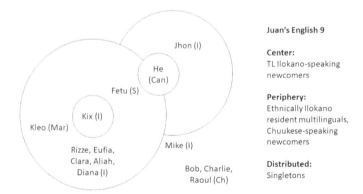

Figure 4.1   English 9 class dynamics

Table 4.2   Students in English 9

Pseudonym	Years in Hawai'i	Relative arrival	Ethnicity (L1/HL)	Audio-recorded	Interview
Kix	1–2	Newcomer	Ilokano	Y	Y
Eufia	1–2	Newcomer	Ilokano	Y	N
Rizze	1–2	Newcomer	Ilokano	Y	N
Clara	Unknown	Newcomer	Ilokano	Y	N
Diana	<1	Newcomer	Ilokano	Y	N
Jhon	6	Long-time resident	Ilokano	Y	Y
Aliah	Unknown	Unknown	Ilokano	Y	N
Mike	Unknown	Unknown	Ilokano?[2]	N	N
Bob	Unknown	Unknown	Chuukese	Y	Y[3]
Charlie	Unknown	Unknown	Chuukese	N	N
Raoul	Unknown	Unknown	Chuukese	N	N
Kleo	HI-born	Long-time resident	Marshallese + Chuukese[4]	Y	Y
He	10	Long-time resident	Cantonese	Y	Y
Fetu	1–2	Newcomer	Samoan	Y	N

Table 4.2 summarizes English 9 students' L1s/HLs, the number of years in Hawai'i (if they agreed to participate in the interview aspect of the study) and whether each student was a newcomer or had grown up in the US. Other columns show what aspects of the study each student agreed to participate in.

Generally, students who were academically stronger and/or more orally active in class (Kix's group, He, Kleo and Fetu) consented to participate more actively in the study, by being audio-recorded and, for some, interviewed about their multilingual practices – though not all the data is included in this book. I do not think this self-selection is a coincidence. There is a connection between being confident in one's class performance and being comfortable with being studied while in class. Moreover, confidence in English class means a student like Kix or Eufia not only participates quite actively, but feels no shame using their L1/HL because with a certain degree of English proficiency, L1/HL use is seen as an interactional choice and does not suggest lack of English proficiency. On the other hand, singletons like He, Kleo and Fetu avoided oral trans-languaging and used their L1s/HLs and other languages less frequently and in other ways, such as stylization, ludic play and creative writing, which can be partly explained by the fact that no one else shared He's and Kleo's HLs or Fetu's L1.

Table 4.3 summarizes English 9 students' responses to the language questionnaire. The first question asked, 'How often do you use another

Table 4.3   English 9 students' responses to the language questionnaire[5]

	Language/s used	How often	Think to self	Talk aloud	Write notes	Use dictionary	Other
Rizze	Ilokano	All the time	X	X			
Clara	Ilokano	All the time					X help translate
Kix	Ilokano	Often	X	X			X talk to friends
Raoul	Chuukese	Sometimes	X	X			
Charlie	Chuukese	Sometimes		X			
Bob	Chuukese	Sometimes	X				
He	Cantonese	Sometimes	X				
Eufia	Ilokano	Sometimes		X			
Fetu	Blank	Rarely			X	X	
Aliah	Ilokano	Rarely	X				
Kleo	Marshallese	Rarely					
Jhon	Blank	Never					
Mike	Blank	Never					

language in English class? Choose one: Never, Rarely, Sometimes, Often or All the Time'. The second question asked students to check all the ways in which they used the language(s) if their answer to the question was Sometimes, Often or All the Time: to think to oneself, talk to others, write notes, translate using a dictionary or 'Other' (with a blank space). The third question asked students to explain their answer to the first. If they used another language at least sometimes, how was it helpful? If they rarely or never used another language, why not? Based on the questionnaire, I ranked students in order of frequency of reported translanguaging.

Except for Eufia (who downplayed her use of Ilokano in this questionnaire yet translanguaged often to do class work, such that I would rank her with Rizze, Clara and Kix), the class appears to be divided into three groups in the chart: (1) self-identified frequent translanguagers such as the Ilokano-speaking students Kix, Rizze and Clara; (2) self-identified 'sometimes' translanguagers, such as the three Chuukese-speaking boys and the singleton He, none of whom actually seemed to speak their other languages aloud, even though one can also translanguage in one's thoughts, which three out of four of them reported doing; and (3) self-identified reluctant translanguagers, such as the Samoan singleton Fetu, ethnically Ilokano students who were English dominant (such as Aliah and Jhon; I am not sure about Mike's age when he immigrated, and he rarely came to class) and Kleo, the only student born *and* raised in Hawai'i.

Regarding the self-identified frequent translanguagers, I noticed that even though they typically reported using Ilokano to socialize and help each other, none reported writing notes in Ilokano or using an Ilokano-English dictionary or electronic translator – which has to do with the less commonly taught nature of their language, even back in the Philippines where the languages of instruction are Filipino and English. Online Ilokano-English dictionaries are rather hard to navigate (i.e. they define isolated words rather than translating phrases/chunks in context like Google translate does for more widely spoken languages such as Arabic and Japanese). On the other hand, oral translanguaging using Ilokano to make sense of English seemed second nature to them, as if they were used to translanguaging in Filipino- or English-medium lessons.

Their responses stand in contrast to Fetu's, who put down that he rarely used another language in English 9 (and did not even state the language on the questionnaire), but reported writing notes and using a dictionary. Although he did not consent to be interviewed, it is more likely that Fetu received schooling in his L1, as Samoan and English are the official languages in American Samoa, and are used in government, education and the media.

Raised in Hawai'i and schooled in English, He said in an interview that he could not read and write in Cantonese. However, he reported on the questionnaire that he thought to himself in Cantonese, and during an interview he also talked about acting as a language broker for his parents in official settings, resulting in Juan giving him excused absences from class.

The three Chuukese L1 boys gave interesting answers because they were somewhat divergent. I believe Bob's claim that they thought to themselves in Chuukese but did not use it in conversation, but Charlie reported that they *did* converse in Chuukese and Raoul reported that they both thought and conversed in Chuukese. It is possible that due to my placing my two recorders with Kix and He, I may have missed Chuukese, which I would identify as such by hearing a language I didn't understand that didn't sound like Ilokano. However, due to varying my seating on each visit, it is my impression that they did not actually speak Chuukese, and I recorded no Chuukese even when two or more of the three Chuukese-speaking boys sat with He, Jhon and/or Fetu. In any case, the vast majority of translanguaging in the class was clearly between Ilokano and English.

Apart from Fetu, four other students reported that they rarely or never translanguaged: Kleo, Aliah, Jhon and Mike. Of these five students, Fetu and Kleo were L1/HL singletons (the ethnically Marshallese Kleo was the only student born and raised in Hawai'i) and the other three were English-dominant Filipinos who had also grown up in Hawai'i. This group of students gave two main reasons for their infrequent translanguaging: not knowing how to speak their HL well, and consideration for the whole class. Jhon wrote, 'I want to know more English and I don't want to use my language in class because some people may not understand'; Mike inaccurately responded, "Cause everyone is just speaking English'; Kleo stated, 'I rarely speak my own language in English class because I don't know how to speak my own language'; Aliah answered, 'I rarely speak another language in class because sometimes I don't remember...'. What all these students had in common was that they reported low levels of oral translanguaging, corroborated by my observations and audio-recordings.

However, out of Kleo, Aliah, Jhon and Mike, I think only Kleo (whom I had a long interview with but who soon left the class to go back to the Marshall Islands for an indeterminate period of time) *truly* found it hard to converse in her HL, as her stepfamily had raised her as an English monolingual while cultivating bilingualism in her two younger half-siblings. However, all four students, who had largely grown up in the US, would have lost at least some ability to use their less commonly taught language (LCTL) fluently in oral speech, particularly for academic purposes, due to many years of English-only schooling and/or limited opportunities to use it in the home due to patterns of interaction (Mirvahedi, 2021). Thus, one way to position themselves positively was to assert an English speaker identity, accompanied by a discourse of speaking English in class so everybody could understand them. Fetu also aligned with this discourse, as a newcomer singleton proficient in English.

In the next sections, I compare the translanguaging practices of the classroom linguistic majority, linguistic minorities/singletons and English-dominant old-timers in more detail, remarking that even students in the latter two groups who were reluctant translanguagers translanguaged *some* of the time, and that the frequently translanguaging Ilokano–English bilinguals refrained from translanguaging at certain times. I conclude the chapter with a practical discussion of how these findings relate to task design and positionality.

4.4 The Translanguaging of the Linguistic Newcomer Majority

4.4.1 The principal language broker

In Section 3.5, I explained that a major theme in this study was socially constructed linguistic and cultural competencies, such as competencies in the forms of academic literacy valued at school, English proficiency, proficiency in an L1 or HL and knowledge of peer languages of affiliation. Of the 31 participating students in this study, only one student had a language repertoire with no immediately apparent vulnerabilities in any of these categories, and that was Kix, largely because of his unusual educational background in Ilocos Norte, the northern province of the Philippines where he was from.

Kix, who had immigrated to the US one to two years previously, describes his life story: After graduating as valedictorian from his elementary school, he was offered a place in a sciences-focused secondary school where all classes were in English except for 'Tagalog class'. While at the English-medium school, he traveled widely through the country as editor-in-chief of the school newspaper, which had a staff of seven and won local and regional titles, ranking third in a national competition in 2017. In one interview, when I remarked, 'Oh my gosh, you're busy' upon hearing about Kix's involvement in volleyball and the Junior Reserve Officers Training Corps (JROTC) at his present school in Honolulu, Kix explained that he had been even busier in the Philippines, when he went to school at 6am daily to put out the weekly newspaper with six others; he also worked on it from 6 to 7.30pm and got home at 7.30 or 8pm. The parallels between Kix and Juan were probably lost on nobody in the class – both were academically accomplished Ilokano males with leader-like qualities and high levels of multilingualism. Kix described his proficiency in English, Ilokano and Filipino as 'fairly equal', and took responsibility for helping others.

4.4.2 Peer scaffolding by the principal language broker

Not only was Kix a member of the ethnolinguistic majority in English 9, but he was also proficient in three languages (Ilokano, English and Filipino) shared by this group of students to varying degrees. Outgoing and intelligent, he served as a central language broker and role model in Juan's class. For example, Excerpt 1 shows him explaining an analogy in Sherman Alexie's novel *Flight* to his classmate Aliah, which is expressed through the metaphor of lifeguards and lifeboats. In the novel, Alexie implies that when a youth suffers adverse experiences, they feel that they are drowning, yet mentors can be like lifeguards and creative outlets like lifeboats.

Excerpt 1 'Lifeguards and lifeboats'

1	Kix:	Like, when you hear about the drowners and like (.) some people (Eufia yawns) are like lifeguards and cartoons are the lifeboats—
2	Female student:	Ngi. *Ugh.*
3	Aliah:	I'm sorry, I cannot listen!
4	Kix:	(laughs) It's like you have hope (.) saying that you have saviors, even though they're just (.) cartoons or people that could (.) yeah. You know what I mean.
5	Juan:	'Kay why don't you explain what you're trying to say in a different way.
6	Kix:	So, if people are readers... if they can infer that those are—if they can infer that the floods are the problems, and they hear that um (.) there are lifeguards inside the boats that could save them— (sighs) OK. Narigrigat ngarud nokua diba (.) kasi (.) like (.) amom no mangeg mo ket kasla adda hope mo nga masagip pelang [*It's harder you know (.) because (.) like (.) if you could hear it feels like there's hope that you could be saved*], unlike, if you don't hear them, like, 'Oh I'm gonna die.' And if you hear that there's life saviors in life boats around, like, you can get hope by being saved. (1.0) You know what I mean?

7	Aliah:	Hope?
8	Kix:	Hopeful.
9	Juan:	So basically no mabasa da [*if they're able to read*] these characters are being saved.
10	Kix:	Yeah.
11	Juan:	Ma-feel da— *They can feel*—
12	Kix:	Like, they're hope. Hopeful.
13	Aliah:	Ohh!
14	Kix:	You know what I mean now.
15	Aliah:	Yes.
16	Juan:	'Kay put that in a sentence!

In Lines 1–3, Kix is losing the group as he tries to explain the extended metaphor, with a female student groaning and Aliah declaring she can't listen anymore. Still, he persists, mitigating his lecture with a laugh and an encouraging 'You know what I mean' (Line 4). Juan suggests explaining it 'in a different way' (Line 5), which Kix seems to interpret as a cue to translanguage. After explaining one scenario (the positive one) in Ilokano, 'Narigrigat ngarud nokua diba (.) kasi (.) like (.) amom no mangeg mo ket kasla adda hope mo nga masagip pelang' [*It's harder you know (.) because (.) like (.) if you could hear it feels like there's hope that you could be saved*], Kix provides the contrasting negative scenario in English, which is a subtle code-switch to juxtapose the two contrasting ideas: 'unlike, if you don't hear them, like, "Oh I'm gonna die"' (Line 6). He then repeats the positive scenario in English: 'And if you hear that there's life saviors in life boats around, like, you can get hope by being saved' (Line 6).

Aliah, grasping the main theme, says 'Hope?' (Line 7), and Kix repeats, 'Hopeful' (Line 8). Next, Juan says, 'So basically no mabasa da [*if they're able to read*] these characters are being saved' (Line 9), which organizes information separately into the story world in English ('these characters are being saved') versus what the reader is doing in Ilokano ('no mabasa da'/they will read). Juan then uses another Ilokano phrase with one borrowed English word, 'ma-feel da' (Line 11), to create a parallel structure: 'If they read' (in Ilokano) 'such-and-such' (in English) 'they will feel' (in Ilokano) 'such and such' (in English) (Lines 9–12), though what the reader will feel is supplied by Kix rather than Juan (Line 12). Aliah next replies 'Ohh!' (Line 13) to demonstrate understanding. In this dialogue, Kix and Juan use pedagogical code-switching to create juxtapositions and contrasts, the way color coding or highlighting words on PowerPoints organizes information more clearly. Thus, both distinct codes and integrated, holistic meaning-making using all the resources in individual language repertoires are important to carry out the task of scaffolding comprehension.

4.4.3 Peer scaffolding among the majority language group

I often observed and recorded the class' Ilokano-speaking linguistic majority translanguaging and code-switching productively[6] and inclusively to meet course learning aims. These included expert–novice interactions as well as collaborations in which students oriented to one another as equals in expertise (Storch, 2002). Excerpt 2 is an example of the latter. As Kix explained in an interview, translanguaging was especially useful for vocabulary clarification.

Excerpt 2 'Suitor'

1	**Eufia:**	(to Rayna) What's suitor miss?
2	**Kix:**	Suitor like—suitor.
3	**Rizze:** *FI	To ligaw. *To court.*
4	**Kix:** *FI	Suitor manliligaw [*suitor*]. (2.0) Court something.
5	**Eufia:** *IL	Ni Romeo? (10.0) Ni Paris ka di? *It's Romeo? (10.0) It's Paris right?*
6	**Clara:** *??	Ni Rosaline di ba? *Of/It's Rosaline, right?*
7	**Eufia:** *FI	Sino kwan ni ano? Juliet? *Who's the whatchamacallit of who? Juliet?*
8	**Rizze:** *IL	Ni Paris. *It's Paris.*
9	**Eufia:** *FI	Saan? *Where?*
10	**Rizze:** *FI	Ayan o. *There see.*

This was a rare occasion when Ilokano students in English 9 used more resources from Filipino (not only Ilokano and English) to translanguage; in fact, more Filipino resources are used in this excerpt than Ilokano ones, starting with the explanation of what 'to court' and 'suitor' are, using the Filipino 'manliligaw' instead of the Ilokano word 'mangarem'. One possible explanation is Clara's presence. Although she did not consent to be interviewed, I suspected she was Filipino dominant because of her friends' shifts toward Filipino when she came to class (her attendance was spotty). Ethnically Ilokano, she could be addressed in Ilokano, but tended to speak back, as well as talk to herself, using more Filipino.

In Line 5 of Excerpt 2, Eufia's switch into Ilokano as she asks who the suitor is, with a 10-second pause, may be a specific appeal to Kix to help her out. However, the next speaker, in Line 6, is Clara, who produces the ambiguous utterance: 'Ni Rosaline di ba?' [*It's/Of Rosaline, right?*]. The 'di ba' is 'right?' in Filipino, but 'Ni' can mean 'Of' (Filipino) or 'It's' (Ilokano), creating two separate meanings: 'the suitor *of* Rosaline, right?'

versus 'the suitor *is* Rosaline, right?' Eufia makes an immediate move to clear this up in Line 7, changing to Filipino again and indicating that she is asking about the suitor of Juliet. Rizze's response in Ilokano is that the answer is Paris (Line 8), and Eufia continues in Filipino asking for the textual evidence (Line 9). Rizze says 'There see' in Filipino (Line 10), presumably pointing to the page.

While Ilokano utterances may indicate specific addressees (e.g. Lines 5, 8),[7] what is interesting is how Eufia switches to Filipino after Clara's clarification check, 'pushing' Filipino as the medium of communication (Line 9) until Rizze aligns (Line 10). Normally, however, Rizze, Eufia and Kix translanguaged to learn in Ilokano and English. Similar to Excerpt 1, Excerpt 2 shows that translanguaging to learn using *both* the whole language repertoire *and* what students orient to as distinct codes is important not only as students work out the topic content but also as they highlight different parts of utterances for pedagogical purposes and negotiate inclusive code choices based on others' needs.

4.4.4 The majority language group's wider multilingual identities

Translanguaging among the Ilokano-speaking majority extended into their language of affiliation, Korean, which they knew bits of through K-pop and K-dramas.[8] One way they used Korean productively (even though they didn't have the proficiency to converse in this language) was by trying out stylized forms of address such as 'big brother' on each other, as seen in Excerpt 3. This is a dialogue that occurred in a multi-class poetry workshop, attended by Kix and Eufia's friend Konan. Konan, in the same grade, was a Visayan who spoke Ilonggo and Filipino and was also a fan of K-pop and K-dramas. He did not speak Ilokano, so the three conversed in Filipino and English.

Excerpt 3 'Oppa'

1	Kix: *KO	(to Konan) Oppa…?
		(to Konan) Big brother?
2	Konan:	'Oppa?'
		'Big brother?'
3	Kix: *FI	Ilang taon ka na?
		How old are you?
4	Konan:	[Hyu:::ng. Why oppa?
5	Eufia:	[Hyung. Oppa is older than you.
6	Kix:	How old are you?
7	Konan:	I'm more comfortable—
8	Kix:	How old are you?
9	Konan:	Fifteen.
10	Kix:	O di I'm fourteen.
		Oh see I'm fourteen.

11	Konan:	So why do you—why do you—why do you call me 'oppa'? When you're a man?
12	Kix:	Oh right.
13	Eufia:	(chuckles)
14	Konan:	Call me 'oppa' when you're a girl.

For most of this workshop, the three had translanguaged between Filipino and English as they worked on bi/multilingual poetry. Toward the end of the period, Kix called Konan 'big brother' in Korean, but used the wrong term for his own gender. In Filipino, it doesn't matter what the younger person's gender is, as all older male siblings/cousins are called 'kuya' and all older female siblings/cousins are called 'ate'. In Korean, the younger person's gender makes a difference, so there are four options: 'oppa' (big brother, girl-to-boy), 'hyung' (big brother, boy-to-boy), 'noona' (big sister, boy-to-girl) and 'unnie' (big sister, girl-to-girl). Noticing that he is being corrected but not understanding why, Kix thinks Konan doesn't know which one of them is older, and asks Konan's age (Line 3). Konan and Eufia both provide the right word, 'Hyung' (Lines 4–5), overlapping when they say it, but Eufia adds the wrong explanation (Line 5). Kix keeps asking how old Konan is (Lines 6–10) until Konan explains why the vocative is incorrect (Line 11). As can be seen, English and Filipino are used to negotiate the right form in Korean and the reason why.

When Kix and Eufia discussed how to say things in Korean between themselves, the primary language they used was Ilokano rather than Filipino or English, which are the languages they use in Korean metalinguistic discussion with Konan.[9] In Excerpt 4, back in Juan's class without Konan, Kix and Eufia try to figure out how to transcribe sounds using the Korean alphabet.

Excerpt 4 'Tangjinjaem'

1	Eufia:	(singing BTS song) Yolo yolo yolo yo / Yolo yolo yo / Tangjinjaem tangjinjaem tangjinjaem—anong tangjinjaem? *(singing BTS song) Yolo yolo yolo yo / Yolo yolo yo / Tangjinjaem tangjinjaem tangjinjaem—what's tangjinjaem?*
2	Kix:	*Tangjinjaem?*
3	Girl:	*Tangjinjee. (sic)*
4	Kix:	Um (.) one day something.
5	Eufia:	Tangjinaem ah. (laughs)
6	(overlapping singing in the group)	
7	Eufia:	Wrong pay ta Romanized ne! *You spelled the Romanized wrong!*
8	Kix:	Where?
9	Eufia:	T (.) apay a T iti impan na D koma? *Why did you put T instead of D?*

10		(interrupted by a brief visit from the substitute)
11	**Kix:**	Which one?
12	**Eufia:**	Tangjinjaem. Tangjin—
13	**Kix:**	Where?
14	**Eufia:**	Deta ni. Deta ni tangjinjaem. Dapat T deta. Mabalin kadi ti T wenno D? (to substitute) Yes mister. *There. There's tangjinjaem. That should be T. Is T interchangeable with D? (to substitute) Yes mister.*
15	**Kix:**	That's T.
16	**Eufia:**	Ya pero D. (laughs) Yeah [isu ngarud tangjinjaem konak ngarud itay. *Yeah but D. (laughs) Yeah [that's why, I told you earlier to refuse (it).*
17	**Kix:**	[I thought T's like this. D's this.
18	**Eufia:**	Wait. (2.0) D. Tas iti P (.) kasdiay. *Wait. (2.0) D. P would be like this.*
19	**Kix:**	No that's B.
20	**Eufia:**	Saan B kata ni. *Then B would be like this.*
21	**Kix:**	Yeah, P.
22	**Eufia:**	(disagreeing tone) B:::
23	**Kix:**	B is (.) [that. P is this.
24	**Eufia:**	[Kasta aya. Kasta P. (1.0) Saan a kastoy? *[Like this. Like P. (1.0) It's not like this?*
25	**Kix:**	Is this the same?
26	**Eufia:**	Saan a kastoy? Ah yeah yeah yeah kastoy. *Is this the same? Ah yeah yeah yeah the same.*
27	**Kix:**	Diak man ammo. *I have no idea.*
28	**Eufia:**	Saan baka pronunciation. *It might be the pronunciation.*
29		(singing *Tangjinjaem* again; the student teacher, Rayna, joins in)

While these students do not have the proficiency to converse in Korean, terms learned from global K-pop culture are socially meaningful for them, and they are curious about the language, as shown by Excerpt 4 in which they translanguage in Ilokano and English (languages in which they have generative proficiency) to solve problems encountered in Korean learning to the best of their ability. When I interviewed Kix about why he wanted to learn Korean, he explained, 'When I was young, but I never had the chance—I wanted to learn more languages rather than speaking in English, Ilokano, Tagalog'. I asked him if he liked Korean music because it was popular, but he revealed his reasons were more personal:

No, it's actually (.) my fascination in—um so, Korean music for me, I like the beats and stuff, and like, even though I cannot understand all of it, when I read the songs I notice that there's some words and lyrics that usually connects to what everyday life would be.

I then asked, 'What kind of topics do you connect to your everyday life?' and he said, 'So (2.0) mostly it's love, um (.) troubles and—yeah. It's like hardships and stuff in life'. However, he said he couldn't speak for his friends as to why they liked the music. Tellingly, Kix did not want to be restricted to languages deemed 'natural' for him to acquire. Youth's multilingual potential does not always need to be associated with L1s/HLs plus English – students can have rich discussions using *non-English* L1s/HLs/L2s (e.g. Excerpts 3 and 4) about the grammar, vocabulary, pronunciation or pragmatics of a third language/fourth language (L3/L4) etc. of affiliation (Leung *et al.*, 1997).

4.4.5 The majority language group's translanguaging in the presence of people with different language repertoires

I now come to Ilokano L1 students' translanguaging in the presence of peers who did not speak Ilokano. In a group in which everyone could comfortably speak Filipino if not Ilokano, as in Excerpts 2 and 3, Filipino-English translanguaging helped to include everyone. If there were non-Filipino peers present and interaction patterns were inclusive, English was the 'base' language with asides in Ilokano and Filipino (see Mendoza, 2020a: 171–172). Otherwise, Ilokano and Filipino were used more often with less regard for the social needs of the non-speaking peer(s). This is seen in Excerpt 5, a dialogue that occurred when Rizze and Eufia were sitting with He, who had a not-too-subtle crush on Rizze. Note that He would not understand the bits in Filipino and Ilokano.

Excerpt 5 'Friend-zo::ne, friend-zo::ne'

1	**Eufia:** *FI	Ano He? [*What He?*] He's wife. (giggles) She said (.) she's your wife.[10]
2	**He:**	Yeah you wish.
3	**Eufia:**	Aw::w.
4	**Rizze:**	Ouch. My heart.
5	**Eufia:**	Friend-zo::ne, friend zo::ne.
6	**Rizze:** *FI	Mahal ko yan. *I love that one.*
7	**Eufia:** *FI	Hindi na ata kita crush, mahal na kita. *You're not much crush anymore, I love you now.*
8	**Rizze:** *IL	Di kanta ti 'much better sayo'? *What was that song again—'much better for you'?*[11]
9	**Eufia:** *FI	(sings) Di na ko nag aasa... *(sings) I don't hope anymore...*
10	**Rizze:** *FI	(dramatic tone) Sana di na lang ako nag dala ng chokolate. Ay love letter sayo. *If only I hadn't brought chocolate. Ay a love letter for you.*

11	**Eufia** and **Rizze:** *FI	(singing) Kung hindi mo din ako sasagutin / Pwede bang sainyo'y wag mo na akong papuntahin *If you're not gonna answer me / Then don't come round courting me*
12	**Eufia:** *FI	Sana di na lang ko (.) hala. Sana (.) ano? *If only I hadn't (.) uh-oh. If only (.) what?*
13	**Eufia** and **Rizze:** *FI	(singing) Systema natin ay ganun pa din. *Our system's the same-old-same-old.* (song continues)
14	**Eufia:**	You looking at me.
15	**He:**	I'm looking at the paper!

First, Eufia tells He that Rizze called herself his wife, which he recoils against, causing Eufia to say 'Friend-zo::ne, friend-zo::ne', i.e. your crush only wants to be your friend (Line 5). This is ironic because it is He who has the crush on Rizze, and the girls know it. In Lines 6–7, Eufia and Rizze recite cliché lines from Filipino soap operas in front of him, then Rizze asks Eufia in Ilokano (their default language) how a Filipino song by hip-hop artist Skusta Clee went (Line 8). The girls proceed to sing the song, and Rizze recites another cliché romantic line (Line 10) in Filipino, from Filipino dramas, about regret – putting her own spin on it by mentioning bringing chocolate as the thing she regrets doing for He, as she has the reputation as the one who brings chocolates and other snacks to class. The girls keep singing (Lines 11–13) until Eufia snaps out of it by saying to He, 'You looking at me' (Line 14) in English. He was likely doing so because he was trying to figure out the nature of what they were saying, whether it was ill-intended or not, in their language, which he referred to as 'Filipino' in an interview, unaware that it was two languages.

The use of Ilokano for in-group talk, English for out-group talk and Filipino for stylized in-group cultural references (if not wider inclusivity) can be compared to different uses of the same languages in other excerpts, suggesting that translanguaging constellations (Rajendram, 2021) vary across groupings, tasks and social actions. However, it is clear which students translanguaged the most in oral interaction – the students whose type of plurilingualism (Ilokano, Filipino and English trilingualism plus Korean as a language of affiliation) was in the class majority.

4.4.6 Exceptions to the majority language group's embracing of translanguaging

I now come to the Ilokano-speaking students' translanguaging not between themselves but with the teacher. They used Ilokano with Juan outside of (not during) class time, but tended to address his regular substitute, Ed, in English. Only once did I record a student (Eufia) asking Ed a question in Ilokano, about a vocabulary word. During an interview with Kix, I asked him why this was in his case.

Excerpt 6 L1/HL use as a sign of closeness

1	**Anna:**	How about Mr Ed why do you talk to him in English mostly?
2	**Kix:**	I don't know. It's just that (.) when I'm here yeah? So when I'm talking to older, or more mature people in the class or in the school, I often speak to them in English—
3	**Anna:**	Unless you have a close rapport like Mr Juan.
4	**Kix:**	Unless I have a close rapport.
5	**Anna:**	That makes sense.

Even though it is I who suggest the reason (Line 3), Kix immediately accepts my suggestion (Line 4). I do not really doubt his answer, because in my interviews with him, we use English readily without much thought about Filipino. Chan (2016) has shown that Hong Kongers can opt for English as the language of communication in the workplace even when other language choices are available such as Cantonese or Mandarin – not only when non-Chinese-speaking colleagues are in the group but also when Chinese interlocutors do not know each other well. One reason for this is that code choices can index sociopolitical sides, while English has many possible social meanings *apart* from its meaning as a colonizer's language, one of which is side-neutrality if the other choices are between Cantonese versus Mandarin or Ilokano versus Filipino, signaling things such as regional background, social class or political affiliation. Similarly, this is why I don't address Kix in Filipino: (1) it is the hegemonic national language that oppresses his L1, Ilokano; (2) he speaks it more fluently than I do, having grown up in the Philippines; and (3) it would be ridiculous to expect him to speak 'my' language when I don't even speak it as well as he does. Since we can both communicate in English, we use English, which also indexes the more formal context of the research interview.

In terms of what speaking Ilokano would index when Ed was teaching, I observed that Ed did not seem to have the English proficiency to understand course texts and lead students to deconstruct them. Therefore, while Ilokano was a way for some students to show Juan they were thinking deeply about the material, and to seem like competent bilinguals themselves, using it in Ed's presence might suggest one shared his lack of English proficiency, which was remarked on in subtle ways (e.g. once, Kix corrected Ed's pronunciation under his breath when Ed was reading the morning announcements, though Ed's pronunciation of the word was right).

These musings are impossible to prove with a participant statement,[12] as no one will admit to thinking this way in an interview, but I have spent enough time in the classroom to perceive that the enabling force allowing Ilokano students in English 9 to draw on their L1/HL in academic work was the model set by Kix, for whom the model was Juan. When Ed, whose English did not extend into academic domains, was teaching,

Kix did not translanguage much (also for reasons of social distance, as he explains), and as a result, this inhibited translanguaging at regular speaking volume for his group of friends as a whole. While Ilokano students' translanguaging went *beyond* their shared L1 to encompass Korean, a language of affinity, I argue that it is being in the class linguistic majority and the legitimation of Ilokano-English translanguaging for academic purposes by an academically fluent bilingual teacher and peer leader that allowed them to embrace and express their identities as multilinguals more broadly, including with a language of affiliation not part of the official curriculum.

Moreover, when Ilokano students engaged in playful talk in Ilokano or Filipino, the teacher, unlike He in Excerpt 5, was aware that the content was harmless because he understood the languages. As Juan said in an interview: 'English speakers do that all the time. I cannot take that away from them'. However, speakers of languages Juan did not know could *not* count on him knowing what they were talking about, and the smaller the number of speakers of their languages in class, the more exclusive it would seem to use these languages in conversation at regular volume. This brings me to the translanguaging of students who had little to no proficiency in Ilokano.

4.5 The Translanguaging of Linguistic Minorities/ Singletons and English-Dominant Old-Timers

4.5.1 Translanguaging observably less

In this section, I examine how the translanguaging of linguistic minority and singleton students, as well as that of an English-dominant Ilokano HL speaker, was both *observably less* and *qualitatively different* than that of the Ilokano L1 students who were relative newcomers. Only one other language had multiple speakers, and that was Chuukese. However, regardless of where I placed my recorders in a small class of 14 students, they picked up no Chuukese as far as I could tell, which I would identify as a language I did not understand that wasn't Ilokano. On the language use questionnaire, Bob reported that they thought to themselves in Chuukese but did not use it in conversation, but Charlie and Raoul put down that they spoke Chuukese in class. Researcher ethnocentricity aside, it is nevertheless clear that Chuukese use was minimal at most, in contrast to extensive oral translanguaging in Ilokano at normal speaking volume in group work (but *not* in talk out to the whole class, unlike in ESL 9/10, when Filipino use for this purpose undermined the authority of the non-Filipino-speaking student teacher; see Chapter 5).

One possible reason is that English 9 involved extensive reading and literary analysis of Western genres (plays, novels); the book by Sherman Alexie, a Native American novelist, still belongs to the US 'coming of age' genre. Only during the poetry workshop, led by a visiting poet from the Visayas in the Philippines, did students explore Pacific Islander oral literary traditions from Pacific Islander poets, and these traditions are not nearly as well-maintained in the US-colonized Philippines as they are in Micronesia, the Marshall Islands and the forcibly annexed Hawai'i. The group discussions in English 9 that students engaged in, on a day-to-day basis, would inevitably reveal whether one had done the reading homework, which could be substantial (dozens of pages every night). For this reason, Micronesian students, whose accustomed literacy practices did not align as closely with textual literacy practices valued at a US or Philippine school, may have felt inhibited to participate in such discussions, regardless of what linguistic resources were used.

When it came to the language singletons, only once did I hear them use a non-English language in oral speech, and on this occasion it may have been a *parody* of the translanguaging frequently undertaken by the Ilokano-speaking students. While language crossing with Korean, an integral part of Kix's and Eufia's identities, occurred regularly for them, I only observed something remotely similar on the last day of data collection (May 2) as I was walking around the classroom giving out Pocky sticks as a token of appreciation for the class' participation in my study. On that day, Fetu, Mike and He sat together, the first two having identified as rarely or never translanguaging on the questionnaire I had administered earlier in the data collection. As Juan made a comment about Pocky, the three boys began to engage in ludic (playful) stylization.

Excerpt 7 'Am-eri-kan'

1	**Juan:**	These are American Stick-O's, guys.
2	**He:**	Ah, we know that, mister. We know that it's American Stick-Os.
3	**Mike:**	American.
4	**He:**	Am-eri-kan!
5	**Fetu:**	(mock belligerence towards He and Mike) Shut up I'm Am-eri-kan! You are Chinese, you are Philippine! You ain't Am-eri-kan. I am the only Am-eri-kan heah [*i.e., here*]
6	(boys laugh)	
7	**He:**	No. That's France. No Italy.
8	**Fetu:**	Hey?
9	(boys laugh)	
10	**Fetu:**	Pan tschwow (?)
11	**Mike:**	Are you—
12	**He:**	=Bonjour!

In Line 5, Fetu plays the jingoist claiming to be a 'real' American, with a stylized toughness that seems to remind He of a French or Italian accent (Line 7), possibly indexing for him 'Western' jingoism more broadly. Fetu then attempts to mimic the sound of a foreign language (Line 10), but it is so bizarre I cannot tell what it is. Mike, an English-dominant Filipino student, seems to begin to ask (Line 11), but is interrupted by He's 'Bonjour!' (Line 12).

What do Fetu's 'pan tschwow' (Line 10) and He's 'Bonjour' (Line 12) suggest? In contrast to the Ilokano-speaking students' regular language crossing in Korean, these *transient* utterances do not really matter in terms of what language(s) they are; all are interpreted as foreign, and therefore funny. The boys' purpose is simply to share a chuckle, which when connected to their responses to the language questionnaire and the moment of the recording, might possibly be interpreted to mean that they find it amusing how non-English languages could be the focus of someone studying an English class.

I now come to occasions when English-dominant students and class language minorities embraced translanguaging, which was not in everyday oral conversation.

4.5.2 Translanguaging qualitatively different

Fascinating data emerged on the rare occasions when He and Fetu translanguaged in serious ways. This happened in the same domain: the multi-class multilingual poetry anthology. Fetu, for example, used Samoan in his poem 'I am a va'a':

In American Samoa, in the past, there were two giants
lua lapoa who are brothers, uso
Their names were Matafao and Pioa
but they always argued
Later on, Matafao and Pioa passed away
on the same day
and became the two biggest mountains in American Samoa
They are the most important mountains of all time
because they're big, tall and beautiful
like my parents who always fight when it comes down
to financial and family issues
I am a va'a who is still rowing to find answers
to help my parents

Some of the Samoan words in the poem have no English translations; these include the giants' names and 'va'a', which has metaphorical significance related to spiritual journeys and is not just any canoe (the same word exists in Hawaiian and Tahitian). However, 'uso' is a translation of the word that came before, 'brother(s)'. 'Lua lapoa' is 'two big'. Interestingly, 'lua' (two) is a cognate of 'dua' (two in Ilokano), though

Ilokano-speaking students would likely not realize this from context alone. Language that most of the class does not understand has a poetic effect; the words command attention *precisely* because of lack of semantic information.

Indeed, He knew this fact and capitalized on it in the poetry anthology. On May 2, as English 9 students signed five copies of the book for Juan's friend, also a teacher, He asked Juan a question as the copies were being passed around.

Excerpt 8 Chinese name or English name? (Part 1)

1	He:	Oh should I write my Chinese name or my English?
2	Juan:	Ha?
3	Fetu:	Chinese name.
4	He:	English or Chinese?
5	Juan:	OK. Can I ask you something. Why are you asking that question?
6	He:	I don't know. I just asking.
7	Juan:	There should be a reason why you started asking that question.
8	Fetu:	Everything happens for a pur[pose—
9	Juan:	[You <u>chose</u> it. Choose it. >How do you wanna write it, English or Chinese, that's your choice. That's your name.< (2.0) I love that question. I dunno, I just love it.

Juan's 'Ha?' (Line 2) is not 'What did you say?' in brusque English but Filipino for 'What did you say?' in a regular tone. This is understood by Fetu and He, the former suggesting that He sign his Chinese name (Line 3). Instead of also suggesting that He showcase his Chinese heritage, Juan asks He why he asked that question (Line 5). In reply, He says he doesn't know (Line 6), and Fetu starts to joke around (Line 8), but Juan cuts Fetu off with a passionate, quickly spoken statement: 'You <u>chose</u> it. Choose it. >How do you wanna write it, English or Chinese, that's your choice. That's your name.<' (Line 9).

Two minutes later, Juan checked back to see what He chose:

Excerpt 9 Chinese name or English name? (Part 2)

1	Juan:	Did you write it in Chinese?
2	He:	One special book.
3	Juan:	One special book in Chinese, that's good. Why don't you make all of it special? [i.e. sign the others in Chinese][13]
4	Fetu:	Hurry up He. I'm gonna write my name in Chinese too.
5	Juan:	See Summer [a girl in another class] wrote it in Chinese too.

In effect, He has decided to create a limited edition copy of the anthology that has his Chinese signature in it. Although Juan suggests making them all special by signing them all in Chinese (Line 3) and points out that someone else wrote their name in Chinese (Line 5), I see what He is trying to do: the existence of the English-signed copies heightens the value of the 'one special book' (Line 2) signed in Chinese. The same effect cannot be achieved by signing his English name in one book, and his Chinese name in all the others. He is aware of the social meanings created by majority and minority languages in the school, and plays with them effectively. And yet, whenever he visits Guangdong with his family, which he told me he did from time to time, his Chinese signature would be unremarkable.

As this study is not a study of code-meshing in translingual writing (Canagarajah, 2011), the reader may wonder why I am discussing Fetu's poem and He's signature in this section on the translanguaging of minority language students and singletons. Researchers who promote translanguaging in classrooms often use instances of oral mixed language use as the most common 'evidence' of translanguaging's many social and academic benefits, but this may put undue pressure on linguistic minorities and singletons, judging them by the standards of the linguistic majority, and expecting them to showcase their languages in oral speech at regular volume when it is pragmatically infelicitous to do so. Again, the choice *not* to speak a language does not necessarily indicate that the language is devalued in class or by the speaker, but might simply be due to the fact that some languages are less useful for sociocognitive (i.e. thinking aloud together) and pragmatic purposes when few group members or classmates understand them. As Bob's, He's, Fetu's and Raoul's responses to the language questionnaire suggest, these languages could still be useful in note-taking or self-talk.

Compared to classroom majority languages, classroom minority languages have different affordances in the linguistic ecology (rather than being lingua francas for collaborative thinking aloud) precisely because *few*, rather than *many*, people understand them. On the rare occasions when they are used, their very sight or sound commands attention: 'Something special is happening or being shared, look/listen!'. Also, classmates' lack of knowledge of classroom minority languages can lead to curiosity, and it is often necessary to ask the speaker/writer for a translation when they use these language resources. Even though they don't speak the majority language, they have language knowledge that is rare in the class.

Another student whose translanguaging was restricted to the poetry anthology was Aliah, an English-dominant student who spoke Ilokano as a HL. Aliah wrote a poem called 'Nanang Who', inspired by Sandra Cisneros' poem 'Abuelito Who' – Cisneros being a Latina author who grew up in the US with a transnational identity, like Aliah's. This transnational identity is referenced in Aliah's poem through both content and language.

Nanang Who

The text was my ticking bomb clicking
Quick tears streamed down for you
For you, who picked me up with wrinkly
old skinny arms that made me laugh
that I purposely jiggled so you could laugh, too
For you, who made me fine toasted sugary
bread and honey
who joked impolitely to make me happy
whenever I'm gloomy
who walked me to school every day
who I had to help walk across the house
For you, who sometimes told me 'Haan ka pay mangan, annako
ngamin nag lukmeg kan,' and I responded 'Wen, nanang'
but I still ate because food is life. For you, who let me sleep
between Tatang and you, to whom I said 'I love you, Nanang Violet.
I'll see you next year ah, and be careful' and who responded
'Aysus, appo ubbing umay-kayon ah.'
But the next day, the text
makes my heart drop
strikes the heart of every loved one
'She tripped and hit her head on the ground'

In poetry writing, Aliah saw a purpose for drawing on Ilokano.[14] She used her HL to write about a grandparent, creating a work as moving as Cisneros'. Furthermore, the modality of writing allowed Aliah to put her best foot forward when using Ilokano: she could produce the language at her own pace, check for grammatical correctness, revise sentences until they looked the way she wanted them to, and did not have to be judged on her intonation or pronunciation.

4.6 Summary

While being in the classroom language majority made it easier for Ilokano-speaking students to translanguage to learn, I do not think that this was the main reason they did so, but the *precedent* established by Kix and Juan, academically proficient English–Ilokano–Filipino trilinguals who led and/or legitimized translanguaging in academic work. As Juan's regular substitute, Ed, could not do this due to lack of academic English proficiency, whenever Ed was supervising the class as students worked on activities pre-planned by Juan (Table 4.1), Kix did not translanguage nearly as often, and as a result, neither did anybody else.

In contrast, linguistic minority students, singletons and English-dominant students (including those who spoke Ilokano as a HL) were less observable translanguagers who also evaluated the idea of translanguaging less positively. However, this did not mean that they never drew on languages other than English. A few did when the use of their L1/HL was pragmatically appropriate and offered them a positive identity such as 'multilingual poet', even when their L1/HL was in the class minority, or even when they were not fully fluent in it. However, in all these cases, the student (He, Fetu or Aliah) was already quite proficient in English, and so their translanguaging would likely be regarded as a language choice, not a 'fallback' due to lack of English resources.

When it came to the Chuukese-speaking students who used their L1 the least in English 9, pedagogical adjustments in the form of a deliberate, teacher-led translanguaging design (García et al., 2017) likely had to be made to encourage them to translanguage more. For example, making the class learn and use pragmatic phrases in all students' languages (e.g. greetings, colorful words and 'Can I go to the bathroom?'), decorating the classroom walls with such phrases in students' languages and translating key curricular terms and passages into students' languages to display on the walls (e.g. 'metaphor', 'ode' and quotes from Alexie, Shakespeare, etc.), to the extent that these are translatable – using electronic dictionaries and family/community linguistic knowledge – might have increased attendance and participation among students who were not only linguistic minorities but linguistically *minoritized* in the class, creating more systematic spaces for their languages. And while Juan was a competent and critical educator, students might have performed spoken word and oral poetry more during the poetry unit, aside from publishing a poetry anthology, to engage these students in potentially familiar literacy practices.

To sum up, while translanguaging pedagogies should invite *positive dispositions* toward multilingualism ('translanguaging stance'), *planned activities* that draw on students' languages as learning resources ('translanguaging design') and *spontaneous adjustments* to students' language practices during teaching and learning ('translanguaging shifts'; see García et al., 2017), equitable translanguaging spaces cannot be created without consideration of distinct languages. Because of linguistic majorities and minorities (Allard et al., 2019), and the varying extents to which the teacher's language repertoire overlaps with those of individuals or groups of students, people associating themselves with models who represent desired types of bi/multilingualism and proficiencies in distinct languages, as well as students' positionality in relation to activities that bring out their (lack of) language competencies in different domains, distinct languages must be taken into account for the teacher to practically implement 'drawing on the whole language repertoire to learn' among the class as a whole. This is because an essential aspect of getting *any* student to translanguage – and the means will vary from student to student – is an activity that is pragmatically appropriate given class language demographics, and allows that student to present their language and literacy skills in an asset-oriented rather than a deficit-oriented light.

Notes

(1) An asterisk marks a lesson taught by Ed, Juan's regular substitute.

(2) Mike was definitely Filipino, but I do not know what language(s) he spoke at home.

(3) Bob is a student whom I regret not reaching out to more actively, as he consented to be interviewed at the start of the study, but did not come to class that often, and in the end I did not interview him (see note on researcher ethnocentricity in Chapter 3).

(4) In her interview, Kleo told me she had one Chuukese grandparent. She left to go back to the Marshall Islands about halfway through the study.

(5) Diana, who had not yet joined the class, is not included.

(6) By 'productively', I mean in oral speech. As a peer reviewer noted, translanguaging in *thought* is impossible to account for observationally. Therefore, on the questionnaire, I offered 'think to self' as an option for students to report how they translanguaged in class, besides 'talk aloud', 'write notes', 'use a dictionary' and 'other'. Students may always be translanguaging (i.e. thinking in multiple named languages while doing what looks from the outside like using one, or while being silent), but we must also allow for participants' understandings of what they are doing as using their whole linguistic repertoires or using distinct codes. See Ruuska (2016) for an excellent treatment of how translanguaging in thought might also be researched in comparison/contrast to observable oral translanguaging.

(7) However, only video data (gaze) would confirm this, pointing to one of the limitations of this study.

(8) Leung *et al.* (1997) distinguish languages of affiliation from languages of inheritance, pointing out that even if one inherits a language, one may not affiliate with it. In contrast, one may deeply affiliate with a language that one did not inherit.

(9) This metalinguistic discussion reflects what Swain and Watanabe (2012) called 'languaging': multilingual, multimodal negotiation of forms that learners are working to produce in a target language.

(10) See Georgakopoulou (2006) for a sociolinguistic treatment of the phenomenon of adolescent female friend groups creating ongoing hypothetical narratives about men they know.

(11) A song in Filipino by the hip-hop artist Skusta Clee.

(12) Analyses are corroborated with participant statements where interview data about the dialogues are available. This is the case in roughly a quarter of the excerpts (eight out of 27): Excerpts 6, 8–9, 10–12, 18 and 20.

(13) In a follow-up email, I asked Juan what he thought of He's question. Juan wrote back: 'It was an interesting question because non-English names are often anglicized when people move to the U.S. … I interpreted He's question as his desire to reclaim part of his identity'.

(14) As can be seen in classroom dialogues like Excerpt 1, Aliah's use of oral Ilokano was receptive; she could understand her peers' bilingual Ilokano-English talk in peer tutoring during literary analysis, but replied in English.

5 ESL 9/10: Connecting Translanguaging and Critical Language Awareness

In this chapter, I examine Kaori's English as a second language (ESL) 9/10 class in terms of the translanguaging of students in the Filipino first language (L1) majority, including an interactionally dominant group of 'loud' Filipino boys, quieter Filipino boys, Filipino girls and singletons. I explore classroom dynamics in terms of two phenomena, 'doing ridiculous' (Jaspers, 2011) and code-switching as metalinguistic commentary (Rymes, 2014), to suggest that the key to addressing imbalances in interactional turn-taking within a linguistically diverse class is not so much to promote translanguaging over English (as students can take advantage of a language their classmates don't know), as it is to address the underlying linguistic insecurity of all students, especially the interactionally dominant group of students, across various aspects of their language repertoires. This helps students make interactionally inclusive rather than self-preserving moves toward one another and their teacher, positioning each other as competent academically, linguistically and socially across languages and the whole of individual language repertoires.

5.1 ESL 9/10 Class Activities

Kaori's class was for ninth- and tenth-grade students whose World-Class Instructional Design and Assessment (WIDA) scores were between 1.8 and 2.5, meaning they had not yet exited the ESL designation. With 1 on the 5-point WIDA scale described as 'Entering', 2 as 'Emerging' and 3 as 'Developing', students who have scores of about 2 speak in 'phrases or short sentences' and demonstrate 'emerging expressions or ideas'.[1] They know only general language in English rather than vocabulary related to academic subjects, and cannot yet speak or write an expanded range of sentences of varying linguistic complexity.

In ESL 9/10, there was no textbook, but materials included short stories, poems, verbal analogy worksheets and teacher-made Power-Points and handouts. Table 5.1 shows what the class did on each day I visited from January to early May. Major themes and course learning

Table 5.1   Sampling of lessons in ESL 9/10

Jan. 17	Civil Rights Movement; Martin Luther King Jr and the National Association for the Advancement of Colored People (NAACP)
Jan. 24	Verbal analogies, synonyms and antonyms, e.g. light : dark :: dry: wet
Jan. 31	*The Gold Cadillac* by Mildred D. Taylor, about an African American family's struggles for socioeconomic mobility. In the climax of the story, their lives are in danger when they go on a road trip in a nice car the father bought.
Feb. 7	Analyzing story structure in *The Gold Cadillac*, including inciting incident, rising action, climax, etc.
Feb. 21	Correcting grammar in recent compositions on laptops; verbal analogies practice; poetry writing according to the five W's structure (Who, What, Where…).
Feb. 28	Kaori recruits volunteers for the March 2 multilingual conference, a professional development workshop, at the school; students discuss perceptions and stereotypes of ELLs; poetry writing related to identity.
Mar. 7	Poetry-writing workshop by local poet Celeste Gallo (pseudonym), who did the workshop with Juan's class on the same day.
Mar. 28	Continue working on identity poems to be published in the multi-class poetry anthology (including Juan's English 9 class).
Apr. 4	Electing a class representative to speak at the poetry book launch; writing emails to thank photographers (students in a visual arts class who took ESL 9/10 students' photos for the anthology).
Apr. 11	Voting for the book cover of the anthology; lesson on the concepts of 'tone' and 'mood' featuring movie trailers.
Apr. 18	Introduction to argumentation; whole-class debate on the pros and cons of having cellphones.
Apr. 25	Analysis of an article about a law in Hawai'i banning use of cellphones while crossing the street (study of argumentation).
May 2	Preparing for poetry anthology book launch at the Honolulu Public Library; writing personal notes on bookmarks students will distribute at the reading.

aims included US history, such as the civil rights movement, and experimentation with various meta-genres such as narrative, descriptive and argumentative writing. Students also contributed bi/multilingual identity texts (Cummins & Early, 2010) to the school's multi-class poetry anthology, first described in Chapter 3. The anthology was launched at the Honolulu Public Library one weekend in May.

Starting in February, the student teacher Rayna took over the class. Like Juan and Kaori, she explicitly told students that they should feel free to use non-English languages to help each other learn, and never scolded them for using these languages. This involved a positive stance toward bi/multilingual language use in the classroom, but no explicit translanguaging design (García *et al.*, 2017). Interestingly, when Rayna implemented the same classroom language policy that Juan did, the result was very different due to various positionality factors, including Rayna not speaking students' languages and her relative lack of experience with interactional positioning as a teacher.

Although I obtained Rayna's permission to record those lessons she taught, I did not formally interview her. Part of the reason was that she struggled with disciplinary issues arising from teaching a class of loud male teenagers. I could see her making similar mistakes I made as a student teacher with regard to triggering their insecurities with discourses of academic and standard language, which was why I suspected they acted out so much. In retrospect, I believe it would have been better to have asked her whether or not she wanted to be interviewed about classroom interactions, rather than assuming that it would be too awkward for her; it might have benefited us both in terms of opportunities for reflection. For example, my promotion of translanguaging likely made it even harder for her to manage the class, as she did not speak Filipino.

On the other hand, I was able to interview Kaori about her life story and teaching background at the start of the data collection and gathered her feedback on the findings toward the end.[2]

5.2 The ESL 9/10 Teacher

As ESL department head, Kaori managed the changing placements of about 450 students ('443, to be precise') in the school English language learner (ELL) program, which she said she was 'always updating'. She came to Hawai'i about 20 years before the study to finish her Bachelor of Education and do a masters, during which she met her husband and decided to stay. Back in Japan, she had worked for five years at a school that prepared students for a university entrance exam, a job she enjoyed, but she said it was more oriented to grammar than 'practical things' or literature – 'I loved to read'. Hence, she sought a career change to teach beyond test preparation.

After becoming a certified teacher in Hawai'i, she worked as a substitute teacher in another Filipino-dominant area of Honolulu, and then as a 'regular' teacher at an elementary school near Waikīkī; however, working at that school made her realize that she enjoyed teaching older students more. As a result, she applied to and was hired at her current school. At the time of the study, she was a veteran at the school, having taught there for 13–14 years: 'When I started, I taught all the different levels [of ESL]'. At this school, she found what had been missing in her first teaching context, which she returned to in our second interview:

> Civic involvement. That's a part of language learning too. So without knowing what's going on in the community, not just yourself—that's y'know, becoming part of the community. … And also (.) holistic approach, I guess? Not just language learners. You know, my goal is to graduate—help them graduate from high school, but not just language. … That's why I found that teaching at the high school and teaching at the language school is a totally different job.

Given the prevalence of Filipino students in her class, Kaori not only recognized the importance of language to her students' sense of self, but also highlighted the importance of considering others' needs. She explained:

> I encourage them to use first language (.) in class, and I don't punish them. But at the same time, I want—I wanna give the equal opportunity so equal chances, to, you know, speak—to (.) benefit from these privileges. ... I really have to, so—look at it too, because I don't want other non-Filipino students to feel intimidated or, like if, treated unfairly or so. Yeah. So don't get that same opportunity to use, you know, first language.

While Rayna, the student teacher, did not voice this concern, I believe she also felt it, as classroom management became difficult for her in this class composed mainly of vocal Filipino boys. A Korean American who came to Hawai'i during high school and was pursuing teacher certification in her mid-twenties, Rayna could not tell Filipino languages apart, much less know what students were saying, though she encouraged students to use their home languages if they needed to. In this chapter, I show how this well-meaning encouragement, combined with the boys' English anxiety, which she sometimes unintentionally provoked, had an impact on their bi/multilingual oral classroom practices, which in turn impacted the classroom experience for Rayna and the other students.

5.3 The ESL 9/10 Students

There were 17 students in ESL 9/10 in 2018–2019 and, as with English 9, a few came or left partway through the year. One vocal student, Flow-G, and most of his group[3] of 'loud' Filipino boys – Cookie, Aaron, Ricky, Kok, Skusta and Simon – were present throughout the school year (all except for Simon). At the periphery of the class were quieter Filipino boys (Luke and Kyrie), Filipino girls (Juliana, Mariel, Ruby and Jennifer) and singletons such as Kaiea (Marshallese), Binh (Vietnamese) and Summer (who was joined by another Chinese girl in April). Skusta, who was originally 'one of the gang' of Filipino boys, became marginalized from January to May as the others made fun of his English performance. Figure 5.1 shows the class' social groups from my perspective, again with letters being shorthand for students' L1s/heritage languages (HLs) – except this time, I put 'F' (Filipino) for all Filipino students since they used this as their lingua franca. The arrow shows how Skusta was expelled from the dominant group of boys over time, whereas two other male Filipino students, Luke (who wanted to be a 'good' student and generally avoided misbehavior) and Kyrie (who was very quiet) did not belong to this group in the first place.

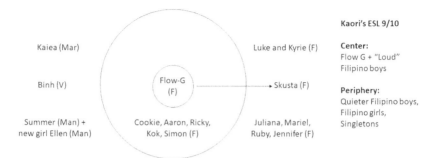

Figure 5.1   ESL 9/10 class dynamics

In Table 5.2, I summarize ESL 9/10 students' demographic information and home languages (if known, i.e. if they agreed to be interviewed).
It can be assumed due to placement procedures that the class consisted
of relative newcomers.

As with English 9, individual students' reported willingness to use
languages other than English in ESL 9/10 varied widely. Table 5.3 summarizes the answers of 14 out of 17 students, not including Binh, who
left the class early in the semester, Ellen, who came toward the end,
and Simon, who had limited attendance. Many of the Filipino students

Table 5.2   Students in ESL 9/10

Pseudonym	Years in Hawai'i	Country of origin	L1(s)	Audio-recorded	Interviewed
Flow-G	1–2	Philippines	Ilokano and Tagalog	Y	Y
Aaron	Unknown	Philippines	Unknown	N	N
Ricky	Unknown	Philippines	Unknown	N	N
Cookie	1–2	Philippines	Ilokano and Tagalog	Y	Y
Kok	1–2	Philippines	Ilonggo	Y	Y
Skusta	1–2	Philippines	Cebuano	Y	Y
Simon	Unknown	Philippines	Unknown	N	N
Luke	Unknown	Philippines	Unknown	N	N
Kyrie	<1	Philippines	Ilokano and Tagalog	N	N
Juliana	<1	Philippines	Ilokano and Tagalog	Y	Y
Mariel	<1	Philippines	Unknown	Y	N
Ruby	<1	Philippines	Unknown	Y	N
Jennifer	<1	Philippines	Unknown	Y	N
Kaiea	Unknown	Marshall Islands	Marshallese	Y	N
Binh	Unknown	Vietnam	Vietnamese	Y	N
Summer	Unknown	China	Mandarin	Y	N
Ellen	Unknown	China	Mandarin	N	N

Table 5.3   ESL 9/10 students' responses to the language questionnaire

	Reported language/s used	How often	Think to self	Talk aloud	Write notes	Use dictionary	Other
Aaron	Tagalog	All the time		X			
Flow-G	Tagalog	Sometimes	X	X	X	X	X (reading)
Ricky	Ilokano and Tagalog	Sometimes			X	X	
Cookie	Ilokano and Tagalog	Sometimes					X (help friend)
Kok	Tagalog	Sometimes					X (not stated)
Luke	Tagalog	Sometimes	X				X (not stated)
Kyrie	Tagalog and Ilokano	Sometimes				X	
Skusta	Tagalog, Bisaya and Ilokano	Sometimes		X			
Summer	Blank	Sometimes		X			
Juliana	Ilokano and Tagalog	Sometimes			X		
Ruby	Ilokano	Sometimes			X	X	
Mariel	Ilokano and Tagalog	Sometimes			X	X	
Jennifer	Blank	Never					
Kaiea	Blank	Never					

identified more than one language other than English (LOTE) while those in Juan's class did not, a response which may have arisen because this class had more ethnolinguistic variety in terms of Philippine languages.

The chart can be broken down into the following individuals/groups for analysis, based on gender, ethnicity and levels of oral participation: (1) Aaron, Flow-G and Ricky, who appeared to be ringleaders among the Filipino-speaking boys (e.g. Excerpts 17 and 19); (2) Cookie, Kok, Luke, Kyrie and Skusta, other Filipino-speaking boys, all of whom were vocal except Kyrie; (3) the Chinese singleton Summer, who had a hearing disability and was very quiet, but participated well enough in class activities (though she sometimes read what appeared to be Chinese fiction on her phone when apparently bored); (4) the Filipino-speaking girls Juliana, Ruby, Mariel and Jennifer, who often sat together, though Ruby was also friends with Cookie; and (5) Kaiea, who did not say much in class but was an avid reader of English young adult (YA) fiction. She produced some very fine poetry for ESL 9/10. In addition, Kaori mentioned that Kaiea used to be chatty before her Marshallese-speaking friend moved to another class.

Within the groups, there were individual differences. For instance, of the three ringleaders among the Filipino boys, only Aaron reported that he used another language 'all the time', and that his only use of this language was to 'talk aloud'. In contrast, Flow-G reported doing every kind of translanguaging, and was the only student in the study who checked all the boxes. Ricky seemed to play the 'good boy', answering that he wrote notes and used a dictionary, but didn't talk aloud, in Ilokano and Tagalog (though I recorded him speaking these languages and did not observe him writing notes or using the dictionary much). As I will illustrate using the data that follows, Flow-G was the true leader of the class – naughty but also able to answer the teacher's questions in English, with high trilingual proficiency in English, Filipino and Ilokano, at least for general conversational purposes, though use of the last was limited in this class. Aaron, admired for his athletic ability, had a reputation as a 'tough' boy with Ricky as his sidekick, but their academic confidence did not match Flow-G's. Joined by four or five others, they formed the class' loud majority. The other Filipino-speaking boys had individual differences as well. Cookie and Luke were eager to please the teachers, and Cookie did not ignore the girls. Kok, an Ilonggo speaker (though he only put 'Tagalog' on the questionnaire), seemed to eventually sympathize with Rayna, who tutored his brother Konan in Korean during breaks or after school. However, he only showed this disposition in minor ways like saying 'Bye miss' and 'Take care' at the end of class. Kyrie was the only quiet Filipino boy, and tried his best. Skusta, the Bisaya/Cebuano-speaking boy who was originally one of the gang, was eventually ostracized due to his reading challenges,[4] which made him seem less proficient in English than the others.

The rest of the chart shows the data for the girls and singletons. Summer's response is odd, as I did not hear her speak a Chinese language aloud, or speak much at all, but saw her writing bilingual notes and using an electronic dictionary. Ruby and Mariel reported taking bilingual notes and doing dictionary work, and I saw them use their phones to Google things related to classroom activity. Indeed, such multimodal communication was used when students could not find the words to express their thoughts in English. Among these students, only Jennifer answered on the questionnaire that English was appropriate for class even with speakers of one's L1/HL: 'I always speak inside the class an English language and I also talk outside the room a Tagalog language'. As for Kaiea, she said (corroborating Kaori's comment about her Marshallese-speaking friend who left): 'I never use another language in this class because I don't have Marshallese classmate and I think it's helpful for me to must understand English and know how to speak English'.

5.4 'Laissez Faire Translanguaging'

While Rayna often explicitly told students to 'feel free' to use Filipino, Ilokano, Marshallese, Vietnamese, etc., to learn, she did not draw on their languages in any systematic or pedagogical way (e.g. García *et al.*, 2017; Woodley & Brown, 2016). In other words, while translanguaging was permitted in this class and in English 9, we might call it 'laissez faire' translanguaging (Mendoza, 2020a). Not surprisingly, given that there were three singletons and everyone else shared Filipino, almost all of the translanguaging aloud in oral speech that occurred when invited was in Filipino (with the exception of stylizations in other Philippine languages). While Rayna supported translanguaging, the lack of English spoken by the Filipino-speaking majority *to each other* was concerning in that they did not seem to practice English enough in English class, or appear confident to try it out with each other. One morning in February, a third through the audio-recording period of the study, I tallied utterances directed out to the class rather than to immediate neighbors for 25 minutes (Table 5.4). Most to all of these came from Filipino-speaking boys.

The trend is clear: about two-thirds of public talk is in English (120 versus 76 utterances), yet the students' public talk to *each other* is in Filipino rather than English about two-thirds of the time (73 versus 32 utterances). The vast majority of English utterances were directed to *Rayna* – which I observed left her drained as her attention was commanded by so many students at once. In addition to this large amount of Filipino talk to the class, which singletons like Kaiea and Summer could not understand, there was constant chatter to immediate neighbors in Filipino, and three utterances in Filipino directed to the Filipina educational assistant, to whom I gave the pseudonym Teresa.[5]

Field notes I took during this session included the following observations. First, if the non-Filipino students did speak, what they said could not be caught above the din. Second, English statements, mostly coming from the Filipino-speaking boys, directed to Rayna struck me as rather rude, and showed little consideration of the needs of the rest of the class: 'MISS! MISS! MISS!' 'WHAT IS THIS MISS? WHAT IS THIS?' 'HE'S SEARCHING YOUTUBE MISS! HE'S SEARCHING YOUTUBE!' 'MISS, I'M DONE! I'M DONE MISS!' 'MISS, I'M DONE ALREADY! SHARE?'

When I talked to four Filipino boys who agreed to be interviewed, they gave various answers as to why they used so much Filipino in class. Together, these responses showed how mirth and camaraderie in Filipino were mixed with English anxiety, and as I began to suspect how the former compensated for the latter, I discerned differences in how the boys dealt with this tension given their positions in the class. I present the interviews in chronological order, starting with Cookie's on January 31.

Table 5.4   Filipino versus English talk

Filipino to others	73
Filipino to teacher	3
English to others	32
English to teacher	88

Excerpt 10 Speaking Filipino in class (Cookie's perspective)

1	**Anna:**	May huling tanong ako sayo. *I have one last question for you.*
2	**Cookie:**	Oo miss. *Yes miss.*
3	**Anna:**	Bakit ang lakas lakas ng mga boses n'yo sa klase? (Cookie laughs) Like ah (.) bakit minsan minsan parang lahat kayo gusto mag ah (.) magsalita hindi na kayo nakikinig sa isat' isa? *Why are you guys' voices so loud in class? (Cookie laughs) Like ah (.) why is it sometimes it's like you all want to ah (.) talk even though you aren't listening to each other anymore?*
4	**Cookie:**	Parang kwan lang man miss, pag nagsasalita kami, para lang maagawan yung attention ng teacher ay (.) ganon. *It's only like you know miss, when we speak, we talk just to get the teacher's attention (.) like that.*
5	**Anna:**	=Oo nga. Bakit mo ginagawa yon? *=Yeah that's right. Why are you doing that?*
6	**Cookie:**	(snicker) (XXX) yung ganon parang ganon. *(snicker) (XXX) it's like that kinda like that.*
7	**Anna:**	What?
8	**Cookie:**	Yung katabi ko kasi miss, pag nagsasalita miss—umaapaw na din miss. *My neighbor see miss, when he speaks—boiling over already miss.*
9	**Anna:**	Oo, pero bakit mo ginagawa yon, bakit parang may kompetensiya kung sinong pwede ah (.) kayang agawin yung attention ng teacher. *Yes, but why are you doing that, why is it like there's a competition of who can ah (.) is able to catch the teacher's attention.*
10	**Cookie:**	Di ko alam eh miss. Di ko alam. … Parang (.) parang kwan lang miss, yung (.) parang natutul—kung inaantok kami sisigaw ka. Para mawala yung antok mo. *I don't know miss. I don't know. … It's like (.) it's like miss, like sleep—if you're sleepy you'll shout. So your sleepiness goes away.*

Cookie gives two explanations for why they talk so loudly: his neighbor is like a kettle of boiling water (Line 8) and they shout to keep themselves awake (Line 10). Such answers could show an attempt to lead the researcher 'up the garden path' (Jaspers, 2011: 1273), but I had to be satisfied with them.

The next week, I tried Kok and Skusta, two friends who were interviewed together on February 7, though Kok later participated to some degree in Skusta's exclusion. They also gave somewhat avoidant answers, humoring me when I confronted them about this borderline misbehavior.

Excerpt 11 Speaking Filipino in class (Skusta's and Kok's perspectives)

1	**Anna:**	Tinanong ko din to kay Cookie, bakit ang lakas lakas ng mga boses n'yo sa English class? *I was asking this to Cookie too, why are your voices so loud in English class?*
2	**Skusta:**	(Pretending to scold Kok) Oo nga e. *(Pretending to scold Kok) That's right.*
3	**Kok:**	Sila po miss. *It's them miss.*

4	Skusta:	Sila lang po.
		It's just them.
5	Anna:	Sila lang? Sino yung 'sila'?
		It's just them? Who's the 'they'?
6	Skusta:	(amused voice) Sila Fl—Cookie.
		(amused voice) Fl—Cookie.
7	Anna:	O malakas din kayo.
		Hey you guys are loud too.
8	Kok:	Hindi.
		No.
9	Anna:	Bakit minsan naman na (.) a:hhh (.) like ah—nung isang, nung isang klase parang ang, ang, like lahat na lang sumasagot tapos mga sagot parang mga (.) kung ano-ano na lang sinasagot? Like, 'The moon is round (.) and the sun is square.' (Kok laughs) Bakit lahat kayo gumaganon, bakit naman?
		How come sometimes (.) a:hhh (.) like ah—that one, that one time it was the, the, like everyone was answering and then the answers were like (.) just about everything? Like, 'The moon is round (.) and the sun is square.' (Kok laughs) Why do you guys all do that, why?
10	Skusta:	Sakin, 'because of the gravity of the earth.' (Kok laughs) Ako, doon ako sa science ako pinakamadaldal. At-chaka sa kwan. Math. Doon ako pinakamadaldal.
		For me, 'because of the gravity of the earth.' (Kok laughs) Me, it's in science that I'm most chatty. And also in what's-it. Math. There I'm most chatty.
11	Kok:	Ano miss (.) patawa lang po.
		It's like miss (.) just for laughs.
12	Skusta:	Oo, patawa lang—
		Yes, just for laughs—
13	Anna:	Patawa.
		Just for laughs.
14	Kok:	Para hindi naman boring minsan. Kasi minsan boring.
		So it's not boring sometimes. Because it's sometimes boring.
15	Skusta:	Opo miss.
		Yes miss.

Kok and Skusta first claim that it is not they but others who are loud (Lines 3–4), such as Flow-G or Cookie (Line 6). I contest this (Line 7) and Kok disagrees (Line 8), which leads me to narrate an event as vividly as I can, struggling a little for the words in Filipino (Line 9), at which point they appear to remember that they sometimes partake in the clamor themselves, including shouting nonsense answers to verbal analogies. This leads Skusta to give my 'Why?' an idiomatic answer in Filipino English[6]: 'Because of the gravity of the earth' (Line 10), which roughly translates into 'just because'.

The interview ends with them saying that they do it because they're a little bored and want to have a laugh, which could have been what Cookie meant when he said they shout to keep themselves awake (rendering his answer more reasonable after Kok and Skusta's interview). Their teacher, Kaori, did not object to this in one of her own interviews, saying, 'They're still kids. So sometimes I have to give some leeway (.) to be (.) a kid. You know, I'm OK for them to goof around once in a while. But not all the time'. (In Juan's class, I observed students could be loud, especially the boys Kix, He and Fetu, though answers to the teacher's questions tended to be earnest, suggesting that the boys in ESL 9/10 were playing with Rayna. In other words, there seemed to be a gendered dynamic to this behavior, though differences in the two teachers' experience and authority was another factor.)

While Cookie, Kok and Skusta represented 'just being kids', my interview with Flow-G two weeks later, on February 21, suggested there was more to this behavior. By late February, I saw that he was the most multilingually proficient student, also in Kaori's own assessment: 'He has more language than others too. And people kind of look up to him'.[7] In my interview with Flow-G, he acknowledged that no one but Teresa used Filipino in ways relevant to classroom tasks, and on the rare occasion that the boys did so (e.g. three utterances in Table 5.4), it was to address her. Later in the interview, I introduced the same issue I had discussed with the others:

Excerpt 12 Speaking Filipino in class (Flow-G's perspective)

1	Anna:	Bakit mo ginagamit ang Tagalog sa English class, kung hindi—hindi—ibig sabihin mo hindi siya para mag-aral? Bakit ganon? *How come you use Tagalog in English class if not—if not—you said it's not to study? Why like that?*
2	Flow-G:	Hindi po miss, pag ano po (.) kasi minsan (.) pag English po ako minsan ganon (.) mali po ganon. Mali po. Tapos minsan tatawanan nila ganon. *No miss, if it's (.) because sometimes (.) if I use English sometimes it's like (.) it's like wrong. It's wrong. Then they laugh like that.*
3	Anna:	Ahh. So (1.0) I mean (1.0) you're saying na (2.0) hindi mo kinakausap ang mga kaibigan mo sa Ingles kasi siguro tatawanan (.) [pagtatatawanan ka? *Aah. So (1.0) I mean (1.0) you're saying (2.0) you don't talk to your friends in English because maybe they laugh (.) will laugh at you?*
4	Flow-G:	[Yon miss. Pagka magkamali ka miss, ganon. *[That's it miss. When you make a mistake, like that.*
5	Anna:	Tagalog ginagamit n'yo kasi—hindi kayo, like, hindi ah (.) mahina ang Tagalog. (sic) *You guys use Tagalog because—you're not, like, not ah (.) weak in Tagalog.*
6	Flow-G:	Opo miss. *Yes miss.*
7	Anna:	Ganon pala? *Is that so?*
8	Flow-G:	Opo miss. [Tatawa tawa— *Yes miss. [Laughing and laughing—*
9	Anna:	[Paano mo alam yon? *[How do you know that?*
10	Flow-G:	Nag-gaganon din po kami minsan miss. Naguusap-usap din po kami sa English. Tapos kung may nag-kamali po ganon tatawan-tawanan po ganon. *We do that sometimes miss. Sometimes we're talking in English too. Then if someone makes a mistake then they laugh at them like that.*

11	**Anna:**	… So paano ba sabihin to sa Tagalog—so how do you feel about that? Anong ah—anong ah—
		So how do you say this in Tagalog—so how do you feel about that? What's ah—what's ah—
12	**Flow-G:**	Nahiya rin miss. Shy. Nahiya rin. Parang ngayon ayaw ko na ulitin ganon.
		End up shy too miss. Shy. End up shy. It's like now I don't want to do it again.

Flow-G's explanation for their high levels of Filipino use is straight-forward: they use Filipino with each other to avoid being teased about one's English (Lines 2–6). Later, I ask him how he knows this (Line 9), and he explains that they also use English sometimes but make fun of someone who makes a mistake, and when this has happened to him, he felt too shy to do it again (Lines 10–12). It is remarkable that Flow-G is the *strongest* Filipino–English bilingual in the class, and yet he still feels this way. His anxiety appears to arise because the group is not focused on communicative competence but native-like accuracy in English (as I will demonstrate in other excerpts in this chapter and Chapter 6), i.e. no matter how perfectly well you can express yourself, if something is pronounced with an accent or contains a grammatical error, that pro-vides grounds to make fun of your English. If a common activity in class is to make light of things, then the boys must avoid being the target of humor as well.

I documented an example of this during another lesson, when Aaron and Kok were sitting next to each other, each with a laptop in front of him as they corrected grammar in their poetry for the multi-class poetry anthology.

Excerpt 13 Past tense of 'climb'

1	**Aaron:**	Miss, what is 'climb'? (2.0) Ow, I mean in the past tense? (2.0) Climbed.
2	**Kok:**	(whispers) Past tense, 'climbed' ba?
		(whispers) Past tense, 'climbed' is it?
3	**Aaron:**	Past tense nang 'climb.'
		Past tense of 'climb.'
4	**Kok:**	Anong climb?
		What climb?
5	**Aaron:**	Climb ED yeah?
6	**Kok:**	Hindi. I-N-G. I-N-G nga. (2.0) >Double-m pala, double m.<
		No. I-N-G. I-N-G. (2.0) >Double-m actually, double m.<
7	**Skusta:**	Eh gagi.
		Eh jerk.
8	**Unknown student:**	Ah climbing.
9	**Aaron:**	Baliw to!
		This crazy ass!
10	**Kok:**	What? (to Rayna) Miss!

While Aaron was on the right track and only sought confirmation that 'climb' was a regular past tense verb (Line 5), Kok gave him a wrong answer (the ING form) and, as an afterthought ('Double-m pala' [Double-m actually]; Line 6), took the prank further to see if Aaron would believe the past tense of climb was 'climmbing'. Overhearing, Skusta called Kok a jerk (Line 7) and Aaron reacted roughly (Line 9). Such interactions, however, were in Filipino and could not be perceived by Kaori and Rayna.

I believe that these Filipino boys in ESL 9/10 genuinely wanted to learn, as are many students who are marginalized by standard language regimes at school, which they no doubt play a part in.[8] In the case of these young men in the study, they were often too anxious to translanguage – defined as using their whole language repertoires to think aloud and make meaning – but the resources they avoided were from English, because it was their English use and not their L1 use that was stigmatized in their context; that is, avoiding English use meant avoiding being the butt of a joke, and being discursively constructed as less competent in English. Instead, they used Filipino to code-switch into unsanctioned activities that turned the balance of social power in their favor.

In the following two sections, I discuss two of these activities: (1) 'doing ridiculous' (Jaspers, 2011) and (2) using Filipino as the *medium* through which language competencies (and identities) were discursively constructed without Kaori or Rayna knowing. In other words, the 'loud' Filipino boys were not inhibited to speak Filipino, being in the class linguistic majority and given that their teachers supported translanguaging, but they could often not think aloud using English with one another, either on its own or in translanguaging, due to the scrutiny applied to their English by their peers (i.e. by each other). Of course, they still made an earnest effort to speak English to their teachers, and actively (perhaps too actively) solicited teacher help and assistance to learn.

5.5 'Doing Ridiculous'

The term 'doing ridiculous' comes from Jaspers' (2011) study of working-class male high school students in Flanders, Belgium, but the same phenomenon was documented in a high school ESL class in Hawai'i by Talmy (2008). Flanders, the northern part of Belgium, has Dutch as an official language. In the 19th century, Dutch used to be subordinate to French (i.e. Dutch L1 speakers who were second language [L2] speakers of French were discriminated against in the higher professions and in the education system); however, a Flemish movement in the 1930s led to Dutch becoming the dominant language, necessary for professional advancement in the same ways that French once used to be. In recent decades, many immigrants have arrived in Flanders, mostly from North Africa and the Middle East. In the classroom Jaspers observed, the official language was Dutch, and the class' dominant group consisted of a Moroccan majority while the subordinate group had Arabic, Turkish, Berber and white working-class Dutch students. The Moroccan majority had 'good vernacular competence in Dutch' (Jaspers, 2011: 1268) and knew how to make their talk more academic or more casual depending on the situation, though they still struggled with academic language. They spoke ethnolectal varieties of Dutch, influenced by Moroccan Arabic, yet had a wide range of Dutch pragmatic competence – in that they could identify and style a wide range of Dutch dialects and registers, which allowed them, especially the boys, to do what Jaspers called 'doing ridiculous', hijacking lessons and thwarting the teacher's intentions through witty verbal repartees.

These Moroccan Dutch students also made fun of the ways of speaking of the classroom minority students, pointing out those students' (other kinds of) non-standard Dutch, while the minoritized students could not fight back, as many of them 'lacked the skill for witty repartee [in *any* dialect of the official classroom language] and were effectively marginalized in public classroom talk' (Jaspers, 2011: 1275), unable to draw on the *other* languages they knew that were not very useful in this setting. Finally, the Moroccan Dutch students knew they did not speak Dutch like middle-class white people. And they did not care – to them, it was too 'nerdy' and unnatural to do so. It was more that they wanted to be recognized as proficient in *Dutch*, which they defined as their formidable command of Dutch. By and large, they were well positioned to socially construct themselves as the 'legitimate' Dutch speakers, being in the class majority and in control of the linguistic capital in that environment.

In Talmy's ethnography of a secondary ESL classroom in Hawai'i, there were both newcomers (called 'FOBs' or 'Fresh Off the Boat') and students who had grown up in the US but spoke other languages at home (called 'Lifers'). The Lifers were fluent in Hawai'i English, but struggled with academic reading and writing. Although Lifers had ethnolinguistic markers in their speech that indicated their difference from the 'white US mainstream', they rejected the ESL label by positioning the newcomers as the 'real' ESL students. To do this, they, especially loud male Lifers (similar to the Moroccan Dutch students in Jaspers' study) repeated newcomers' English pronunciation, goofed off in class and engaged in wry metacommentary in Hawai'i Creole (Pidgin) – the way a sports announcer makes comments as a game or a race is unfolding, about what is happening, only in this case 'what is happening' is what is happening in class, linguistically speaking. That is, these Lifer students, particularly the vocal male Lifers, used the class majority non-English language (Hawai'i Creole) as a *medium* to evaluate their peers' English and general academic competencies, discursively constructing each other's language abilities and classroom identities in that other language or dialect without teachers being able to (fully) understand.[9]

When interviewing Cookie, Kok, Skusta and Flow-G, I asked about their tendency to 'do ridiculous' and engage in these discursive positionings in Filipino, noting that they also positioned themselves as competent English users by using English primarily in talk addressed to the *teacher as the only ratified participant* (even when that talk was silly, and displayed their wit to their peers as unratified participants; see Goffman, 1981). I referred them back to the lesson on verbal analogies, e.g. 'light : dark :: dry : wet', a vocabulary-building exercise for standardized tests.

Excerpt 14 Verbal analogies

1	Rayna:	What would be an antonym of wealth?
2	Skusta:	Health (.) uh wealth (.) uh wet.
3	Rayna:	What does wealth mean?
4	Cookie:	I don't know miss. Wealth—I don't know (.) wealth.
5	Skusta:	Healthy like that?
6	Rayna:	It's not healthy.
7	Boy:	...Height is you're tall.
8	Cookie:	Like the—the water is wet.
9	Kok:	Why is 'water is wet'?
10	Rayna:	>So wealth means you have a lot of money.<

In this excerpt, Skusta, Cookie, Kok and possibly a fourth boy had no idea of the meaning of 'wealth', yet instead of looking it up in a dictionary, waiting for someone else to answer, saying 'I don't know' or asking Rayna to explain, they spoke up by grasping at *any* kind of association to participate and show what they *did* know in English – whether rhyme or a proverb ('health is more important than wealth'), alliteration (health and height both begin with H) or pronunciation ('wealth' sounds like 'wet' with a Filipino accent). Soon this became a source of comedy. When Rayna said, 'This is what I want it to look like', Cookie stammered in Filipino-accented English, 'It *lok* like (.) it *lok* like (.) it *lok* like—' and Flow-G interrupted, 'Itlog!' (egg).[10]

There are better ways to deal with this situation. Rayna, who was still a novice teacher, could have asked students to study the words beforehand, had them review in small groups and finally ask different individuals/groups to answer the questions on the projector in a whole-class review, with her own metacommentary and explanations on test-taking skills, rather than jumping into a whole-class activity that publicly tested students on words they might or might not know. By the second half of the exercise, the Filipino boys were guessing randomly. In this way, they demonstrated 'trying' and some knowledge of English, as well as a sense of humor. When Rayna asked, 'Car goes on the road and ship goes on—', the Filipino boys, latching onto each other, answered conceptually related words that were not the answer: 'Earth!' 'Ship!' 'Spaceship!' 'Beach!' 'Kalawakan!' (outer space) and 'Water!'. Nothing was heard from other students. (This is the exercise I was referring to when I asked Kok and Skusta why they answered that 'The moon is round and the sun is square'.) The Filipino-speaking boys did not even attempt a reasonable guess – since to try to answer the question in earnest would probably result in a wrong answer – but demonstrated alternative forms of mastery by seeing who could be the funniest, most creative or most verbally dominant in showing what English they *did* know.

In a later class that also involved verbal analogies, Rayna tested words previously taught, but it appears students had not bothered to study them (or at least, none of the students who spoke up). On this occasion, she presented a matching exercise on the projector, with five words on the left and five words on the right.

Excerpt 15 Verbal analogies review

1	Rayna:	Do you guys remember these words? Let's see if you guys remember these words. So what does 'synonym' mean?
2	Cookie:	Same. Similarities!
3	Student:	Opposite!
4	Rayna:	Yeah, similar meaning. What does 'lurk' mean? Or what is its synonym?
5	Cookie and Juliana:	C.
6	Rayna:	What does 'lurk' mean?
7	Student:	Hide.
8	Juliana:	Hide.
9	Student:	Hide from someone.
10	Rayna:	Similar to—
11	Various students:	E.
12	Other students:	C.
13	Rayna:	Embarrassed?
14	Various students:	C. C. C.
15	Cookie:	C! Humiliate!
16	Student:	Drowsiness is sleepiness.
17	Student:	Sleepiness. D!
18	Various students:	D! D!
19	Cookie:	Splendor is stupidness!
20	Rayna:	Splendor is to—
21	Student:	Majesty! Majesty!
22	(class breaks off into many simultaneous shouts, giving the final answer by elimination)	
23	Student:	Just like what I said.

24	Rayna:	So some—only two people I think got everything correct.
25	Cookie:	>=About (.) I correct yeah? But I mean—I did pass it yeah?<
26	Student:	Yeah me too.

Several points are noteworthy here. First, not everyone remembers that synonym means 'same' and antonym 'opposite', rather than vice versa (Lines 2–3). Then, a few students get the first question, 'lurk', right – but there is disagreement: E ('hide'; correct) and C ('embarrassed'; incorrect) are both proposed (Lines 6–12). For item two, the answer is C, 'embarrassed' = 'humiliated'. After several people say C (Line 14), Cookie shouts it (Line 15) as if to claim it for himself. For the third item, a boy answers at normal volume that drowsiness is sleepiness (Line 16), which others take up by shouting the same (Lines 17–18).

With two pairs of words remaining, Cookie makes a guess, but he gets them switched around (Line 19). Rayna signals his answer is incorrect by repeating the question, 'Splendor is to...?' (Line 20), so another student yells the right answer: 'Majesty! Majesty!' (Line 21), while the rest of the class seizes the correct answer to the last item by shouting it out (Line 22), and unfortunately it is 'ignorance' = 'stupidness'. Cookie then claims, in a rapid voice denoted by pointed brackets, that he still passed (Line 25), and another student asserts that he did too (Line 26). While few of the answers seem to have been recalled, these are highly expressive moves by students to perform task competence and position themselves positively.

In short, even when students are 'doing ridiculous', their emotional involvement in interactions reveals how high-stakes these interactions are for them. Of additional concern is the oft-accompanying practice of using the classroom majority non-English language as the *medium* through which language competencies and identities are discursively constructed, beyond teachers' full level of understanding. I call this 'code-switching as metalinguistic commentary'.

5.6 Code-Switching as Metalinguistic Commentary

Metalinguistic commentary is a wider social phenomenon going beyond classroom contexts, as sociolinguists note that people socially construct language competencies by talking about what they (or others) have just said, or tend to say (e.g. Coupland, 2003; Eckert, 2008; Irvine *et al.*, 2009; Sandhu, 2015). In ESL 9/10, Filipino-speaking students used code-switching into Filipino, the primary language of metalinguistic commentary, to discursively construct competencies in both English and HLs. Recall that self-stylization (Canagarajah, 2012) does not require extended stretches of discourse to be produced in a HL. Below is an example in which the Filipino boys, many of whom identified Tagalog and/or Ilokano as their L1 in Table 5.2,[11] discursively constructed their proficiency in Ilokano *through* Tagalog (Filipino).

Excerpt 16 Heritage languages and self-stylization

1	FLow-G: *FI	Ilokano ako gago.
		I'm Ilokano dumbass.
2	Aaron: *FI	Pero sakin ka nagtatanong pag Ilokano gago.
		But you ask me how to say things in Ilokano dumbass.
3		(laughter)
4		Pero yung iba hindi ko naintindihan.
		But the other things I didn't understand.
5	Male student: *FI	Ako rin Bisaya e. (4.0) Nakaintindi din ako kasi Binibisaya.
		Me too for Bisaya. (4.0) I can understand because they used Bisaya.
6	Aaron: *FI/*IL	Ilokano sa bahay. Pag 'oo nga', 'wen ngarud.'
		Ilokano at home. To say 'oo nga' ['yes' in Filipino], 'wen ngarud' ['yes' in Ilokano].
7	Male student: *IL	Manganen kano?
		Did you eat yet?
8	Aaron: *FI → *IL	Pero tinatanong mo, 'ngangankan ka na?'
		But to ask, 'did you give birth yet?'

In this dialogue, several boys position themselves as knowers of Ilokano, and one as a knower of Bisaya (Line 5), the lingua franca of the Visayas, also called 'Cebuano' (the ethnic language of the Cebuanos). This is ignored by others, who keep on showing knowledge of Ilokano through self-stylization and framing 'what I know in Ilokano' using metacommentary in Filipino (Lines 7–8). While Aaron makes the qualifying statement that he doesn't understand everything in Ilokano, even though he is Ilokano (Line 4), he illustrates how 'yes' is different across Tagalog and Ilokano (Line 6), after which another boy shows he knows a greeting in Ilokano (Line 7). Next, Aaron gives a different sentence in Ilokano (Line 8). As Johnstone (2013) notes, neither individuals nor groups need to speak a language/dialect extensively to claim heritage ownership of it, or an expert identity with regard to certain of its features. In Excerpt 16, Ilokano is legitimized as a subject of interest whereas Bisaya is not, and Filipino, which these boys seem more dominant in, is legitimized as a framing mechanism to demonstrate bits of Ilokano knowledge; in this case, it is not discursively necessary to converse in Ilokano to show one knows the language.[12]

While this dialogue is relatively harmless (despite the fact that the Bisaya-speaking student's contribution was not acknowledged and non-Filipino students could not understand what was being said), others were more troubling. In these cases, Filipino was used to make others look academically or linguistically incompetent in English class, below the teachers' full level of understanding.

For example, I return to the song by Filipino rapper and hip-hop artist Skusta Clee that Eufia and Rizze were singing in Chapter 4 (Excerpt 5). This song goes (translation): *If you're not gonna answer me / Then don't come round courting me.* One morning in ESL 9/10, as students were working individually, Flow-G created alternative lyrics on the fly – demonstrating no small degree of verbal skill to fit them into the rhythm of the song – to make announcements about his peers.

Excerpt 17 Alternative lyrics

1	**Flow-G:**	(sings) Kung si Ricky ay hindi maka-pasa::
		Hindi bigyan ang pera niya::
		Kasi hindi (tapping on table) naman siya nakapasok
		Sa iskul niya, nagtatambay lang siya kung saan-saan.
		Para hindi na siya mag-a::ral, sayang lang ang ba::on (a boy laughs) ni Ricky
		(Juliana laughs)
		(sings) If Ricky can't pass
		Don't give him his money
		Because he didn't (tapping on table) get to attend
		In his school, just hanging around wherever
		Since he didn't learn, lunch money wasted (a male student laughs) *of Ricky*
		(Juliana laughs)
2		(Flow-G apparently notices Skusta sleeping)
		(sings) Kung si Skusta ay natutulog la::ng
		Huwag mo na lang siya papasuki::n.
		>E wala naman talaga siyang ala::m< (drumming)
		Kung hindi matulog at wala naman ibang alam gawi::n.
		(Flow-G apparently notices Skusta sleeping)
		(sings) If Skusta's only going to sleep
		Then don't make him come to school.
		>Eh he doesn't really know anything anyway< (drumming)
		If he's sleeping and doesn't know how to do anything else.
3	**Rayna:**	You're bothering him.
4	**Flow-G:**	No miss. I'm not bothering.
5	**Rayna:**	You had his name in your song.
6		(Flow-G doesn't reply.)
7	**Skusta:**[13]	(sitting up and singing) Kung si Skusta ay natutulog
		Huwag mo nang gisingin baka naginip yan.
		(sitting up and singing) If Skusta is sleeping
		Don't wake him, maybe he's dreaming.

Flow-G's code-switching as metalinguistic commentary, which is also ludic translanguaging (Li, 2011), allows him to observe aloud that Ricky skips class and Skusta doesn't understand much, below the teachers' full level of awareness. Even though Rayna suspects that Flow-G was teasing Skusta because she heard Skusta's name in the song (Lines 3, 5), she doesn't know exactly what he said.

The co-occurrence of ludic translanguaging with code-switching shows that switching into L1s/HLs leads to conversations or jokes with a restricted audience, though these are not necessarily disrespectful of peers, and can even lighten the mood and build rapport. Regarding these moments, Juan said in an interview: 'those conversations are not hurtful, you know? I don't think it's going to cause um (.) destruction (.) within the classroom or to another student, because native [monolingual English] speakers do that often, so, like, I cannot take that away'. He has a point, and because ludic translanguaging often co-occurs with culture-specific content, not allowing it in L1s/HLs would deprive multilingual students from doing activities that monolingual English-speaking students engage in to build rapport and joke around in non-problematic ways. At the same time, mocking or disrespectful statements are harder to police when spoken in languages the teacher does not understand. Since banning these languages entirely would 'throw the baby out with the bathwater', so to speak, classroom management and respectful relations are necessary to ensure that students deploy their linguistic resources in kind ways.

At other times, it was not a student but Rayna who was on the receiving end of the code-switching into linguistically exclusive practices. For example, Filipino was used at the end of one lesson to orchestrate bluffing that undermined her attempts to elicit sharing poems students had written. In Excerpt 18, 'charot' is Filipino slang for 'just kidding'.

Excerpt 18 'Charot'

1	Rayna:	Two or three people want to share? I think all of your poems are good. Volunteers?
2	Kok:	Miss look. Empty.
3	Rayna:	OK, Simon.
4	Simon:	No, no miss.
5	Rayna:	No? Any other volunteers?
6	Kok:	Is empty miss.
7	Aaron:	I wanna share it!
8	Rayna:	OK share it Aaron. Go ahead.
9	Cookie:	Charot!
10		(Students chuckle. Aaron is silent.)
11	Rayna:	Anybody? (softly) Anybody, anybody?
12	Male student:	Charot.
13	Cookie:	Miss.
14	Rayna:	Why do I ask you guys to share? Because I know you guys <all have voices.> [*Voices* is the title of the multi-class poetry anthology.] You guys have *power* to talk about your...self. (this last word is said with some hesitation) You can say *no* to wrong things. Right? So who wants to share?
15	Cookie:	(2.0) Me.
16	Rayna:	OK Cookie.
17	Multiple male students:	Charot.
18		(laughter)
19	Rayna:	Are you being silly?

20	Male student:	We said charot miss.
21	Rayna:	Cookie?
22	Cookie:	Pass miss pass.
23	Rayna:	Guys. Anybody? We just wasted one minute. (Apparently sees Flow-G raise his hand) Flow-G is sharing. So everyone, look at Flow-G. Listen to Flow-G. Show your respect to Flow-G.
24	Flow-G:	Never mind miss.
25	Rayna:	°Why?°
26	Flow-G:	Si Cookie na lang miss. *How about Cookie after all miss.*
27	Rayna:	(disappointed) Flow-G.
28	Cookie:	Bakit ako? *Why me?*
29	Rayna:	Please. (1.0) Please. Yes, Simon do you want to share? (1.0) Guys! Show (.) your (.) respect (.) when somebody's sharing their work. So everyone look at Simon, listen to Simon, show your respect to Simon.
30		(Simon starts to read)

When Rayna asks students to share, the first to reply is Kok, and the answer is negative (Line 2). Simon either raises his hand or is nominated by Rayna when she says, 'OK, Simon' (Line 3), but then Simon immediately says 'No, no miss' (Line 4). Aaron then declares in a bright and cheery voice, 'I wanna share it!' (Line 7), but when Rayna says, 'Go ahead' (Line 8), Cookie shouts 'Charot!' (Line 9). As students chuckle, Aaron is silent (Line 10). This is the start of Rayna's begging; her voice softens as she repeats, 'Anybody? Anybody, anybody?' (Line 11). A male student replies, apparently to her face and at normal volume, 'Charot' (Line 12). Rayna reminds them that she values their *voices* (Line 14), which is the title of the multi-class poetry anthology, and which they are ironically using to disrespect her at this moment.

Cookie then volunteers next, but the same thing occurs with him – when she gives him the floor, he is silent and the others say 'charot' and laugh (Lines 15–18). Rayna then asks, 'Are you being silly?' (Line 19), while a male student replies, 'We said charot miss' (Line 20), as if that means anything to her. She reminds them that they wasted one minute (Line 23), then seems to see Flow-G's hand go up, and calls on him next. He says, 'Never mind miss' (Line 24). When she asks 'Why?' softly (Line 25), he addresses her entirely in Filipino to suggest that Cookie should go instead (Line 26), which Cookie protests in Filipino (Line 28). This negotiation is restricted only to Filipino speakers, since the words are meaningless to non-Filipino-speaking students and Rayna.[14] Rayna says in a disappointed voice, 'Flow-G' (Line 27). She then makes an appeal to 'show respect' (Line 29) when someone is sharing their work, even though what they are actually disrespecting is her invitation to share work. Finally, Simon shares his poem (Line 30).

Excerpt 18 shows that use of languages other than English, which Rayna supported ideologically if somewhat reluctantly in practice for reasons like what happened here, *cannot* be democratic or inclusive if the language(s) are used by an individual or group to express themselves to the fullest extent without regard for the needs of others when they do so – just as (playful) English should not be used in this way by English L1 speakers. Code-switching, in this case, positioned Rayna as the one who was linguistically lacking something, even if the 'loud' Filipino students were less confident in their English. In other words, linguistic practices in the classroom naturally render vulnerable those with a partial under-standing, whether or not anything bad is being said, and people who have had many multilingual encounters can get used to this experience to some extent. During moments like these, I cannot assume that non-Filipino students felt linguistically 'incompetent', but their silence is telling, in that they at least didn't seem to see themselves as ratified participants in the discussion about who would share their poetry.

Nor could a student consider himself 'safe' if he felt competent in both English and Filipino, because with many peers experiencing English anxiety, demonstrating English proficiency could be seen as showing off or overreaching. This was something that Luke, who was new in April and not part of Flow-G's group of friends, learned the hard way. On April 4, Rayna asked students to elect a speaker to represent the ESL 9/10 class at the upcoming launch of the multi-class poetry anthology at the public library. What was supposed to be a simple conversation regarding who wanted to co-introduce the book with representatives from other classes went out of control because of a 'triggering' instance of positioning.

Excerpt 19 Electing a speaker for the poetry book launch[15]

4:00	Rayna explains how one person will represent their class at the poetry book launch.
4:30	Rayna says, 'I want you guys to volunteer if you want to share your poem.' People raise their hands and Rayna writes down their names on the board: Juliana, Flow-G, Aaron…
4:50	Aaron: 'Miss, what's that?' Luke: 'Babasahin mo doon sa mga maraming tao.' [*You're going to read there in front of many people.*] Aaron: (not realizing what he volunteered for) '=Hala![16] Oh no! Just joking miss!' (classmate laughs) Rayna: 'Aaron if you are being silly I cannot have you on the list.'
5:10	Aaron keeps shouting 'Just joking miss!' with others laughing. Aaron: (to Luke, who has volunteered) 'Tanga tatanongin ka nila bobo.' [*Dummy they're going to ask you questions idiot.*] Luke: 'Ayaw mo?' [*You don't want?*] Aaron: 'Pagkatapos babasahin tatanongin ka nila, puro English!' [*After your reading they'll ask you questions, all in English!*]
6:50	Boys jokingly call out Kyrie's name (Juliana's brother still in the 'silent stage' of English acquisition) as Rayna elicits volunteers.
7:20	Rayna tells them to write their pick on a slip of paper, choosing from names on the board.

7:50	Cookie: 'Kyrie, Kyrie, Kyrie!' Unknown boy: 'Luke, Luke, Luke! Luke, gago [*bastard*].' Cookie: 'Sige sige sige.' [*Fine fine fine.*] Unknown girl next to Cookie: 'Pangalan lang?' [*Just the name?*] Cookie: 'Luke. Luke Luke Luke Luke.' Girl: 'Si Luke? Juliana na lang.' [*Luke? How about Juliana.*] Cookie: 'Bahala kayo diyan.' [*It's up to y'all.*] Luke: 'Gusto mo mag basa? Ayaw ko na!' [*Do you want to read? I don't want to anymore!*] Unknown girl: 'Tapos Luke na lang.' [*Then Luke after all.*] Cookie: 'Luke na lang. Luke.' [*Luke after all. Luke.*] (snickers) Aaron: (presumably to Luke) 'Tapos di ka makasalita. Volunteer volunteer ka.' [*Then you won't be able to talk. You 'volunteer volunteer.'*]
9:50	Rayna: 'So let's reveal (.) who is going to present for our class.' Luke is the clear winner (7/15 votes, with the other eight votes divided between three people). Cookie bursts out laughing and cheering every time Luke's name is announced by Rayna; at one point, he announces 'Isa dalawa tatlo apat lima anim!' [*One two three four five six!*] The other boys react similarly to Luke's election, loudly drumming on the table.
10:22	Luke's name is pulled yet again. Boys: 'Hala hala!' Juliana: (singsong voice) 'Hala!'
10:30	There is also one vote announced for Kyrie. Someone quips, 'Habol Kyrie.' [*Catch up Kyrie.*]
11:20	Luke: 'MISS! I DON'T KNOW HOW TO SPEAK ENGLISH!' Rayna: 'But you wanted to do it.' Cookie: 'You don't know how to speak sabi yata sa English naman.' [*You don't know how to speak I think you said it in English after all.*] Rayna: 'Why did you raise your hand?' Ricky: 'Yeah.' Luke: 'I was joking miss.' (class laughter) Luke: 'No, miss...' (cheering) Rayna: 'Luke, you have to decide now.' Luke: 'Miss I don't know promise.' Anna (researcher): 'He wants to.' Luke: 'No, I don't know.' Rayna: 'So, Luke is going to represent our class!' (Class cheers.)
12:40	Luke: 'Miss, please!' Aaron: 'Another vote miss. Another vote!' Rayna: 'I cannot tell if you're serious or being silly.' Overlapping talk; multiple students insist on another vote.
13:10	Kaori: 'Can you be quiet!? If everybody's talking, [students suddenly fall silent] we cannot decide anything. Right? One person at a time. Right? You know, I'm so *glad* (.) Luke (.) she's a—he's the newest, right? But he wanted to read, I think yea—his poem's good, it's OK for him to *go* for it. But uh (.) also, what he has to do at the library? Not just reading, but he has to explain. So maybe you know, this is my suggestion. Aaron I'm sorry but I'm talking. (3.0) So *if*, maybe somebody can help him too. So maybe you know, he can read, if some—if he has to say about the project, maybe if one person can be with him, and you can explain to him too. What do you think?' (Kaori keeps talking about the poems, explaining that they should read each other's poems and then decide among themselves which poems they'd like to have read out at the launch) Actually, everybody did a good job. OK? Everybody has y'know chance. But I don't—we don't wanna force (.) anybody who doesn't wanna read. Right? 'Cause it has to be some (.) willingness, 'cause you have to present. So, what d'you think?' (She tells them she will print out the poems so they can discuss it.)
15:50	Aaron: 'Buti na lang bro. (1.0) Buti na lang Luke.' [*Good thing it happened bro (i.e., Kaori saved your skin). (1.0) Good thing it happened Luke.*]
15:55	Kaori: (loudly) 'LUKE IT'S OK! You can read, but we can help. That's fine.'
16:00–16:30	Rayna elicits people to volunteer to help; Kaori calls on girls first to put their hands up, then boys.

While the class appears to turn on Luke until he is abashed and withdrawn, note that *Aaron*[17] is the one who is embarrassed at the start of the dialogue, as he unwittingly volunteers to give a speech in English at the public library. His panic is met with laughter from his peers; on top of that, Luke, a new boy who has confidence in English, asks him what the problem with speaking in public is (5:10). Aaron then uses harsh language with Luke, telling him only a fool would want to go up and answer all those questions in English, and the other boys make the situation worse by suggesting that Kyrie, a boy who hasn't yet gone beyond the silent stage of second language acquisition, should be their speaker (6:50). Instead of defending her brother Kyrie, Juliana takes part in the mirth of making inappropriate nominations (e.g. 10:22). At 7:50, an unknown girl suggests voting for Juliana, who has relatively strong English proficiency, but Cookie tells her to vote for Luke, who is by then passionately recanting. At 11:20, Luke yells out: 'MISS! I DON'T KNOW HOW TO SPEAK ENGLISH!' It is then that I cannot help speaking up, saying 'he wants to', which in hindsight might not have been the best thing to do, since Luke's desire to represent the class appears to have been taken down thoroughly. As Rayna announces that Luke is going to be their speaker, students cheer.[18]

Note the silence of the singletons in this excerpt – I do not think they were among the cheerers, as they could not follow the social metacommentary about the election. When Filipino students call for another vote immediately after the result of the first, Rayna says, 'I cannot tell if you're serious or being silly' (12:40). Here, Kaori intervenes (13:10). First, she validates Luke's desire to speak for the class, praising him for volunteering even though he was a new student. Despite not understanding what Aaron said at 5:10 – 'Pagkatapos babasahin tatanongin ka nila, puro English!' [*After reading they'll ask you questions, all in English!*] – and despite telling me she didn't know what was going on in this conversation, Kaori, somehow, responds directly to the issue of English anxiety and tries to shepherd the class into cohesion and mutual support. She does this swiftly, with as much positivity and as little drama as possible: suggesting that students assist each other to speak, telling them they all did a good job writing poems and reminding them that the presenter has to be willing to present, ending with 'what do you think?'. Aaron comments to Luke that Kaori saved him (15:50), while Kaori assures Luke, 'LUKE IT'S OK! You can read, but we can help. That's fine' (15:55). Then, when Rayna asks for people to volunteer to help Luke, Kaori calls on girls first to put up their hands, giving them an opportunity to be heard in this moment *and* at the reading (16:00–16:30).

I now summarize the implications of these dialogues by discussing how translanguaging is *not* a K–12 teacher's only concern. Teachers are more broadly concerned with learning, and what's more, not only about subject knowledge – but learning how to be a member of a learning community (see Kaori's comment about 'community' at the beginning of this chapter).

5.7 Summary

Flow-G in ESL 9/10, Kix in English 9 (Chapter 4) and to some extent Aaron in ESL 9/10 have something in common: they were recognized implicitly or explicitly as class leaders. As bi/multilingual role models, their influences *rippled out* and affected others' identities, as peers were positioned as tutees (Excerpt 1), confident and cosmopolitan speakers of a language of affinity (Excerpts 3–4), 'one of the gang' (Excerpts 10–12), competent speakers of a HL (Excerpt 16), academically incompetent (Excerpt 17), language insiders/outsiders (Excerpt 18) or linguistically overreaching (Excerpt 19). In the case of Kix and Flow-G especially, these students were the 'center of gravity' in their respective classes because they had the most linguistic, cultural and academic capital *overall* out of all the students present – in the majority non-English language (Ilokano or Filipino), in English, in languages/codes of affinity (Korean in English 9 or Filipino hip-hop in ESL 9/10) and in 'academic' literacy practices valued at school. Therefore, they had a strong influence over the language standards that could be applied in that particular classroom ecology. While Aaron had social sway at times (Excerpt 19), what this study is most concerned with are language standards set by people who have fairly consistent authority to determine them in that setting: 'Who in each class presents themselves and is recognized as a valued model of bi/multilingualism? What counts as a legitimate instantiation of a code? What are the social processes through which these understandings are mutually constructed? What are the consequences for people? And what are the implications for teaching and learning in plurilingual, English as a lingua franca classrooms?' (Chapter 3).

In a specific setting such as a classroom, what does or does not count as language competence is largely determined by standards relevant to the setting: who is there, what their repertoires look like and what language competence means to them (Blommaert, 2007; Blommaert *et al.*, 2005). Consider the absence of white monolingual English speakers in either class; no one spoke 'standard' American English, but there were English standards with social consequences. Rayna, a native Korean speaker, overheard Korean stylization in the English 9 class, but it was not a Korean class. In English 9, bits of Korean, regardless of their degree of authenticity, signified cosmopolitanism for Filipinos rather than a minoritized 'ESL identity', and the use of Ilokano alongside English was normalized in academic work among the Ilokano-speaking majority, supported by the Ilokano-speaking teacher. In ESL 9/10, Filipino-accented English was perfectly unmarked English, but, as I will demonstrate in Chapter 6, this was not so with Bisaya-accented English.

As I have argued in Mendoza (2020b), teachers should look for students in the class who are bi/multilingually proficient in English and the class majority language (e.g. Androutsopoulos, 2015; Malsbary, 2013), as they are central language brokers, and recruit these students as positive influences on their peers, while mitigating their language dominance in other ways – e.g. when Juan encourages a language singleton to express himself in his HL in Excerpts 8–9, and when Kaori attempts to diffuse a language-based power play even when she did not share any language with students apart from English. Each class leader (and there can be multiple ones) is a focal point of setting-specific linguistic and interactional norms; sometimes, the norm is not even to display language competence but to downplay it to avoid seeming like one is 'above everyone else' (Excerpt 19).

In addition, even if a teacher does not speak students' language(s), it is important to intuit what is happening socially to manage students' linguistic anxiety. This is particularly important with regard to English if it is the class lingua franca, and not only with the least English proficient students and classroom language minorities/singletons, but also with the most English proficient students and the classroom language majority. In fact, it is perhaps *especially* important with the latter students, because if they can largely determine the language standards and interactional norms in that particular ecology and have a substantial effect on others, whether they do so in inclusive ways depends on their own self-esteem.

Notes

(1) https://wida.wisc.edu/sites/default/files/resource/Performance-Definitions-Expressive-Domains.pdf.

(2) Juan and Kaori read the findings chapters at the same time that the manuscript went through peer review as part of conditional publication.

(3) The centrality of students such as Kix, He and Flow-G in this study is illustrated by a number of data forms, such as *observations* (e.g. if Kix didn't translanguage when Ed was teaching, others wouldn't as well), *recordings* (e.g. these students leading the discussion or scaffolding, as in Excerpts 1 and 21) and *teacher comments* (e.g. Kaori saying in an interview that Flow-G had more English proficiency than others, and that they looked up to him).

(4) Skusta's reading challenges, which will be presented in more detail in Chapter 6, could have arisen from a lack of exposure to print literacy, a learning disability such as dyslexia, or both.

(5) Teresa was not often in the class when I visited, though she was on one or two occasions which are mentioned in this chapter. I did not interview her, but by conversing with her casually once, I learned she spoke several Filipino languages and English.

(6) I am grateful to Jayson Parba for this information.

(7) These language skills were bilingual. There were moments when Flow-G could entertain the Filipino students, in Filipino and hence without teachers' understanding of what was being said (see Excerpt 17).

(8) For a discussion of why working-class males from various racial and ethnic backgrounds can be averse to adopting 'proper' school language since it threatens their masculine identities (making them feel powerless, stupid, etc.), see Young (2004) and Willis (1981). However, this does not mean that they are immune to insecurity about white middle-class language norms, which they cannot help internalizing to some extent. This is why they still need to distinguish themselves from others, e.g. recent immigrants or linguistically minoritized classmates (Jaspers, 2011; Talmy, 2008).

(9) This is not to say that teachers who do not know students' language(s) should *forbid* translanguaging, but that teachers need to assuage students' linguistic anxieties and manage power dynamics in the classroom ecology to ensure that people use language(s) inclusively.

(10) The secondary school linguistic ethnographer Ben Rampton (2006) points out that when a class is going off track, one sign of it happening is that students no longer pay attention to the *meaning* of words, but rather to their *sounds*: what puns with what, what can be twisted into what. This throws off teachers' linear scaffolding of students toward understanding a concept through asking a series of questions, as the actual propositional content is ignored by students in favor of wordplay.

(11) All but Skusta and Kok, who were from the Visayas and Mindanao, respectively. These students would be seen as coming from the hinterlands of the country, a topic that will be taken up further in Chapter 6.

(12) Newcomer Ilokano-speaking students in English 9 seemed to have more Ilokano proficiency than newcomer Ilokano-speaking students in ESL 9/10. It is possible that in the Philippines, ESL 9/10 students became Filipino dominant due to being raised and educated in a Tagalog-dominated society, whereas English 9 students were more bilingual in Ilokano and Filipino and developed academic literacies across languages. Layers of subtractive bilingualism and how they relate to social class, not only after immigration but also *before*, require more study.

(13) Skusta's on-the-fly lyrics do not match the rhythm of the song, pointing to his lesser proficiency in Filipino than Flow-G's.

(14) I argue that these interactions are impolite for two reasons. First, Rayna appears to experience it as impolite. There is paralinguistic evidence she is intimidated, such as her voice going soft in Line 11, her hesitation with 'your...self' in Line 14 and her softly spoken, almost heartbreaking 'Why?' in Line 25. Second, there is Juliana's comment in a March 7 interview about the boys' use of Filipino: 'Hindi po niya maintindihan kung ano po pinaguusapan. Alam po ni Ms Rayna kung binabastos na siya' (She can't understand what's being said. Ms Rayna knows when she's already being disrespected).

(15) I do not present a transcript here but describe events in chronological order by combining notes I took during the observation and after listening to the audio recording. I believe presenting the data in this way gives the clearest picture of what happened over a more extended span of time (see a similar method of recording translanguaging data in Blackledge & Creese, 2017).

(16) This is 'oh no' in a number of Pacific Islander languages, including Hawaiian.

(17) In an interview, Kaori mentioned that Aaron and Flow-G seemed to be the ones the other boys looked up to the most, although Aaron was somewhat 'kolohe' (naughty). Nevertheless, she praised Aaron's ability to ask critical questions. Aaron was also a star basketball player.

(18) Ultimately, the speaker at the event was Juliana.

6 Identity Trajectories of Individual Students: Multidialectal Translanguaging and Expanded Notions of 'Academic' Literacy

While the previous two chapters focused on each class as a whole, in this chapter I explore the linguistic identity trajectories of two students, Jhon in English 9 and Skusta in English as a second language (ESL) 9/10. My purpose is to examine an under-researched form of translanguaging, namely, multidialectal translanguaging. An examination of this under-researched form of translanguaging points to the need for (1) asset-based views of classroom participants' linguistic and cultural repertoires *within* and not only across named languages (González *et al.*, 2006) and (2) expanded notions of 'academic' literacies (Hornberger & Link, 2012). At the end of the chapter, I discuss why it is not bi/multilingual language practices *per se* but the above two elements of translanguaging theory in education that have great potential to challenge linguistic hierarchization and standardization.

6.1 Identity Trajectories in Classrooms

Every student's academic and social identity in a particular class emerges from a combination of factors operating on multiple timescales – from interactional choices made by others in an unfolding conversation, to classroom relations developed over a school year, to the narrative of a student's educational career, to generations of systemic oppression or privilege (Wortham, 2006). Longitudinal changes in national language-in-education policy can impact the education landscape, for better or worse, for various groups of learners. For example, a study by Mortimer and Wortham (2015) illustrated how the perceived academic competence of an individual student can be impacted by a shift in national language policy and what 'counts' as academic language. Guarani, an indigenous language in Paraguay, was largely banned in Paraguayan schools until

1992, when a new constitution promoted Spanish–Guarani bilingual education. Up to this point, Guarani had been associated with a rural identity, poverty, lack of education and coarseness, but the policy shift led to the emergence of a new kind of Guarani-speaker stereotype, of a positive nature: the bilingual Guarani academic.

This stereotype affected students' academic identities as early as the elementary level, as shown in one class studied by the researchers. In this class, one of the students, Manuel, was highly proficient in his home language, Guarani, in contrast to his classmates who spoke Spanish at home. Manuel was able to claim a competent academic identity due to discourses operating on different timescales:

(1) His elementary class was seen by adults as a smart, well-behaved, cohesive cohort (six years).
(2) He graduated as one of the top students (one to two hour ceremony).
(3) His mother identified him as naturally intelligent and studious (his lifetime).
(4) There was the change in national education policy about two decades before, in 1992.
(5) When students read about the guarango/a, or uneducated Guarani-speaking country bumpkin, they rejected this stereotype by using Manuel as a counter-example (a school day).

Mortimer and Wortham (2015) point to the importance of the fourth discourse as the catalyst for the others, as it was the emergence of an academic Guarani–Spanish bilingual identity in the public imagination that made the marshalling of the other discourses possible. (Unfortunately, however, this ideal bilingual academic was construed as a 'balanced' bilingual who did not mix languages in academic performance – i.e. two monolinguals in one person.)

Wortham and Reyes (2017) argue that classroom processes such as identity formation can be studied using cross-event discourse analysis to see how identities emerge across linked speech events across different timescales. They state: 'These links are implicitly or explicitly created by participants in discourse, and the analyst's job is to trace these links' (Wortham & Reyes, 2017: 72). To do so, ethnographers need to pay attention to 'cross-event configuration of indexical signs' (Wortham & Reyes, 2017: 79), such as utterances and linguistic forms, and provide evidence that research participants find them meaningful markers of identity.

In this chapter, I explore how discourses are drawn on to construct classroom identities with regard to indexical signs that involve *dialects* rather than languages. Some of these discourses relate to what counts as 'academic' literacy practices in English-dominant countries. Other discourses about academically legitimate dialects and literacy practices are carried over from the country of origin (Valdés, 2001). To illustrate, I use the cases of Jhon in English 9 and Skusta in ESL 9/10.

6.2 Jhon

Born in Ilocos Sur (southern Ilocos),[1] Jhon was a 15-year-old student in English 9 who had lived in Hawai'i for six years, since age nine. In a one-on-one interview, he said he spoke both English and Ilokano at home, and although he spoke English better, he could still have a conversation in Ilokano. On the classroom language use questionnaire, Jhon's attitude toward translanguaging was unequivocally negative, as he wrote 'Never' in response to the first question of how often he used languages other than English in class. Despite his dispreference for oral translanguaging in deconstructing texts, he still agreed to participate in all aspects of the study, and it was during the individual interview that I attempted to probe into the reasons for his response to the questionnaire.

Jhon was fully aware of others' extensive Ilokano use in English 9, and when I asked him how often he heard languages other than English in class, he replied, 'Every time'. I next asked him what languages he heard, and he named three – Ilokano, Filipino and Chinese – even though my recordings and observations indicated that Filipino was used infrequently and Chinese not at all unless one counted the rare instance of stylization.[2] Thus, I suspected that Jhon was positioning himself as even more English oriented than most others. I tried to probe into this positioning further, asking when He (Jhon's friend in the English 9 class) used Chinese and with whom, to which Jhon replied, 'He teaches me sometimes', but said he forgot the words he learned from He. Rampton (1995) has shown that teenagers often teach each other a few words in different languages, typically swear words or sexual words, and are content to remain perpetual beginners in this sense. Alternatively, Jhon might have been making up a vague example to support a minor fib, but it was impossible to tell.

I next asked Jhon about other languages he knew, and he replied that he spoke a little Filipino and Spanish from the Philippines. Then, I inquired into his literacy practices, and he responded (like many a heritage speaker) that he wasn't good at reading and writing in Ilokano. What was most telling was his response to the question of what language or languages he *wanted* to learn if he could take a language class; he answered 'Spanish', even though he did not provide further details as to why. What came across, from a number of his answers, was alignment with language hierarchies (downplaying his Ilokano proficiency and emphasizing proficiency and interest, however emergent, in more prestigious Philippine languages) and with normative classroom language practices. This could be seen in his expressed preference for an English-only policy in English 9.

Excerpt 20 Jhon explains why he uses English only

1	Anna:	(reading from his questionnaire) You say you never use [other languages] because you wanna learn English. [Jhon: Mm-hm.] Can you explain that? Like uh (.) what do you mean by you don't—you always use English because you wanna learn more English. What do you mean by that?
2	Jhon:	I dunno, I just wanna be (6.0) <u>good</u> at it.
3	Anna:	Do you think that speaking Ilokano or (.) any other language prevents you from learning English?
4	Jhon:	Mm-hm.
5	Anna:	How?
6	Jhon:	You::u (.) might (.) forget some (2.0) 'cuz if you keep speaking Filipino then (.) it's gonna be your habits. Or, it's gonna become your habit and then [Anna: OK] you might forget—
7	Anna:	You might forget what the word is in English [Jhon: Mm-hm] if you use another language. >What if you use both words together?< Doesn't it help you remember—each one helps you remember the other?
8	Jhon:	=Yeah.
9	Anna:	If you use both words together, right? Why not use both words together?
10	Jhon:	Too hard for me. :-)
11	Anna:	Too hard! How is it too hard?
12	Jhon:	I dunno. :-)
13	Anna:	What about um—but you also said you wanted to (.) um (.) because some people may not understand. D'you think it's important that everybody understands what you're saying?
14	Jhon:	Yeah.
15	Anna:	Yeah? Why is that?
16	Jhon:	Because they might (.) think that you're like, saying bad things to them, or...
17	Anna:	Could they know what you were saying based on the way it <u>sounds</u>? ... Sometimes the way it sounds is, people are just like asking the question about the homework or something. So, why would they necessarily think that [you're saying bad things]? Would they always think that?
18	Jhon:	I dunno. :-) When Kix them—when Kix talks Filipino and then He couldn't understand, so...
19	Anna:	But is Kix saying something bad about He?
20	Jhon:	No it's just that (.) He couldn't (.) um, participate in the discussion if he— yeah.
21	Anna:	Could Kix say something in Filipino and then say something in English to He? And then say something again in Filipino to Rizze and then say something in English to everybody? And then could everyone participate then?
22	Jhon:	Mm-hm.
23	Anna:	So (.) does it stop He from participating? :-)
24	Jhon:	No.
25	Anna:	No. So why—
26	Jhon:	(makes a sound like a cross between a snicker and a sigh)
27	Anna:	Maybe you can think about it that way?

While I come close to arguing with the research participant in this excerpt, I felt it was worth having a few minutes' discussion to try to bring Jhon around to a different point of view regarding the 'need' to speak the dominant societal language all the time. I still maintain the opinions I expressed in Lines 7, 17 and 21 about (1) the usefulness of using languages together to learn new things in various languages – in other words, Ilokano *helps* you learn English, so that the two languages complement each other, rather than competing; (2) how people can usually tell whether talk in another language is ill-intentioned through contextual cues; and (3) how class participants should actively bridge their language differences in inclusive multilingual talk, which Faltis (2001) calls 'joinfostering'. Conversely, I understand Jhon's exasperation (Line 26), as what remains unspoken in this dialogue was the occasional abuse of Ilokano and Filipino in class, as in Excerpt 5, in which Eufia and Rizze used these languages in front of He, playing out a mock romantic story that made him uncomfortable.

Thus, Jhon not only supported an English-only policy due to language hierarchies and ideologies of 'appropriate' language use in class, but more reasonably, because he had seen Juan's flexible classroom language policy taken advantage of, to the detriment of a friend. I also asked him whether people expected students to speak English in a US high school, and he shook his head no, even though he said later in the interview that those who did not speak English well could be made fun of (see Chapter 5). I also asked whether his parents advised him not to speak Filipino languages at school, but he shook his head, so I summarized, 'You just don't feel like it', and he confirmed, 'Yeah'.

Reflecting on this exchange, I am hesitant to make conclusions about direct causal relationships between heritage language use and social well-being. 'Forcing' Jhon to speak Ilokano or Filipino in a school setting does not seem to contribute to a better identity positioning from his point of view, nor do I take his words to mean that he doesn't value his linguistic and cultural heritage. In fact, when I asked him when he used Filipino languages, he said he used them outside class with friends and family. Of course, there is

> the need for not only teachers, but also students, to interrogate the language ideologies that push them to perceive majoritized language practices as appropriate in school and minoritized translanguaging—their own and others'—as antisocial, suspicious, or perhaps valuable only for communication within linguistically minoritized homes and social arenas. (Beiler, 2021: 133)

On the other hand, one cannot pressure a student to use a heritage language in class, even if others are doing so; this is putting students into cultural boxes and doesn't respect individual preferences. Teachers can and should legitimize all languages and dialects for academic work (Seltzer & García, 2020), but making the fullest range of options available to the class is not the same as making every student use everything in their repertoire as a rule. What is more important to consider is *positioning*. Thus, I now come to why Jhon's professed 'English-only' policy was so integral to his classroom self.

Jhon was not an academically strong student, but he was invested in a positive classroom identity, and had a habit of pretending to 'think aloud' – but not actually thinking aloud, which would involve real stumbling or struggling in self-talk or negotiation of meaning, which he avoided doing. For instance, Juan began the unit on *Romeo and Juliet* with a worksheet that scaffolded students to go from a common-sense understanding of tragedy as 'bad things happening' to the Western literary definition of tragedy: a series of events ending in the fall of the main character, from a state of well-being to a state of ruin, due to a fatal flaw. In the first lesson of the unit, students worked in pairs to brainstorm examples of tragedy according to everyday, non-literary understandings. One of my two recorders captured the brainstorming between Jhon and He. Since the only language they shared was English, the conversation took part in English, but I noted a difference between the extensive languaging (i.e. thinking aloud; see Swain, 2006) by He and the absence of it on Jhon's part.

Excerpt 21 Tragedy

1	**He:**	Like (.) shooting. Um, gun shots.
2	**Jhon:**	Yeah.
3	**He:**	Car bang—no. (1.0) Car crash. Gun is (.) gun shots. Murderer. Mur::der. And (.) car crash. ... (reads from worksheet instructions) 'If you had to explain the concept to someone who had never heard it before, how would you do it?'
4	**Jhon:**	How would you do it or say it?
5	**He:**	(8.0) How would you do it I don't know.
		(Half a minute later)
6	**He:**	Tragic is a (3.0) horri—what? Horrible. (Tapping) Things (.) that—
7	**Jhon:**	(reading instructions) 'Make sure to keep this quick write around—'
8	**He:**	Happen around... (continues to think aloud as Jhon continues to read out instructions)

In this excerpt, as in other small-group discussions recorded throughout this study, Jhon faked thinking aloud to grapple with ideas and problem-solve (Vygotsky, 1980), as can be seen in the pre-packaged comment 'How would you do it or say it?' (Line 4), which in another discussion might have been an insightful contribution, but only leads to an eight-second pause of confusion on He's part (Line 5) because the question is irrelevant to the discussion. Second language acquisition scholar

Merrill Swain (2006) calls the process of thinking aloud to problem-solve 'languaging', and translanguaging researchers have described it in similar ways (e.g. Li, 2018). Paralinguistic features in the excerpt show that He, unlike Jhon, is doing just that: He's speech contains pauses and elongated words (Line 3), and he taps on the table as he thinks (Line 6). When He reads from the worksheet, he focuses on the question being asked ('If you had to explain it to someone who had never heard it before…'; Line 3), not on other details as Jhon does ('Make sure to keep this quick write around…'; Line 7).

Granted, what is being asked by the worksheet is very doable, but Jhon still avoids directly engaging with it. This was not one-off behavior. Although Jhon seemed to realize that languaging was a social expectation in English class, he often made a pretense of doing it rather than truly engaging in it, for example by muttering indistinguishable words during such small-group discussions, framed by an audible 'Cool' or 'OK' or 'I see this'. Excerpt 21 took place on April 11. On February 7, when Jhon was working at a table with Kix and Aliah, Kix lost patience with this tendency of Jhon's and blatantly said, 'You're such a fake'. Ten minutes before the end of that period, Kix told Aliah a story about Jhon coming to school wearing fake glasses on the day the yearbook photo was taken (presumably a previous school year), with the implication that Jhon had done such a thing to project an intellectual, bookish image, and that this bluffing was something that had been going on for a while. When students like Jhon, who are uncomfortable showing what they don't know, pretend to language, it defeats the purpose of languaging: to articulate your understanding, *including its limits*, so you and your groupmates can correct and build on each other's thoughts and scaffold each other's learning.

In addition to avoiding thinking aloud to avoid loss of face (as genuine languaging would have revealed what he did not see or understand in literary analysis), Jhon seemed to compensate for his academic limitations compared to his academically strong Ilokano first language (L1) peers like Kix and Eufia by defending his preferred language policy as a US-raised English speaker. This was likely his way of claiming a more positive linguistic identity, balancing the language scales, so to speak, between him and other Ilokano–English bilinguals in the class who were relatively newly arrived and had stronger academic reading and writing abilities. Thus, when it comes to the issue of how the more Ilokano-proficient students' academic translanguaging positioned Jhon (i.e. as not adept in literary analysis), and how Jhon's preferred English-only policy positioned them (i.e. as not functioning in English only), the question arises how positive positionings might be achieved for everybody.[3]

While it was text-oriented multilingual translanguaging in the class poetry anthology that led other students like Aliah, Fetu and He to translanguage for the only recorded time in this study, in Jhon's case, his 'time' for observable[4] translanguaging came in a different situation.

On April 25, there was a drama workshop led by a visiting pair of actors – primarily by the male actor, Mr Nick, assisted by his colleague Ms Marie (pseudonyms). This workshop, which prepared students to recite two or three lines from a character in *Romeo and Juliet* as a formal assessment, took place entirely in English. I did not pick up any other language used by Mr Nick and Ms Marie, but they were evidently kama'āina and spoke Hawai'i English, and Mr Nick rendered Juliet's nurse's lines in a Pidgin accent. Thus, one could observe the workshop was multidialectal, and this could have appealed in particular to local students, who would rarely have seen Pidgin or Hawai'i English represented in their regular language arts curriculum. However, it was evident that *all* students in the two or three classes who took the workshop together had fun, and the workshop leaders gave good tips for public speaking in general.[5]

The session began with Mr Nick at the front of the room. 'All right. Good morning (.) boys and girls. ... I like what I saw yesterday, Ms Marie liked what she saw yesterday, and you guys are doing well. And we're (.) we're gonna improve on that today'.

First, he showed students how to use the 'off' position, standing still with one's head down, with Ms Marie, his partner, demonstrating. She stood in this position, then turned 'on', reciting a few of Romeo's lines with expressive posture and gesture: 'But soft, what light through yonder window breaks? / It is the east, and Juliet is the sun!' – and turned off again. Students then practiced turning on and off without saying anything, pulling faces and getting into poses based on different scenarios Mr Nick read out to them (e.g. receiving a puppy, smelling a fart).

After this warm-up, Mr Nick told them they would each be performing a few lines from their *Romeo and Juliet* character that day, in front of the class. They first needed to say, 'I'm [name] and I am doing the line of [character]', then turn off, then turn on to perform their line, then turn off again. Before these individual performances, students had 15 minutes to practice with a partner. In the pair rehearsals, I saw a different side of Jhon as he worked with his partner, He. Like every pair, Jhon and He took turns delivering lines they had memorized, Jhon first.

Excerpt 22 Worms' meat (Part 1)

1	Jhon:	Hi. My name is Jhon (.) and I'm doing the line of Mercutio. (7.0) Ah! A scratch. But 'tis enough. Help me to some house, or I shall faint. Aargh! Zounds! A dog, a rat, a cat! To scratch a man to death. They have made been—they may have :-) worms' meat of me. A plague both your houses! (laughs)
2	He:	Mine is shorter than you.
3	Jhon:	Your turn.
4	He:	Hi, my name is blah blah blah; I'm doing the line of blah blah blah.
5	Jhon:	(laughing) Capulet.

6		(He delivers a few of Juliet's father's lines, competently but not with Jhon's degree of expression)
7	Jhon:	(with bravado) Hi, my name is Jhon! And I am doing the line of Mercutio. (6.0) Aah! A scratch. 'Tis enough. Help me to some house, or I shall faint. (1.0) Ah!
8	He:	=Ah!
9	Jhon:	Zounds! A dog.
10	He:	A dog.
11	Jhon:	A rat.
12	He:	=A cat.
13	Jhon:	A cat. To scratch a man to death. Ah!
14	He:	=Ah.
15	Jhon:	They may have worms—they made worms' meat of me. (He laughs) I cannot say all that line. Plague both your houses!
16	He:	Bow!
17	Jhon:	How can I bow, I'm dead?
18	He:	(laughing) Go down and bow down and die.
19		(Jhon laughs; Rayna arrives and scolds He for sitting)

In this excerpt, we see He, an academically strong student, barely taking the activity seriously, perhaps because it is not a traditional form of literacy; in fact, he is more distracting than helpful to Jhon, echoing the one-line exclamations (Lines 10, 14) for fun rather than checking the script for the line his partner is having trouble with ('they have made worms' meat of me'), and sitting when he should be standing (Line 19). In contrast, Jhon is giving it his all, languaging to himself about the line he needs to work on (Lines 1, 15). The two continue rehearsing with the line He needs to practice.

Excerpt 23 Worms' meat (Part 2)

1	He:	Hi, my name is (.) blah blah blah—
2	Jhon:	(annoyed voice) Do it nice::ly!
3	He:	Hi, my name is blah blah blah. I'm doing the line of Lord Capulet. And you already know my name so why I even have to say it?
4	Jhon:	[The audience.
5	He:	[(recites his line)
6	Jhon:	Hi, my name is Jhon. And I am doing the line of (.) Mercutio. (6.0) Ah! A scratch! But 'tis enough. (1.0) Help me to some house. I shall faint. Ah!
7	He:	=Ah!
8	Jhon:	Ah!
9	He:	=Ah!
10		(He laughs; Jhon laughs; both laugh)

11	Jhon:	Ah! Ugh. Ah! A cat—stop laughing! (5.0) A scratch. 'Tis enough. Help me to some house, or I shall faint. Ah! A dog, a rat, a cat! To scratch a man to death. Ah! (He laughs) They made have worms (2.0) they made—
12	He:	Worms' meat out of me.
13	Jhon:	No:: (.) they made worms' meat of me. They made worms' meat of me! A plague both your houses.

In this dialogue, it is even clearer that He sees little point in the activity ('You already know my name so why I even have to say it?'; Line 3), while Jhon reminds him why they should care ('The audience'; Line 4). The next time Jhon tries to rehearse his line, He is even more distracting, and soon they are both laughing (Line 10). Jhon tries to continue, interrupting himself momentarily to tell He to stop (Line 11). Finally, He repeats the line he should have been helping Jhon with (Line 12), but he gets it wrong due to anticipating a modern, rather than archaic, sentence structure – 'made worms' meat out of me' – so Jhon has to correct it himself: 'made worms' meat of me' (Line 13).

After this dialogue, Jhon and He each had time to deliver his line twice more. The recorder captured Jhon languaging: 'I'm gonna check my line. Don't know that part. (paper ruffling) Yeah, they have made worms' meat of me. They have made worms' meat of me'. As Mr Nick called the class to attention, he could still be heard repeating the phrase. The performances went well: no one broke down and students clapped encouragingly for each other. Jhon gave one of the most expressive performances despite still getting the worms' meat line slightly wrong.

Jhon's confidence with Shakespeare continued into subsequent lessons, such as the next week (May 2) when Juan asked students to get into pairs and act out the scene of Romeo and Juliet's first meeting. This can be an awkward scene for ninth graders to perform, as it is a romantic one, and to reduce the awkwardness as much as possible, Juan put students into same-sex pairs except for two friends, Eufia and Fetu. As Juan described the activity, Kix shouted, 'Oh my god!' while He announced in Hawai'i Creole, 'I like be Benvolio' (even though one could only be Romeo or Juliet). As the pairs dispersed around the room to rehearse, Jhon, in contrast to his partner Kix, was heard to drawl in an easygoing manner, 'Ah::l right. Ah::l right'.

During Kix and Jhon's performance, Kix stopped when he heard a classmate giggle. Looking at Juan, he complained, 'Mister!' while Fetu said, 'Kix, you got this'. As Kix and Jhon continued, some girls giggled, and so did Jhon. Kix flinched and seemed relieved to step down. It struck me how a change in literacies – that is, from 'traditional' literary analysis (Excerpts 1 and 21) to dramatic performance (Excerpts 22–23) – could cause a shift in identities from 'capable' to 'struggling' student, or from 'concentrating' to 'lackadaisical' student; how He, for instance, did not take drama seriously, whereas Jhon did, when it was vice versa during literary analyses in which these two friends worked together. Kix, one of the most academically strong students in the class, needed to be coaxed and encouraged to perform the romantic scene (even though he played Romeo), while Jhon took up playing Juliet as nonchalantly as you might pick up a sandwich. Even though Jhon did not embrace multilingual translanguaging, he embraced multimodal translanguaging (text, oral recitation and drama) and multidialectal translanguaging – being given lines from Shakespeare and bringing them to life. Jhon was arguably enabled as a multimodal, multidialectal translanguager by the relatively fluid translanguaging (rather than low/high diglossic contrast) Mr Nick and Ms Marie demonstrated between Hawai'i English, modern American English and Shakespearean English when they led the workshop – which allowed Jhon to link his English 9 student identity to the intellectual capital of Shakespeare.[6]

Thus, even though Jhon did not feel comfortable translanguaging between Filipino languages and English, for reasons which one might guess but can never fully understand, he skillfully translanguaged in a heteroglossic theatrical performance. Just as the bilingual Guarani academic stereotype led to Manuel's socially constructed identity as an intelligent student in Mortimer and Wortham's (2015) study, the workshop by local actors who spoke Hawai'i Creole and seemed used to performing Shakespeare paved the way for Jhon to present himself as a skilled actor and a capable student in at least some literacy activity in English 9 – for example, he knew how to use pauses for dramatic effect and create contrasts in his voice more than others – fleeting as these advantages may have been. While Wortham and Reyes (2017) describe identity trajectories as solidifying over time, this would not have been the case with Jhon's empowered identity as an actor, because multilingual, multidialectal oral poetry and theater workshops are few and far between in language arts classes that focus primarily on textual literary analysis.

Next, I turn to the case of Skusta, whose translanguaging was between Filipino dialects. I show how this situation is more difficult to turn around than Jhon's, even for a brief time, due to the lesser availability of models to legitimate different dialects and diverse literacy practices in immigrant languages, and teachers' lack of knowledge of sociolinguistic features between these dialects that affect students' identity positioning in non-English languages.

6.3 Skusta

Born in Mindanao, Skusta was one of two Filipino students in ESL 9/10 (the other, Kok, was from the Visayas) who did not come from Luzon, the northernmost third of the Philippines and the most economically developed region where the two most widely spoken languages, despite great ethnolinguistic diversity, are Filipino and Ilokano. The

Visayas and Mindanao are ideologically constructed as 'boondocks' – a word in American English that is borrowed from *bundok*, Filipino for 'mountain'.

I interviewed Skusta and Kok together on February 7, and their responses to my questions about their language knowledge and use showed that they constructed themselves as linguistically deficient even when the other Filipino students in the class were not present, and even though they knew more languages than their Filipino classmates. For example, they reported that they sometimes spoke Kok's L1, Ilonggo (a Visayan language) and Skusta's L1, Cebuano/Bisaya/Visayan (the lingua franca of the Visayas and Mindanao), which were cognate languages, to each other and understood each other, but used Filipino with the other boys. They also talked about their own Filipino accents in somewhat deprecating ways; according to Skusta, 'Yung mga bisaya, matigas mag-salita' (Visayans, they speak rough), to which Kok agreed softly: 'Oo miss' (yes miss). (While I did not have the Filipino proficiency to fully perceive accent differences when students spoke Filipino, I knew that they existed, and could recognize certain socially marked examples.)

In terms of their schooling back in the Philippines, they said their teachers taught in a mix of English, Visayan and/or Ilonggo. According to Kok, 'Yung klase po namin (.) Ilonggo po (.) pero yung pagsulat namin Ingles dapat' (Our classes (.) in Ilonggo (.) but have to write in English). In other words, there appears to be diglossia between the Philippines' official languages and regional languages that can lead to under-development of students' L1s for academic reading and writing if they are not Filipino or English, even though these home languages are used in translanguaging to plan written and graded products in the official languages. Skusta then made a wry comment: 'Grabe doon sa Pilipinas may seventy-five pero English. Atchaka Pilipino' (It's extreme that in the Philippines you get 75% but in English. And Filipino). As the term 'grabe' ('extreme') roughly translates to 'Fancy how...', I understood him to mean 'Fancy those people who brag about an English- and Filipino-medium education even if their average is 75%' (cf. Sandhu, 2015, on discourses regarding English- versus Hindi-medium education in India).

When I asked why they used Filipino in their current ESL 9/10 class, Kok explained: 'Ah (.) kasi po yung iba hindi po nakakaintindi sa akin' (Ah it's because the others don't understand me) to which Skusta added, 'Oo, minsan hindi namin masalita ng maayos' (Yes, sometimes we can't say things properly), attributing misunderstanding to their Filipino pronunciation rather than to the fact that the others didn't speak Visayan languages.

Compared to the others, however, they were the most multilingual. When I asked them how many languages they spoke, gesturing with my hands to indicate levels of proficiency, as it was hard for me to say this in Filipino, Skusta said he was most confident in Bisaya, then Tagalog/

Filipino, then Ilonggo, then Ilokano and English. Kok mentioned Ilonggo, then Tagalog/Filipino, then English, then Ilokano.

When they brought up those who were 'magaling sa (good at) English' at their school, I asked who these people were, and they mentioned those in the Junior Reserve Officers Training Corps (JROTC) and sheltered for-credit classes – in this study, students like Kix, Eufia and Rizze. Kok and Skusta explained that they left the JROTC because they had difficulty understanding what people were saying in the club, and were challenged by the regular presentations and essays. When it came to recreation, they said that they would go to a public park to play basketball with the other boys, or swim at the beach. Skusta listed the clubs he was in back in the Philippines, which he talked about longingly, including boy scouts, badminton and chess.

The two young men were frank about how challenging it was to follow lessons in ESL 9/10, as Kaori and Rayna didn't share any languages with the students apart from English. When I asked what percentage of words they understood in English class, suggesting 50% or 80%, Kok said, 'Forty-five percent'. After I exclaimed, 'Talaga? Parang nakakagulat yon' (Really? That's kind of surprising), Skusta said that for him it was 50-50. They told me they wished the teachers could speak more slowly: 'yung dahan-dahan lang na salita' (the slow kind of speech), said Kok, to which Skusta quickly agreed: '=Oo po miss ganyan, maintindihan namin nang maayos' (=Yes miss like that, we'll understand it well).

On the language use questionnaire, both boys had answered that they 'sometimes' used languages apart from English to think to themselves or communicate with others during class; Skusta put 'Tagalog', 'Bisaya' and 'Ilokano', while Kok put only 'Tagalog'. Indeed, most of the talk I heard was in Filipino, so apart from the occasional stylization, I don't believe much Bisaya or Ilokano was used.

Although Skusta was fluent in Filipino, he had an accent that was sometimes negatively marked. The most telling example took place one morning when several students (Ruby, Luke and Simon) were new and Rayna facilitated self-introductions, asking students to take turns introducing themselves and things they liked to do.

Excerpt 24 Playing cheese

1	Rayna:	So when someone asks you what is your—what you like to do, what is your answer?
2	Two male students:	Play basketba::all.
3	Male student:	Homework.
4	Rayna:	So you can say I like (.) to::o something… I want you to share something that you're proud of. … So should we start from Skusta? What do you like to do. Something that you're proud of.

5	Skusta:	(mumbles an indistinguishable response)
6	Rayna:	So for example it can be sports. It can be basketball, or it can be (.) volleyball, or it can be playing video games, some kind of activities.
7	Skusta:	I like to play (.) ch/ɪ/s.
8	Male students:	(repeating) Cheese.
9		(laughter, Filipino boys and Juliana)
10	Kok:	Skusta likes chess.
11		(more laughter as students repeat: 'Chess!' 'Cheese!')
12	Male student:	I like to play cheese o.
13	Male student:	Me too.
14	Cookie:	Cheese, eating cheese.
15	Rayna:	I don't think it's funny.
16	Female student:	Yeah.
17	Rayna:	I don't think it's cool—'cuz it's not funny to me. Do you want me to laugh at you when you make mistake?
18	Male student:	No miss.
19	Rayna:	We are not showing respect, yah? Let's show respect. (She elicits more answers; 'I like to play cheese' muttered surreptitiously)

Note how Rayna frames this activity as one in which people share things they are good at. When Skusta mumbles an answer, she provides several options that he can say, including 'sports', 'basketball', 'volleyball' and 'video games' (Line 6). Instead of choosing among these options, Skusta ventures an authentic answer, but with some evident uncertainty as to how to pronounce it, as shown by the pause in 'I like to play (.) ch/ɪ/s' (Line 7). The other boys pounce on this in a series of latching turns (Lines 8, 12, 13, 14). Juliana also laughs, but doesn't say anything (Line 9). Interestingly, Kok, who was recorded teasing Skusta about his grammar earlier in the period, comes to his defense here ('Skusta likes chess'; Line 10), and so does an unidentifiable female student (possibly the new girl, Ruby), who says 'Yeah' (Line 16) after Rayna tells them it isn't funny (Line 15). Still, 'cheese' continues to be commented on quietly even as Rayna moves on (Line 19).

While I originally saw this as a pronunciation mistake, which is what Rayna interprets it to be when she discourages making fun of others' mistakes (Line 17), it is a systematic rule of Visayan to transform /ɛ/, as in 'dress', into /ɪ/, as in 'kit', which makes 'ch/ɪ/s' vaguely sound like 'cheese'. Dark-skinned Visayan characters on Filipino television – sidekicks, servants and clowns – demonstrate this racialized vowel shift when speaking 'accented' Filipino and English. However, Filipino-accented English can remain unmarked on the same shows, for example, 'measure' (two lightly stressed syllables in American pronunciation) versus 'M/ɛ/ZH ur' (stronger stress on the first syllable in Filipino English) versus 'M/ɪ/ZH ur' (also a strong stress on the first syllable in Visayan English).

Another liability, apart from his accent, that led Skusta to be gradually ostracized by the other Filipino boys in ESL 9/10 from January to May as a student who was not academically competent, was his challenge with the printed word.

Skusta struggled far more with phonetic text decoding than the other students in ESL 9/10, even though his spoken English communicative proficiency was much the same as anyone else's and he was socially competent. It is beyond the scope of this study to examine whether this was because of a condition such as dyslexia or whether it was because of lack of print exposure in his educational history, but given that his school in the Philippines was sufficiently well-resourced to provide a range of extra-curricular clubs, and given that Kok did not have this problem, and from observing Skusta's many coping mechanisms to avoid directly dealing with print activities, I suspect some individual text processing factors were involved. For his part, Skusta often attempted to save face by positioning female classmates – such as Juliana and Summer – as less academically competent or, paradoxically, as helpers, as he relied on them for answers.

I present three examples of this positioning in chronological order, starting with a small-group activity on February 7 involving mapping the story structure in Mildred D. Taylor's *The Gold Cadillac*. In this excerpt, as in Excerpt 19, I do not present a transcript but combine field notes and audio-recorded data to outline class events in chronological order.

Excerpt 25 'Hi Summer'

21:30	The class counts off in groups of three or four. Ricky, Skusta, and Juliana (Filipino) and Summer (Chinese) are assigned to work together. As Ricky sits down next to Summer, he puts his face close to hers and says, 'Hello.' Summer, startled, replies, 'Who are you?' The Filipino kids chuckle and repeat 'Who are you?' to each other.
22:10	Skusta says 'Hi Julia↑na↓' in a seductive voice, followed by 'Hi Sum↑mer↓' in the same tone. Summer repeats, 'Who are you?' and laughs uncomfortably.
23:00	The second time Skusta says 'Hi Sum↑mer↓' creepily,[7] she again repeats, 'Who are you?'
23:15	Skusta says 'Zaoshang↑ hao↓' ('good morning' in Mandarin) with the same creepy intonation, and Juliana giggles.
23:30	Skusta says 'Hi <u>Sum</u>↑mer↓. (2.0) Zao<u>shang</u>↑ hao↓. (2.0) Where <u>you</u>↑ from↓?' in the same creepy voice. Juliana giggles again.
23:40	Ricky: (to Summer) 'Will you be my Valentine's date?' (Filipino kids laugh) Skusta: 'Summer, say yes!'
24:00	Skusta: 'Summer, do you have a date on Valentine's Day?' Instead of answering, Summer sighs loudly. One of the boys imitates Summer's loud sigh. Juliana giggles.
24:40	Ricky: 'Zaoshang↑ hao↓.'
25:10	Skusta: (creepy voice) 'Hi Sum↑mer↓. Hi Juli↑ana↓. Do you know what to do Sum↑mer↓?' Anna: 'What are you doing? That's creepy.' Juliana: 'Tinatakot mo si Summer. [*You're scaring Summer.*]'
25:30	Skusta: 'Meron ka na ba pagka-date Sum↑mer↓? (1.5) Si Ricky wala. [*Do you have a date Summer? (1.5) Ricky doesn't.*]' (Skusta asks the question in Filipino; thus, it's really for Juliana and Ricky.) Juliana repeats: 'Tinatakot mo si Summer. [*You're scaring Summer.*]'

25:45	Skusta: 'Paano ba mag basa hindi ako marunong mag basa e. [*How do you read I don't know how to read.*]' (to Summer) 'Can I see the author?' Summer: 'No.'
26:00	Skusta: 'Sum↑mer↓.' Juliana: 'Dinadamotan. [*Being stingy.*]' (i.e., Summer will not let them copy her work)
26:20	Skusta: 'Hi Sum↑me:::r↓.' (Juliana giggles) Skusta: 'Summer, can I hold your hand?' Summer: 'No.' Skusta: 'Why?' (Ricky laughs) Skusta: 'Do you have a boyfriend?' Summer: 'No.' Skusta: 'Why?' Ricky: '='Cuz Skusta likes you.' Skusta: 'Because Ricky likes you.' Ricky: 'Yeah I like you more.' Skusta: 'You like Ricky?' Summer: '=No.'
27:20	Skusta: 'Hi Sum↑mer↓. Sum↓mer?↑' Rayna: (coming by) 'She's translating. If you need to translate anything you can use your cellphone.' Skusta: 'Hi Sum↑mer↓.' Filipino kids laugh. Rayna: 'That was already five minutes. You guys didn't finish any box.'
28:50	Skusta: 'Sum↓me::r.↑' Ricky: 'Love me?' Summer: 'No.' Skusta: 'Summer, do you love me?' Summer: 'No.' Juliana giggles.
29:20	Rayna comes again, sees little progress, and asks, 'What are two events that happened in Part One?' Skusta: 'OK.' Rayna: 'What are they?' Skusta: (reading incoherently) 'To in wer::e eben [events] dat kana has my fader's [father] soo (?) crow (?).' (Juliana laughs at Skusta's answer) Rayna: (gently) 'What? Was that your answer?' Skusta: 'You are beautiful miss.' Rayna: 'What was your answer?' Skusta: 'I'm reading miss.'
30:35	Skusta: 'Sum↓me::r.↑ Sum↑mer↓.' (Juliana giggles) Skusta: 'Summer you are beautiful Summer.' (Ricky sings the words 'beautiful girl' and Skusta laughs) Juliana: 'Beauty pa niya si Summer. O lumalayo na o. [*He even finds Summer beautiful. Oh she's moving away.*]' Skusta: 'Summer? You are beautiful or not?' Juliana: 'Mm. Lumalayo na o. [*Mm. She's moving away.*]'
31:20	Ricky: 'Hoy. Sino sila sa mga characters? [*Hey. Who are the characters?*]' Skusta: 'Si... [*They're...*]' (7.0) Hi Summer! (2.0) Zaoshang hao. (8.0) Why are you mad?' Juliana: 'Pinagtritripan mo kase. [*'Cuz you're harassing her.*]' (lowers voice) 'Pag mag sumbong yan sa— [*If she tells on you to—*]' Skusta: 'Tatay niya. Na Inchik. [*To her father. The Chino.*]'[8]
32:35	Rayna arrives to check their work. Rayna: 'I cannot even understand what you wrote. (1.0) What did you write?' Skusta: (reading) 'Insan dardi are we reach.' (Juliana snickers) Rayna: 'No, that's not an event.' Skusta: 'Oh event OK—' Rayna: 'Yeah—' Skusta: 'Yeah event—' Rayna: 'What did they do?' Skusta: 'OK. (2.0) Hi Summer.'
35:10	Skusta: 'What's the answer, Summer?' Summer: 'No, I don't know.' Skusta: 'How come? You said (.) you have.' Summer: 'I don't know. (chuckles)' Skusta: 'What the (.) place? Oh. (to Juliana) Galit na yata si Summer. [*Summer's maybe angry already.*]'
36:10	Skusta: 'Let's see Summer. You said you have.'
39:30	Juliana: 'Ano number two? Tinakpan niya? [*What's number two? Did she cover it up?*]' Skusta: 'Hindi pa. [*Not yet.*]'
41:40	Skusta: 'Ehh. Tingnan mo Google ito. [*Ehh. Look it up on Google.*]' Juliana: 'Hoy huwag. [*Hey don't.*]'
42:00	Rayna comes by and reminds them they have 10 more minutes in the activity.
43:40	Anna: 'Binasa n'yo ba yung storia? [*Did you read the story?*]' Skusta: 'Opo miss. [*Yes miss.*] But a long time ago miss.'

During this small-group activity, the Filipino students teased Summer in at least three languages, including her own, with comments in Filipino that she could not understand, though she recognized her name. They collaborated to copy her answers, asking each other for them instead of asking Summer herself. Even though there is multilingual language use here, it is not translanguaging to learn, but code-switching into unsanctioned practices below non-Filipino speakers' understanding. Although the Filipino students excluded Summer, none of them seemed to be in a safe space either: Skusta teased Juliana in the same voice that he used on Summer, Juliana giggled whenever Skusta revealed his reading challenges and no one seemed confident enough to venture an answer for the others to check.

This unsettling excerpt suggests how inappropriate language practices can be related to gender relations, and raises questions about classroom management when there is a classroom underlife in non-English languages that the teacher does not understand.[9] Rayna's relative lack of attention to what was going on in the group could be related to her novicehood – i.e. the assumption that all she would need to do was assign work, then put students in groups to check it and they would do so, and also collaborate respectfully and equitably. She didn't seem to be aware of the harassment at this moment, and when she visited the group it was evidently only to check their progress on the worksheet (Excerpt 25). Certainly, I made such mistakes myself during my early teaching career. At other times when she was more aware of male dominance, such as boys talking too much in whole-class discussions, she encouraged female students' bids for the floor (Excerpt 27).

I address these classroom management issues more in Chapter 7, but want to point out here that translanguaging may not necessarily lead to academic or socioemotional benefits – as academic self-confidence, trust, interpersonal relations and authority in literacy activities are factors that affect whether students share their thoughts aloud in any language(s) and what kind of interactional moves they make toward one another. As a novice teacher, Rayna took for granted that students had read (that they even *could* read without assistance) the lengthy story she had assigned for homework, though it may have been too difficult for many of them, and she also took it for granted that, if several struggling students from Language Group A with blank worksheets and a desperate need to save face ended up working with a singleton classmate from Language Group B with a hearing disability but who had done the homework, they would work together supportively. As Kumaravadivelu (2001) puts it:

> [L]anguage teachers can ill afford to ignore the sociocultural reality that influences identity formation in the classroom, nor can they afford to separate the linguistic needs of learners from their social needs. In other words, language teachers cannot hope to fully satisfy their pedagogic obligations without at the same time satisfying their social obligations. (Kumaravadivelu, 2001: 544)

Similar to Jhon, Skusta displayed a reluctance to engage in depth with academic print texts due to what can be understood as anxiety about showing his struggles in front of others. However, while Jhon, who could at least decode what was written, often faked thinking aloud, Skusta's strategies were to deflect the question and to charm others with humor. One thing I marveled at was how he was never disrespectful toward the teacher, no matter how much he suffered academically in class, and even though others were. On the contrary, he tried his best to convey meaning to whoever was teaching, for example by showing pictures on his phone. On the other hand, he sometimes positioned female classmates as helpers or sources of information, especially Juliana, who, being the only female Filipino student in the class until the arrival of Ruby, Mariel and Jennifer, was also on the margins of the network of Filipino-speaking students. Thus, Skusta had a range of pragmatic coping strategies. This could be seen when he and Juliana were working together to brainstorm points for and against cellphone use, in a lesson on argumentative writing:

Excerpt 26 Skusta manages his language brokers

1	Juliana:	(cutting off Skusta singing to himself) —number two?
2	Skusta:	Ikaw na writer a. *You're the writer eh.*
3	Juliana:	Ano? *What?*
4	Education assistant:	Kailangan kayong mag-usap. *You need to discuss with each other.*
5	Skusta:	Ano ba ang English n'yong gusto n'yong—'hindi masaya kung walang cellphone kasi (.) walang ginagawa. Walang kabalaan (?) ng time'? *(using polite 'you') What's the English you want—'it's not fun to not have a cellphone 'cuz (.) nothing to do. No way to pass the time?'*
6	Education assistant:	OK um. We are not happy without cellphones.
7	Skusta:	(to Juliana) Kopyahan mo. *(to Juliana) Copy that.*
8	Education assistant:	We are not happy—without cellphones. Because in some phones, I can watch movies...
9	Juliana:	(reading what she is writing) 'We are not happy without cellphones...'

In Line 2, Skusta reminds Juliana that she is the writer, effectively managing group role assignment so that he does not need to write. When the education assistant arrives[10] and asks them to collaborate (Line 4), Skusta immediately asks him to translate a point about cellphones from Filipino to English, but the only English words he says in expressing this request are 'English', 'cellphone' and 'time' (Line 5). As the education assistant fulfils the request, which has been made with the polite form of 'you', and even adds some ideas of his own, Skusta tells Juliana to write down what the education assistant says (Line 7), which she does (Line 9). Rather than translanguaging to learn, or using the whole language repertoire to think aloud collaboratively or discuss how to express ideas in the target language, this is *relay code-switching*, as Skusta says what he wants translated without having to use much English, the education assistant gives them what to write and Juliana takes down the dictation. These practices get the task done, but they almost certainly do not involve much language acquisition, especially not for Skusta.

The last example of Skusta's reading challenges (out of three, i.e. Excerpts 25–27) illustrates that he was not always able to save face so easily, especially when it was a whole-class activity and others exposed him deliberately. The next week, on April 25, as students came back together after small-group work, anticipating a read-aloud, Flow-G nominated Skusta, followed by others (Excerpt 27). Note that the class studied *The Gold Cadillac* in late January and early February, with Skusta deflecting attention from his reading challenges in the small-group activity with Ricky, Juliana and Summer (Excerpt 25). By Excerpt 27, toward the end of my data collection in late April, it was evidently well known in the class that Skusta had reading challenges, and this is why others nominated him for amusement:

Excerpt 27 Round robin reading

1	**Flow-G:**	Galing si Skusta mag-basa. *Skusta's a good reader.*
2	**Rayna:**	Who wants to be the first reader?
3	**Male student:**	Skusta!
4	**Male student:**	Skusta!
5	**Juliana:**	Me, miss![11]
6	**Rayna:**	Juliana::. 'Kay everyone listen carefully. If you don't listen, you will not know where we are reading.
7	**Skusta:**	OK yeah miss. Listening.
8		(Juliana starts to read. Rayna stops her when she hits key vocabulary, e.g., major, pedestrian.)
9	**Juliana:**	(choosing the next person) Kaiea.
10		(Boys comment as Kaiea is reading: 'Walang marinig. [*Can't hear*]' 'Make loud.' 'I cannot hear miss.')
11		(Kaiea chooses Cookie to read next. Cookie chooses Juliana's quiet brother, Kyrie. Kyrie can't find the place; various people say 'Number nine.' Kyrie still cannot find the place; someone says Kok's name, so Rayna says, 'OK Kok.')
12	**Kok:**	(after reading) Skusta. I mean Flow-G.
13	**Flow-G:**	(reads, then chooses Skusta)
14	**Skusta:**	(reads too fast and in a funny voice) >'Missero Caldwell[12] said da ba:::n was'<
15		(Others burst out laughing)
16	**Unknown student:**	Ang bilis kasi. *'Cause it's too fast.*

17	Skusta:	I can read fast.
18	Rayna:	Uh guys (.) we've been talking about this. It is not funny to make fun of someone. Everyone is learning English. Is your English better than everyone else? ... (to Skusta) 'Kay read one more time, please.
19	Skusta:	'Mister Caldwell said—'
20	Rayna:	Make it a little bit slower.
21	Skusta:	(clear) 'Mister Caldwell said the ban was necessary to make people more aware of the (.) dangers of (.) texting well looking—'
22	Male student:	Well looking. :-)
23	Skusta:	Ah while looking.
24	Rayna:	Mm-hm.
25	Skusta:	'He said (.) "We hold the unfortunate dis-distinction :-) of being—"' (giggles in the background as Skusta reads)
26	Rayna:	What does distinction mean?
27	Male student:	Difference.
28	Rayna:	Next person.
29	Skusta:	°Sino po ba yon?° Summer. *(to self, but using polite form as if to talk to Rayna in his mind)* °Who's that again?° Summer.
30		(The educational assistant goes over to Summer. She starts to read.)
31	Flow-G:	Miss, can you hear?
32	Rayna:	OK, you can stop there. Can you repeat one more time, with louder voice, please?
33		(Summer doesn't read any louder)
34	Rayna:	(in a kind voice) I cannot hear. Louder please.
35		(Summer reads a bit louder)
36		OK. Thank you. It was better, thank you Summer. OK next person.

Jones (2013) critiques such round robin reading activities as having an anxiety-inducing and detrimental effect on students' academic identities. In a graduate university course, she did a demonstration of this effect (pretending it was a 'real' activity) to show in-service teachers how it felt from students' point of view:

> I spontaneously perform the bodied moves of many of my own reading teachers of the past: smooth walk, calm voice, careful surveillance... and overall unwavering presence of power and authority. I control who speaks and who reads. All anxiously await the possibility of their turn. ... It is as if the round robin reading cannot occur without my body moving a certain way, without my head being held high... the taller neck, the slow and steady pacing around the room, the intent gaze on the text in my hands and the brief look at the next student to read. (Jones, 2013: 527)

After 30 minutes of this, she revealed to the class that it was a simulation, meant to demonstrate a point:

'Oh my God. I was so stressed out,' someone says, and everyone laughs. … Students report sweating, feeling hot, noticing their heart rate speed up, shaking legs, and fearing humiliation and being perceived as incompetent. (Jones, 2013: 527)

It is remarkable how seamlessly a teacher can step into an authoritative role, calmly patrolling the classroom and managing power relations. Quoting Bourdieu (2000: 169), Jones explains: 'The magic only works on the basis of previously constituted dispositions [i.e., previously remembered experiences of the same thing in the past], which it "triggers" like springs'. Inherited literacy practices like round robin readings make us behave in ways recognizable across formal education settings, whether loosely termed 'Asian' or 'Western'. According to Jones, there is nothing inherently good about such literacies – a literacy being a communicative practice that has to be taught and learned rather than coming naturally like everyday talk. She implores educators to examine how literacies inherent in schooling reproduce power structures, which in turn reproduce wider discourses in society about who is academically meritorious or worthy of scorn.

Round robin readings reveal, in front of the whole group, who has or does not have text decoding skills and oral fluency in the language of instruction at the level of the course. And when students rather than the teacher get to choose who is to come next, there are social messages in their choices. In Excerpt 27, Juliana nominates Kaiea (Line 9), the Marshallese singleton who had been quiet in ESL 9/10 since the departure of her Marshallese-speaking friend. This is a friendly overture: Juliana knows Kaiea will do well, and she gives her a chance to display her competence in English in this class verbally dominated by Filipino boys.

However, while Kaiea is reading, the boys interrupt by complaining that she is too quiet (Line 10). Ignoring this, Kaiea also makes a judicious choice about the next reader, as she nominates a competent peer, Cookie, to go next, but when he is done Cookie chooses Juliana's brother Kyrie, putting another weak reader on the spot (Line 11). Kyrie cannot find the place in the text, and after some delay, someone says Kok's name, so Kok goes instead. After, he 'threatens' to call on Skusta: 'Skusta. I mean Flow-G' (Line 12). This gives Skusta a start, followed by relief, which is short-lived, as Flow-G unsurprisingly nominates him (Line 13). Skusta turns the situation around with a funny performance (Lines 14–17), to which Rayna responds, 'Uh guys (.) we've been talking about this. It is not funny to make fun of someone...' (Line 18), encouraging Skusta to read slower. Skusta does surprisingly well on the next try, despite pronouncing a word wrong (Line 21), which someone takes the opportunity to point out, in a smiley voice (Line 22). Skusta gracefully corrects himself (Line 23), finishes his turn and nominates Summer, the other person in the class who has difficulties reading aloud (Line 29), so Rayna coaxes the best reading out of Summer, as she did with Skusta, then praises and thanks her (Lines 34–36).

These interactional choices point to students' need to position themselves as linguistically and academically competent, at least relative to others. Such competence is not measured according to an objective standard, but according to traditional school-based middle-class literacies that are imbued with power in both 'Western' and 'Asian' cultures, and according to interactional positionings socially constructed in the moment. This brings up the question of what Skusta's and Jhon's cases illustrate about the need for translanguaging to connect with expanded notions of 'academic' literacy practices – if we want translanguaging to be as transformative an educational theory as some of its proponents claim it to be.

6.4 Summary

This chapter has highlighted the need to investigate translanguaging more with students who speak marginalized dialects of immigrant languages, and those who are challenged by the privileging of print literacies over oral literacies in formal education (Hornberger & Link, 2012; Perez Hattori, 2020). In addition, traditional classroom practices that are high stakes socially if not grade-wise, like spontaneous verbal analogy exercises and round robin readings, may cause stress for students because of individual pressure to perform publicly in academic registers of the language of instruction (Chapters 5 and 6). Although the round robin in the previous excerpt is an oral activity, it is not really an oral literacy, like rap or spoken word poetry, but the oral performance of text decoding skills and a demonstration of oral English fluency. And while it can be anxiety-inducing and challenging, it does not necessarily entail higher-order thinking. As can be seen in Excerpt 27, the students take turns reading aloud, but there are no follow-up questions save for a brief, trite one regarding a synonym match of a word previously memorized (Lines 26–27). This interaction pattern suggests that Rayna could have used the round robin as a way to maintain discipline and control in a class where the verbally dominant group of students sometimes disrespected her (Excerpt 18), thus keeping them on their feet since it was clear that they *did* care about their English oral performance. On a positive note, the round robin interaction order also gave everyone a fair turn to speak, and made room for the girls, who rarely got to say anything in class, even if only to read aloud.

Two points are worth making with regard to how Jhon's and Skusta's academic identities evolved across different timescales and with varying degrees of solidification (Wortham & Reyes, 2017). The first point is that because of the relative stability and higher currency of textual literacy practices in schooling – such as literary analysis and round robin readings – for the most part both students will fight an uphill battle during their entire educational careers, whether in the US or the Philippines, save for fleeting 'contradictory currents' such as the drama workshop led by Mr Nick and Ms Marie, in which a positive identity emerged for Jhon in a particular unit that involved alternative language and literacy practices. The second point is that the emphasis on text-based practices that are high stakes academically and socially prevents both young men from languaging to learn, presumably in class after class, year after year, country after country – from having the confidence to articulate their thoughts aloud, including their struggles and limitations – and hinders educational opportunities, with potential compound effects over time.

Proponents of translanguaging define it as a critical educational practice that challenges linguistic hierarchization and standardization (e.g. García *et al.*, 2021), but the mechanisms of *how* and *why* are rarely investigated through close analyses of unfolding classroom interactions. In this chapter, I hope to have demonstrated that it is not bi/multilingual practices *per se* but language practices that involve *expanded* notions of 'academic' literacies (e.g. the drama workshop and the poetry workshop led by kama'āina that balanced oral and textual literacy, and the multi-class multilingual poetry anthology) that led to this beneficial social effect in English 9 and ESL 9/10, with affordances surely not for Jhon alone but others as well. These alternative literacies can sometimes co-occur with bi/multilingual practices and the valuation of people's entire linguistic repertoires, and I argue that they are empowering particularly when marginalized dialects/accents (in *every* language) are brought into academic activities and when students can use these dialects and accents to 'think aloud' without shame. Hornberger and Link (2012) list the language practices that are more privileged in school, such as monolingual performances over dynamic blending of languages and dialects, written over oral literacies, decontextualized (e.g. textbook academic) over contextualized (e.g. place based) communicative genres and successive rather than simultaneous exposure to different languages, dialects and registers.[13]

When classroom language practices work to balance societal diglossia, they are critical, and this is why multidialectal translanguaging deserves more research attention, even though translanguaging researchers have largely neglected it (Block, 2018). If students are simply communicating bi/multilingually, there is no guarantee that they are overturning any linguistic or social hierarchies or negotiating the threats to face that individual teachers and students with different linguistic and cultural funds of knowledge can pose to each other (Young, 2004), and moreover, they might be doing little to challenge narrow definitions of language, literacy and academic ability.

In Chapter 7, I turn to what all this means for classroom pedagogy.

Notes

(1)   Ilocos is part of *Luzon*, the northern third of the Philippines where there are two main regional languages: Ilokano in northern Luzon and Tagalog (whose official national form is Filipino) in Manila and southern Luzon. Other languages native to Luzon include Kapampangan, Bicol and Pangasinan. In the middle third of the Philippines, called *the Visayas*, and the southern third, *Mindanao*, the main lingua franca is Cebuano – also known as Visayan/Bisaya. Other native languages in the Visayas and Mindanao include Kinaraya, Hiligaynon/Ilonggo and Waray in the former; Maranao, Maguindanao, Chavacano, Subanon and Tausug in the latter. In this study, the Ilokano- and Tagalog-speaking students' region of Luzon is more developed than the other parts of the Philippines not only because the capital is there, but also because the dictator Ferdinand Marcos diverted a lot of government funds to build infrastructure in his home province of Ilocos. (His wife Imelda was Waray Visayan.) Thus, even if these students' families had to take up working-class jobs in the US, they had enough resources to *leave* the Philippines, as did Juan's family and the researcher's. My maternal grandparents were white-collar Visayans whose children only spoke English and Tagalog; my father's family are also Tagalog–English bilinguals. As Valdés (2001) points out, these levels of subtractive bilingualism and linguistic stigmas brought over from the home country require more attention to explain students' identities and language learning in immigrant groups. This is because students recognize and deploy stigmatized dialects to construct their own and others' identities, whereas to cultural outsiders it is simply undifferentiated Spanish, Chinese, Vietnamese, Turkish, etc.

(2)   Rarely did I hear Ilokano-speaking students say something in Filipino (e.g. Clara in self-talk, Eufia or Rizze in stylization), and He did not use Chinese except to sign his name in the multi-class poetry anthology.

(3)   The Ilokano L1 students did not use Ilokano with Jhon in class, which likely had as much to do with their choosing to exclude him from their circle as his expressed language policy, which positioned their translanguaging practices negatively.

(4)   I say 'observable' because it is inevitable for people to translanguage mentally – yet there are at least two requirements for observable/recordable translanguaging to occur: the individual must view it as pragmatically appropriate, and it must place that individual's repertoire in an asset-oriented rather than a deficit-oriented light (Chapter 4). Thus, when a student is described as a 'reluctant translanguager' in this book, I refer specifically to observable/recordable translanguaging, with an attempt to understand, if not to entirely justify, that student's more monolingual communicative preferences.

(5)   In a similarly well-enjoyed March 7 workshop by the visiting poet Celeste Gallo, a kama'āina of Philippine ancestry, students in English 9 and ESL 9/10 practiced oral recitation, but ultimately had to write down their poems for the multi-class poetry anthology (a textual practice), and Filipino cultural references predominated in brainstorming and sharing. On the other hand, Gallo deliberately used Marshallese poet Kathy Jetnil-Kijiner as a model, as well as youth poets of color in the continental US who worked with both oral and print traditions. This shows that many activities that blend students' funds of knowledge with the 'official' curriculum involve tensions between school-based literacies and other literacies, and between majoritized and minoritized literacies in the class or the wider society.

(6)   For this strategy of teachers putting language with symbolic capital in students' mouths through collaborative learning practices so that the language becomes authentically the students', see Jaffe (2003).

(7)   Skusta said 'Hi Sum↑mer↓' with this intonation no less than 20 times in 23 minutes. While it originally sounded sexual (22:10), after plenty of repetition it lost this edge and sounded more annoying than anything.

(8) The term 'Inchik' or 'Intsik' in Filipino is not necessarily a racist slur, and needs to be interpreted in context. While Chinese merchants in the Philippines were heavily taxed during the colonial period, they were not badly off in terms of social class, given the presence of both Spanish and Chinese 'mestizos' (Filipinos of mixed blood). Many Manila elites, including former President Corazon Aquino, are of Chinese heritage. Filipino Chinese speak Hokkien as their heritage language, as do Chinese in Indonesia, Malaysia and Singapore.

(9) While the Filipino boys in ESL 9/10 were very vocal, this kind of harassment of female classmates was not typical, and this case of group bullying was a one-off incident in my study data. However, it was of sufficient concern that I reported it, and Kaori had individual talks with the students involved. I do not know to what extent Summer was negatively impacted by this experience, but Skusta did something else on one other occasion to suggest there was another student who struggled more to read aloud in ESL 9/10 than he did – i.e. Summer, due to her hearing disability (Excerpt 27).

(10) Education assistants in ESL 9/10, who were often Filipinos, were not present in every class. The main one was Teresa, but on that day the education assistant was a male.

(11) Juliana's bid to showcase her reading ability (Line 5) was a response to being teased about her lack of English use in class by Skusta and Flow-G, a turning point as she went from supporting the 'loud' Filipino boys' behavior to ignoring it. Her language identity trajectory in ESL 9/10 can also be explored as an interesting case. However, it is beyond the scope of this chapter, which focuses on the need for translanguaging research to connect to expanded notions of literacy and involve more studies on dialectical translanguaging in classrooms.

(12) Kirk Caldwell, mayor of Honolulu.

(13) In successive exposure, the more prestigious languages and dialects are encountered increasingly in later grades, and the less prestigious ones are used less frequently, whereas in simultaneous exposure, students do not have to stop or decrease using what they already know to do the academic work in new languages, dialects or registers they are learning.

7 Discussion and Pedagogical Implications

This chapter is divided into two parts. In the first part, I discuss how the findings chapters (see the 'Summary' sections of Chapters 4–6) point to the *plurilingual, English as a lingua franca classroom* as a distinct translanguaging context compared to other educational settings that have been featured in translanguaging research, such as heritage language (HL) classrooms (Creese *et al.*, 2014, 2015; Li, 2014; Williams, 1994) or classrooms where all students are part of the same bi/multilingual imagined community and share the same languages when they translanguage (García, 2009; Leonet *et al.*, 2020; Sayer, 2013). This kind of class composition also exists to some extent in English-medium instruction (EMI) classrooms, i.e. classes in which students learn an academic subject in English in a country where English is not the dominant language, but nevertheless share another language as their own (e.g. Lin & He, 2017; Sah & Li, 2020), even though Sah and Li (2020) point out that it is often only this language (the national language) and English that are legitimized in translanguaging, and not minoritized, regional, indigenous or immigrant languages, as has also been observed by Beiler (2021).

In contrast, in plurilingual English as a lingua franca (ELF) classrooms in English-dominant countries, students learn and navigate the class' social life by speaking languages that not all classroom participants understand or have a 'heritage' connection to, while English is the official language of instruction in an English-dominant society. The challenges of this situation must be adequately addressed for teachers to see translanguaging as feasible and desirable when the *only* language shared by all class participants is the language that is the medium of instruction *and* the dominant societal language. Therefore, in this chapter, I outline pedagogical principles for the plurilingual ELF classroom that would meet those challenges, consisting of the following components: multilingual joinfostering (Faltis, 2001); ELF teaching and learning practices; and critical language awareness (CLA).

In the summary of the chapter, I explain how these pedagogical principles point to the need for *teacher-led* activities that show students how to draw on bi/multilingual, multidialectal and multimodal resources to learn and build bridges across individual class participants' linguistic asymmetries. Such *deliberate* translanguaging designs (Hamman, 2018) would reflect possibilities in language teaching tailored to the sociolinguistic context, shaping the classroom culture so that it plays out in ways that are different from the more hegemonic language norms students are used to in their communities and the wider society (Kumaravadivelu, 2001) and restructuring linguistic hierarchies in the ways that García and colleagues have argued for (García & Otheguy, 2020; García *et al.*, 2021; Menken & García, 2010).

7.1 The Plurilingual, English as a Lingua Franca Classroom as a Distinct Translanguaging Context

Translanguaging theory in education originated in Welsh HL classrooms (Williams, 1994) and expanded to encompass bilingual and HL education in English-dominant countries like the US and the UK (e.g. Creese & Blackledge, 2010; García, 2009; Li, 2014). However, a parallel research agenda has existed for longer in EMI for academic subjects in English as a foreign language (EFL) contexts (Lin, 2013), and in bi/multilingual instruction across the regional language, the national language and global English in European contexts (Cenoz & Gorter, 2020; Leonet *et al.*, 2020). A key feature of all these educational settings is that developing bi/multilingualism is the whole point of the program, whether it is a HL program, a dual language program, an EMI program or a Basque–Spanish–English trilingual program, and the languages that the students are seeking to become bi/multilingual in are the same, for example, English and their HL(s), the two languages in the dual language program (English–Spanish, English–Chinese) or English for academic purposes plus students' national language and possibly the regional language as well.

In contrast, in the plurilingual ELF classroom in an English-dominant country, what happens to students' other languages and their place in formal education is less clear. The very act of revealing that one is bi/multilingual in such a class therefore has a different indexicality, or social meaning, if English is the medium of instruction, it is also the single dominant language in the wider society, there is no strong societal imperative to be bi/multilingual in other languages except to pass the language hurdle requirement in secondary and tertiary education, and students use languages from their own backgrounds that their classmates do not speak beyond a few social phrases.

It is not uncommon to see teachers of plurilingual ELF classrooms in Inner Circle English-speaking countries reject translanguaging because they feel it is not relevant to them or their teaching situation. Usually, such rejection is justified with statements like: 'How can I do it, when I'm not bi/multilingual?' 'But I have students who speak 10–15 different languages!' and 'I *do* value students' languages, but the purpose of my course is to teach students (a subject in) English'.

Instead of ignoring these teachers' objections as signs that they are not very open-minded, compassionate or modern in pedagogical outlook, researchers should address their concerns by showing how they can practice a version of translanguaging pedagogy that is appropriate and necessary for their context. To do so, researchers who desire to give pedagogical recommendations for teachers to embrace translanguaging in the plurilingual ELF classroom need to confront *three substantive interpersonal challenges* of teachers and students in such a classroom, challenges not often found in translanguaging research in other contexts. These include (1) how the teacher, even if bi/multilingual themselves, may not be bi/multilingual in the same language(s) as the students (i.e. a linguistic and cultural outsider); (2) how classroom language minorities cannot understand what speakers of the classroom majority non-English language are saying, but are unable to use their own first languages (L1s)/ HLs without seeming exclusive; and (3) individuals' anxiety about their performance in English in a schooling system where English dominates and students from the same ethnolinguistic background have varying knowledge of English and other languages they share, and speak them in different ways.

In bi/multilingual and HL classrooms, and in EMI classrooms in EFL settings, the teacher is usually a member of the same bi/ multilingual imagined community as the students. On the other hand, most 'mainstream' K–12 teachers in English-dominant countries are white middle-class people who speak English as their L1 and may not speak any other language to a substantial degree, reflecting cultural and class dominance. Furthermore, most are women, reflecting the development of teaching into a profession in which caring and compassion are bound up with policing language and manners – all duties primarily assigned to women from middle-class, 'mainstream' cultural backgrounds (Warren, 2015). In Hawai'i, where the dominant cultural group is Japanese American rather than Euro American, many teachers and principals are Japanese Americans who speak 'standard' English as their dominant language, and females with this background (as well as educated immigrants such as Juan, Kaori and Rayna) commonly teach Visayan, Micronesian, Marshallese and Samoan students, among others, again reflecting cultural and class dominance and a general mismatch between the funds of knowledge of most teaching professionals and linguistically and culturally minoritized students. And in every part of every country, it is not uncommon to find teachers who are from a different culture and social class from their learners, because those who tend to become teachers tend to be those who enjoyed school, because their language and literacy practices and funds of knowledge aligned with those taught at school.

Thus, the majority of teachers being from middle-class dominant cultural groups poses a linguistic challenge when such teachers work at schools where most students are from linguistically minoritized and culturally marginalized groups, particularly if the teachers are young and temporary (e.g. on practicum), because their well-intentioned initiatives to bring students' linguistic and cultural capital into the classroom may misfire, as students either ask: 'Why are you inviting this?' or 'What do you have to do with our culture/language?' or use codes that the teacher does not speak to take out their frustration with the system on the teacher.

Pre-service teachers must be aware that flexible language policies inviting translanguaging should be accompanied by intentional and structured classroom management decisions that foster inclusive participation in different languages *and* students' confidence as collective owners of the official classroom language as a lingua franca,[1] otherwise a well-intentioned classroom language policy that seeks to be socially just and equitable but is *not* accompanied by any deliberate, confident teacher-led shaping of the class social atmosphere may result in the teacher losing control of students' bottom-up language practices and, chagrined, turning to a target-language-only policy and traditional literacy practices (e.g. round robin readings, individualized work to keep students on their toes) from then on.

Additionally, there is the issue of language minorities and singletons. In bilingual and HL education, people whose HL is *not* the language being taught (e.g. African Americans in an English–Spanish dual language program, ethnic Japanese and Chinese in a university-level Filipino class) may have an exalted rather than marginalized status as they 'grace' the target language by adding value to it, especially if it is typically only learned by heritage speakers (Mendoza & Parba, 2019). Also, in this context, the teacher addressing the whole class in English-plus-another-language is socially unremarkable, no more than expected. However, in plurilingual ELF classrooms, linguistic minorities and singletons may find themselves at a linguistic and cultural disadvantage when translanguaging is encouraged, or even practiced by the teacher to address the class language majority, because most of this translanguaging is likely to happen between English and another language that they do not understand and did not come to the class to learn (Allard *et al.*, 2019). Teachers using English with the majority non-English language is socially remarkable in two ways: it puts many students' own language on equal footing with English (a good thing) yet puts English and the majority group's language above other languages students speak (a questionable thing). Thus, the teacher cannot use a non-English language without making an implicit political statement – which, in many cases, they should be doing anyway, as translanguaging should not just be focused on getting students to learn effectively but be linked to transformative pedagogy (García & Kleifgen,

2010; García & Li, 2014; Poza, 2017). But what is empowering for one student could be discomfiting for another, as students' needs sometimes conflict (Allard *et al.*, 2019). The point is not *whether* the class community should function bi/multilingually, but *how* languages (including English, the majority non-English language and other languages) can be used to index inclusivity and social responsibility, rather than exclusivity and disregard for others' needs.

'Letting students bring their languages into the class', 'speaking English so everyone can understand', 'doing multilingual things to celebrate diversity' – none of these necessarily entail equity without examination of people's *intentions* or how their actions impact others' needs and identity positions. Students can translanguage in ways that include only those who can understand, or they can do so in ways that include everyone. They can perform playful translanguaging as rapport building or bullying; they can do pragmatic code-switching to manage a collaborative learning activity or an unwarranted classroom underlife; they can use stylized speech to connect with others linguistically or for disrespectful ends. They can translanguage to legitimize minoritized languages and dialects as appropriate for academic learning, or simply translanguage between language forms seen as socially acceptable for academic purposes. There is nothing inherently just about the deployment of an integrated language repertoire or the deployment of non-English languages in English-medium classrooms; on the other hand, encouraging lingua franca dispositions across everyone's whole language repertoires while cultivating critical language awareness (CLA) and appreciation for varied linguistic, cultural and literacy practices as well as *everyone's* ways of using their languages (Hélot & Young, 2002, 2005; Seltzer, 2019a, 2019b, 2020) can develop the classroom culture in the right directions.

A third challenge with encouraging translanguaging in the plurilingual ELF classroom is that students can be particularly anxious about English: not only in terms of how well they do in the class (as in an EFL setting), but also in terms of their academic and social identities more broadly, because English is the dominant language of schooling in a society where it is also dominant. This raises the issue of how resident multilingual students may seek to distinguish themselves from 'FOB' ('fresh off the boat') classmates, whom they position as the 'real' English language learners (Talmy, 2008) – that is, positioning yourself as a competent English user by putting down others' English use. People who support the struggles of multilingual and multidialectal people in English-dominant countries do not like to talk about this phenomenon in which members of linguistically and culturally oppressed groups oppress each other, but it has to be acknowledged as a part of human nature so that educators can adequately address it and guard against it.

This is not to say that students do not experience anxiety about lack of knowledge of other languages apart from English; in this study,

I have shown that students are invested in displaying competencies in non-English languages as well. However, the teacher's job is not only to legitimize multilingualism (languages as resources) but also to legitimize plurilingualism (the notion that individual language repertoires are always in evolution and never finished, reflecting the sum of people's life experiences and constantly evolving communicative needs; see Blommaert & Horner, 2017), and moreover, teachers must *legitimize the full range of students' linguistic resources for academic purposes* (Flores & Schissel, 2014; García *et al.*, 2017; Hornberger & Link, 2012) while *ensuring that students fully include each and every single class member in the functioning of the learning community, regardless of how similar or different others' language repertoires may be and the different ways that people use the class' languages* (Mendoza, 2020b). To lead the class in creating an ecology conducive to learning, teachers need classroom management strategies gained through teacher education, and a commitment to cultivating students' CLA regarding linguistic and dialectal ideologies and inequities through *intentional* teaching practices. I now discuss several of these strategies.

7.2 Use Joinfostering to Facilitate Collaborative Talk

Joinfostering is a pedagogical approach that uses collaborative talk to facilitate content and language learning among linguistically diverse students in English-dominant countries. It was first proposed by Christian Faltis during the exponential increase of linguistic diversity in US schools in the late 20th century, following the 1965 Immigration Act (see Chapter 3). As a teaching philosophy, joinfostering encompasses a gamut of practices which Faltis (2001) observes are essential for effective language and literacy instruction not only for linguistically diverse students but also for relatively monolingual L1 English speakers. On one end of the gamut, there are uncontroversial, student-centered teaching principles that are found in many contemporary approaches to education; on the other end, there is pedagogy grounded in sociopolitically aware CLA (Figure 7.1).

What is interesting about these five principles of joinfostering, which I have arranged in this cline of more and less controversial practices, is how fundamentally different Principles 1, 2 and 3 would be in the presence or absence of Principles 4 and 5, which include seeing family and community languages and literacy practices as resources in students' academic literacy development, rather than a hindrance to students doing well in school; seeing these language and literacy practices as part of the purpose of students' education, rather than something to be remediated through education; and recognizing students' languages and dialects as grammatically complex systems with just as much potential to express deep, abstract and intellectual meanings, culture specific as these may be, as 'standard' English. Few teachers would disagree with the first three

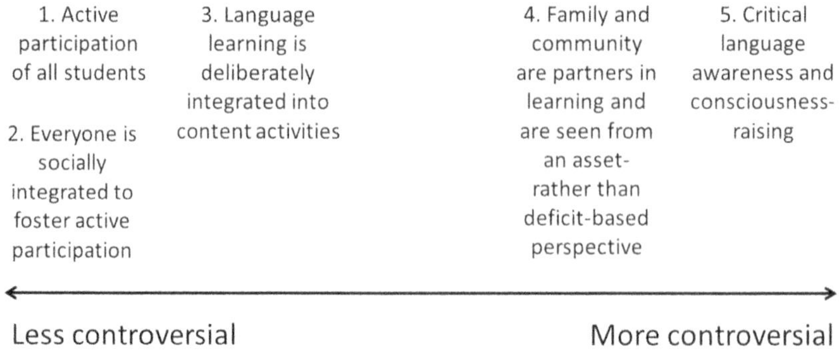

1. Active participation of all students	3. Language learning is deliberately integrated into content activities	4. Family and community are partners in learning and are seen from an asset- rather than deficit-based perspective	5. Critical language awareness and consciousness- raising
2. Everyone is socially integrated to foster active participation			

←──→

Less controversial   More controversial

Figure 7.1   Joinfostering (Faltis, 2001)

principles. The classroom environment should be engineered to foster active participation and social integration so that students learn the target language and content knowledge. Also, few teachers would disagree with the need to manage learner participation in terms of equal turn-taking, student-generated topics and diversity of talk and writing audiences (not just the teacher). Finally, few teachers would disagree that language and content instruction should be integrated and scaffolded systematically.

Yet, whether or not attempts at *implementing* Principles 1–3 would actually garner the student cooperation required for such attempts to 'fly' when teachers invite students to collaborate with one another and scaffold one another's learning across linguistic and cultural differences and asymmetries, depends on the teacher's genuine commitment to the more radical Principles 4 and 5, because this impacts what the students expect as a classroom interaction order and how students treat one another (Yoon, 2008). In fact, I argue that without such a commitment, the first three principles cannot be met, at least not for the class as a whole. Again, I quote Kumaravadivelu (2001: 544), who explains that 'language teachers cannot hope to fully satisfy their pedagogic obligations without at the same time satisfying their social obligations'. Numerous classroom-based studies, including quasi-experimental studies (e.g. Storch, 2002), have found that friendly, collaborative talk patterns support effective learning – that is, learning occurs when an experienced teacher has mastered a 'pedagogical' way of speaking that is also interpersonally warm and engaging, and when these pedagogical ways of speaking are reproduced by students in their small-group interactions, the positive effects are magnified and multiplied. If the teacher models the following acts on a regular basis and creates a supportive learning community, the acts are reproduced in group work (Faltis, 2001: 147–152):

- orienting others to the task and purpose;
- asking follow-up questions, focusing questions and checking questions;

- sharing information;
- correcting others' errors of language and understanding (but being judicious as to which ones to correct, and letting others go);
- repairing miscommunication and sustaining conversation; and
- summarizing/synthesizing what others have said, to show one is listening, and recasting what others say in more 'academic' or discipline-specific ways.

In all these interactions, there are principles of positive interdependence in terms of goals, rewards, labor, resources and roles, as well as student accountability to each other, to the teacher and to the class (Faltis, 2001: 160–164). Yet, I argue that one important condition must be met for these joinfostering strategies to work: these collaborative forms of talk that facilitate learning cannot benefit *all* students unless the class as a whole believes everyone has the right to participate *without having to prove themselves first with regard to academic or linguistic competence*. Thus, the more socially, emotionally, linguistically, culturally and academically secure class members feel, the more inclusive and equitable their 'small culture' (Holliday, 1999) becomes, and the more widely distributed the effects of this 'magic'.

Building a strong sense of community is necessary for certain students to feel more confident, and for stronger students to be humbled by the fact that their performance is boosted by certain factors (e.g. having a higher proficiency in the language being used to teach and learn; being familiar with the cultural topics or literacy practices due to past educational experiences). This makes everyone interact with two moral principles that Faltis (2001) highlights in his book on joinfostering: interdependence and accountability. Students have to wait patiently for one another to get their words out, listen to one another, invite one another to contribute, check understanding with one another and be willing to share their thoughts even if these are half-finished or it is a struggle to articulate them in words that classmates understand, and they must be willing to re-attempt this (or invite a peer to attempt this) even if past attempts did not work so well.

I now turn to how this interdependence and accountability, which are grounded in a good balance of self-esteem and humility, can be cultivated in a linguistically diverse class. 'You can lead a horse to water, but you can't make it drink' – the factors required for students to drink, that is, to participate in learning activities with the ideal dispositions of interdependence and accountability, are (1) security in their academic, linguistic, cultural and social identities, otherwise interdependence and accountability are simply too face-threatening, sometimes to the point that students engage in the opposite behaviors (e.g. isolation, competition, disengagement); and (2) faith that active participation in collaborative meaning-making will lead to their learning, but *only* if they act with interdependence and accountability. These two factors can be cultivated through two strategies: lingua franca norms and CLA.

7.3 Engage in Lingua Franca Teaching and Learning Practices

Strategies for communicating in ELF are similar to those identified by Long (1983) as negotiation-of-meaning strategies that facilitate second language (L2) acquisition. When people are negotiating meaning with a sincere willingness to achieve mutual understanding as equals, they often use facilitative strategies such as repeating what they have just said in a variety of ways until it 'clicks' with the other person, avoiding references they think might be culturally unfamiliar, accepting some misunderstandings by 'going with the flow' of the conversation and engaging in continual comprehension checks and clarification requests. Matsumoto (2018) described similar strategies in ELF communication, in addition to subtle non-verbal checks like nodding and glancing, minimal responses (e.g. 'mhm', 'yeah') and gestures. In addition, in ELF communication, people tend to go with whatever forms emerge as useful for meaning-making, rather than policing each other's language correctness or correcting others' pronunciation and grammar errors.

As discussed in Chapter 2, Friedrich and Matsuda (2010) define ELF not as a variety of English to be acquired, but as a function served by English in communication between multilinguals. When a group of people with different language repertoires use ELF, each person uses the variety/ies of English they happen to know and combines these with multimodal communicative strategies to get tasks done, including learning tasks. Although the nature of the language that emerges is unpredictable, negotiation of meaning and functionality of language take precedence over surface-level forms. Thus, the message implicit in these interactions is that English does not solely belong to 'native speakers', but to all who are using it to get things done.

Of course, it is also the goal of schooling in countries like the US to teach English as a language to immigrant students, to teach subject-specific and academic registers in English (Schleppegrell, 2004) and to do so as clearly and effectively as possible. However, this can be done without devaluing what already exists in students' language repertoires and by building bridges with what students already know and what they have to learn, which increases the potential for family members to support students' learning. Teachers still need to provide students with target input in the form of complete sentences in English, in academic registers and with authentic social meanings, to facilitate academic language acquisition in English (Sah & Li, 2020). However, plenty of research (see Cummins & Man, 2007, for an accessible and comprehensive literature review) shows that academic English acquisition in subject areas is most effectively accomplished by bridging academic language and literacies

Figure 7.2   Bridging pedagogy: The rainbow diagram (Lin, 2016). Reproduced with permission from Angel M.Y. Lin

in English with language and literacy practices with which students are already familiar (Lin, 2016: 98; see Figure 7.2), and that *this 'bridging pedagogy' has to happen with the whole class, with students working together to loop all classmates in – i.e. differentiated instruction for peers, not just with the teacher giving differentiated instruction to 20, 30 or 40 students with unique language and literacy repertoires.*

   Therefore, culturally responsive education does not mean that teachers need to 'know' everything that students and their families know, in terms of languages, cultures and literacy practices. What teachers model for students is *the act of bridging itself*, using funds of cultural and linguistic knowledge that are shared between students and teacher (e.g. bridging discipline-specific and everyday registers of English, using widely recognizable cultural references like Pokémon and Harry Potter to create analogies for academic concepts). In this way, teachers use explanations that make the academic content and language more accessible and easy to learn. When this is combined with a joinfostering classroom culture of interdependence and accountability that requires students to meet each other's language needs (e.g. Excerpt 2; see also Mendoza, 2020b), students will continue the bridging and brokering among each other during in-class group work and collaborative projects, beyond what the teacher can do, using languages/dialects the teacher doesn't know and cultural references of their generation and cultures, to meet the learning objectives – if they see that this bridging is something the teacher encourages and holds everyone responsible for.

In Figure 7.1, everyday oral language in the L1 scaffolds oral academic registers in the L1. This academic oral talk in the L1 can, in turn, scaffold academic L1 written registers, the main mode of high-stakes assessment. Likewise, academic written registers in the L2[2] are scaffolded by L2 everyday and academic oral registers. It is also possible for students to have academic oral discussions in the L1 and L2, using translanguaging and/or code-switching, to scaffold monolingual academic oral and written products in the L2. For example, they can do research (i.e. consult sources) in both the L1 and L2, and then plan an academic essay in the L2, including how to organize it and what target language to use, using translanguaging and code-switching. Therefore, even if certain products need to approximate 'standard' monolingual academic English, they can be better scaffolded through ELF norms and bi/multilingual practices, which lead to more opportunities for deep and meaningful English learning.

In such learning, translanguaging plays a vital role, allowing students to make meaning using their whole language repertoires without paying too much attention to the perceived boundaries between named languages (García & Kleyn, 2016). Code-switching, or deliberate shifts between codes socially perceived as distinct, is a way to separate and organize information, as the teacher or peer tutors explain concepts in ways that scaffold learning (e.g. Excerpt 1; see also Filipi & Markee, 2018; Martin-Jones, 1995). Recall in Chapter 2 that code-switching can also occur between different *registers* of the same language; thus, it can be used between registers by the teacher and between languages by bi/multilingual students in group work. Faltis (1990: 50) explains several functions of such code-switching:

(1) *Conceptual reinforcement/elaboration.* The teacher reads what it says in the text, then switches to another language (or a more accessible register of English) to elaborate, adding background/explanatory details or interesting trivia.
(2) *Review.* The teacher reads what it says in the text, then switches to another language (or a more accessible register of English) to summarize that excerpt in brief. The teacher then asks students questions to check for their understanding, then recasts their contributions in academic English.
(3) *Vocabulary.* The teacher uses another language (or another register of English) to discuss the meaning of key academic terms or concepts.
(4) *Metacognition.* The teacher reads what it says in the text, then uses another language (or another register of English) to discuss the author's language choices in the text, and how they suit the genre and audience. The teacher covers all levels of the text, from its broad

organization to particular details like word choices or the structures of sentences and paragraphs. (Generally, the teacher should get students to notice holistic features of the text first, as *micro*-level details like vocabulary and sentence patterns have to be linked to already-known *macro*-level social factors like genre/text type and audience.)

When reading a text aloud in class, teachers can help students make sense of form and meaning by reading a few lines with them, stopping every now and then and explaining things in an everyday register of English, to (1) call attention to the way language is used in the text at different levels, from key vocabulary to sentence structures to paragraph organization to the organization of discourse in that genre (all of which imply something about the audience, the tone of the writing and the author's position); and (2) prompt students to discover academic ways of thinking in the text, such as classification, cause and effect, comparison and contrast, problem and solution and so on (Cummins & Man, 2007; Haneda, 2009; Wong Fillmore, 1997). As the teacher code-switches to scaffold students' understanding across English registers, students who speak languages/ dialects the teacher does not speak will likely pick up on the strategies and use them to scaffold peers in similar ways multilingually during small-group work. That is, the teacher implicitly models how to tutor in whole-class discussions, so that when students work together, they know how to facilitate each other's learning with open-ended and provocative statements, guiding questions and patience when waiting for others to articulate their thoughts (Mercer, 1997). Of course, the teacher can make these scaffolding strategies more explicit themselves by pointing out what they are doing (e.g. Jacobson & Faltis, 1990).[3]

All these collaborative talk patterns reflect joinfostering strategies 1–3, which have to do with student-centered learning; however, whether students are willing to deploy them encouragingly and helpfully depends on their internalized feelings of academic and linguistic security – or insecurity. Thus, student engagement in joinfostering strategies 1–3 cannot exist without the teacher's subscription to critical joinfostering strategies 4 and 5. If the teacher espouses the fourth and fifth strategies, the class' social atmosphere and interaction order are fundamentally changed. As I explain in Mendoza (2020b: 18), 'Teachers need to get students to negotiate meaning across linguistic and cultural asymmetries as generously as people are apt to do in informal language clubs' and other social contexts where the interaction order is inclusive and supportive.

Once an academic text is collaboratively unpacked using different languages and registers via bridging pedagogy, then students can bi/ multilingually summarize (repack) their understanding of the text in an English everyday register, and also offer their *own* analysis and opinions, finally translating their summaries, analyses and opinions into an academic English register, with teacher assistance or the help of peers in small-group work, for the final assessed product (Lin, 2016). In order to get to that product, teachers can encourage students to write summaries, commentary and opinions using whatever language resources would help them prepare for an assignment like an oral presentation or essay. In everyday learning activities, the teacher can show students how to write from translingual, transdialectal or multimodal notes, modeling how this is done on the board or projector, illustrating that the teacher, too, does not do brainstorming or note-taking in purely academic 'standard' English (Linares, 2019). As students get more and more used to these processes, they can engage in them independently, while the teacher gives encouraging, constructive and individualized feedback on their drafts.[4]

There are so many socioemotionally reassuring benefits to these collaborative practices in which students have to pay attention to their language production *for the product and its authentic audience* – boosting their self-efficacy and self-esteem and drawing their attention to what they should be learning, and away from monitoring classmates' language production in anxious comparison to their own. In such a supportive learning community, one in which languages and dialects apart from 'standard' English are not excluded from important academic tasks, teachers can also consider how to include a wide range of linguistic resources in formally assessed products – like the multi-class poetry anthology in this study that sold 650+ copies on Amazon – to challenge traditional views of what languages and dialects are legitimate for academic purposes in Inner Circle English-speaking countries (Menken & Sánchez, 2019). As for the standardized tests in monolingual 'academic' English, bridging pedagogy is a powerful teaching practice to help students do better on them.

7.4 Cultivate Critical Language Awareness

In discussing the third teaching strategy, critical language awareness, I refer to (1) awareness of language norms as context specific and fluid rather than absolute, which I simply call 'language awareness'; and (2) awareness of language ideologies, hierarchies and inequities in society, such as discourses about what languages or dialects are appropriate in academic and professional domains (often those of the middle-class cultural mainstream), which I call 'critical language awareness'.

Borg (as cited in Svalberg, 2007: 290–291) pointed out that learners can develop language awareness by doing five kinds of classroom activities:

- ongoing investigation of language as a dynamic phenomenon rather than a fixed body of established facts;

- learners talking analytically about language, often to each other – not necessarily in terms of what is right/wrong, but what is working or not working to convey the author's intent (see Canagarajah, 2011);
- involvement of learners in exploration and discovery;
- development not only of the learners' language proficiencies or understanding of how language works, but also their learning skills, promoting independent linguistic analysis abilities; and
- involvement of learners on both a cognitive and an affective level.[5]

The second concept, *critical* language awareness, involves questioning and dismantling language hierarchies related to race, ethnicity and social class to fully value the whole of students' language repertoires, as well as various forms of literacy, as relevant to academic and intellectual work (García *et al.*, 2021; MacSwan, 2000). Teachers and students must not only celebrate linguistic diversity, but also raise awareness about systemic inequalities that privilege some language and literacy practices over others which are *equally* skilled and adept, because the ones that are privileged belong to the middle-class cultural mainstream (Flores & Rosa, 2015). I now use two case examples to show how language awareness and CLA can be taught together.

Cummins (2005: 586) wryly observed that countries are often 'faced with the bizarre scenario of schools successfully transforming fluent speakers of foreign languages into monolingual English speakers, at the same time as they struggle, largely unsuccessfully, to transform English monolingual students into foreign language speakers'. Research in France (Hélot & Young, 2002, 2005) illustrates the national language policies in education that give rise to such a bizarre scenario, within and beyond Inner Circle English-speaking countries. Few countries in the 21st century would deny that foreign language learning is important to participate in the global economy. But national education discourses surrounding language learning go something like this: first, assimilate to the dominant societal language to become a legitimate citizen of the country; then, learn prestigious 'foreign'[6] languages (prioritizing English if it is not the country's national language) to help out the country's economic standing. The first goal is largely successful due to the social pressure faced by immigrants and regional ethnolinguistic minorities, while the second is less so due to the instrumental and rather boring nature of institutionalized foreign language learning, which tends to strip the foreign language learning of its deeper and more interesting cultural, historical and humanizing elements so as not to threaten the official national cultural identity and to promote the language as a tool entirely for instrumental purposes (Al-Bataineh & Gallagher, 2021; Kubota, 1998; Rampton, 2002).

Hélot and Young (2002, 2005) observed that language education programs in France, and the European Union (EU) more broadly, have promoted learning globally prestigious languages of the EU while spreading a discourse that immigrant students' home languages delay their acquisition of French. In response, they implemented a (critical) language awareness program at a small primary school in Alsace to show how languages of unequal status in society could be placed on equal footing to make teachers, students and parents aware of the linguistic and cultural wealth present in their community. I summarize that study here because it addresses the problem of how attempts to value linguistic and cultural diversity rarely go beyond the level of 'good intentions' due to teachers' limited knowledge of students' home languages and cultures and the lack of concrete directives presented to them from the dominant linguistic and cultural mainstream of which they are often a part.

In the French school system, 'modern foreign languages' such as English, German, Spanish and Italian are offered in late primary and secondary education. 'Regional languages' seen as native to France and part of French heritage are also taught, such as Alsatian, Corsican, Provençal, Basque and Breton, even if parents and students tend to prioritize the 'modern' foreign languages for socioeconomic mobility. However, students' bilingualism in 'migrant' languages such as Maghrebi Arabic (which is different from 'standard' Arabic), Turkish, Spanish and Portuguese are little valued, as the people who speak them tend to be low socioeconomic status immigrants. Students are often not able to take classes in these languages or develop literacy in them in formal education contexts.

This is also the case with students in this study: they speak less commonly taught languages that they rarely see represented in formal education settings, and the question arises as to how and why these languages should be valued and used as learning resources. To illustrate some possibilities with a small rural primary school of 84 students in an Alsatian-speaking region of France, Hélot and Young implemented the following project with their teacher colleagues. The project, started in September 2000, involved children from three grades,[7] aged six to nine, who had yet to start learning a foreign language, 12 parents and four teachers. At the school, there were classes on Saturday mornings; on these mornings, each of the parents took turns working with one or more teachers to design a one-, two- or three-week unit on a language they spoke at home or had learned as an additional language. The language lessons (in Alsatian, Japanese, Vietnamese, Malay, Mandarin, Spanish, Finnish, Brazilian Portuguese, Serbo-Croat, Polish, Italian, Turkish, Arabic, Berber, German and English) had to be fun, culturally immersive, hands-on or project-based experiences.

The aim of this initiative was to expose students to a wider range of languages and cultures than formal education would normally allow, making them aware of the richness of languages, cultures, phonetic and writing systems, etc., in their community. As the parents worked with teachers to plan the lessons, with regular preparation and feedback meetings, the teachers also reactivated the knowledge learned the past Saturday during the school week. Students enjoyed listening to parents' cultural and personal stories (e.g. growing up in Vietnam before the war), reading traditional tales from bilingual books, tasting food from around the world, learning various traditions like how to use chopsticks or sit on mats, singing Happy Birthday in different languages, learning about the geography and history of the countries concerned (which they could learn more about in the school library), talking about lifestyles and festivals in different countries (e.g. Lunar New Year and red envelopes), seeing parents in traditional dress, introducing themselves or saying 'please' and 'thank you' in different languages, learning basic vocabulary for colors/fruits/animals, exploring different writing systems and phonetic systems (such as sounds that only exist in particular languages), noticing cognates and parallels between languages (such as German/Alsatian and Portuguese/French) and guessing meaning from context (e.g. a football game in another language). Finally, the parent who taught about Japanese language and culture was a Frenchwoman, showing that it is possible to learn a language at any stage of life.

Hélot and Young (2002) found that the children proved curious and willing to learn about all the languages and cultures from the parents they encountered without making negative judgments, and asked numerous questions about the content they were learning. By the end of the program, they often came to class asking, 'What language are we learning today?' (2002: 106). They also expressed desires to travel and experience firsthand the things they had learned about. Additional benefits were seen with the parents and teachers. For example, parents had 'an opportunity to talk about themselves, to participate in the learning of their children and to share their languages and cultures with teachers and pupils thus providing them with a legitimate place at school' (Hélot & Young, 2002: 106). Such contact between parents and teachers kept the channels of communication open and precluded cultural prejudices from forming, given that it is hard to stereotype or hold prejudices against a community when you have a positive friendship or acquaintanceship with someone from that community (Komorowska, as cited in Hélot & Young, 2002: 106).

The teachers were also positively positioned through the project. They did not need to know anything about other languages and cultures, or need any special training, but simply had to show a positive, welcoming, inquiry-based disposition toward the linguistic and cultural funds of knowledge in their community. Without needing to sacrifice much additional time or energy, they learned a lot from parents which had an influence on their teaching, and 'developed a more global perspective in other subjects through the links made between the various languages [and content] presented' (Hélot & Young, 2002: 107). It is important to note that these linguistic and cultural funds of knowledge eventually came to belong to the school community as a whole, becoming resources for further learning about the world, the nature of different languages or strategies for language learning and intercultural communication.

Hélot and Young emphasize that in language awareness courses and programs, all languages and cultures can support the learning aims, and anyone can be a legitimate representative of a language or culture. Thus, community members *already know everything they need to know* to run an effective program; nothing needs to be handed down from experts, and they negotiate what learning is to occur and how to assess if it was successful among themselves. These projects are not meant to replace language classes where the goal is language acquisition, but bring an added layer of awareness as to *how* and *why* we should be learning linguistic and cultural content: not for neoliberal development or self-advancement but to become a better citizen and community member. After all, learning languages instrumentally is no guarantee of increased tolerance and understanding of others (Byram, 2000: 57). Similar language awareness projects were developed in Australia and Europe from the 1970s to the 1990s (see Hélot & Young [2002: 108] for a review).

Instead of teachers worrying about whether they know enough of students' languages and cultures, they can let go of this anxiety leading to inaction. Like students who have found the right balance of self-esteem and humility in a joinfostering classroom, teachers can shift their focus away from defending themselves against others' negative perceptions of what they lack, and look to what they *can* and *should* be doing:

> [I]t must be stressed here that to work within the objectives of language awareness does not involve the same investment in time as teaching a foreign language does. The competence needed is not the same, one is a matter of sensitivity and curiosity for languages, the other of having sufficient confidence in one's linguistic skills. As teacher educators and researchers, we know that… teachers' lack of confidence in their FL [foreign language] competency is one of the major obstacles to tackle, and however attractive study periods abroad are, they are very costly. (Hélot & Young, 2002: 108)

In contrast, what if schools defined being a 'global citizen' teacher not as someone who is cosmopolitan and well-traveled and has a high proficiency in English and other globally prestigious languages, but as someone who has (critical) language awareness of diversity in their *immediate* surroundings? Who can foster equal valuation and recognition of all their students' languages, literacy practices and ways of translanguaging irrespective of the languages' status, teaching students to value diverse forms of bi/multilingualism? As Hélot and Young (2002: 109) point out, these teachers can draw on the funds of knowledge that are already present and more than adequate to meet their learning aims, inviting students and communities to continually interweave these with the curriculum.

When they progress to the secondary level, students face more serious issues of social stratification and discrimination based on language, particularly students who speak 'non-standard', 'ethnic', minoritized or working-class dialects of the dominant societal language. The main teaching strategy at this level of education is 'a re-seeing and re-hearing of students for their linguistic assets and expertise' (Seltzer, 2019b: 986; see also Seltzer, 2019a, 2020). Too often, they have been burdened with the labels 'English language learner' (for relatively recent immigrants) and 'long-term English language learner' (for those who grew up in an Inner Circle English-speaking country but speak another language at home).

Ofelia García's colleague Kate Seltzer takes up the theory of translanguaging (García, 2009; García & Li, 2014) to understand the role language plays in these students' identities and lived experiences. Seltzer (2019b) argues that students' perspectives on their language and literacy practices yield counternarratives that serve as evidence against strict dichotomies between 'home' and 'school' literacy practices. Over the course of a school year (2015–2016), she partnered with Ms Winter, an eleventh-grade English language arts teacher in New York and a friend of hers who had participated in the City University of New York–New York State Initiative on Emergent Bilinguals (CUNY–NYSIEB) to design literacy activities that would bring about Ms Winter's students' translingual sensibilities and new understandings of their home and school literacy practices. At the end of the school year, students also did better on the statewide standardized English test for their grade (CCERBAL, 2021).

In this year-long study in which Seltzer was the classroom ethnographer and Ms Winter the classroom teacher, the two aimed to bring forth students' translanguaging in skilled linguistic performances, while raising students' awareness of *how* they were translanguaging and eliciting their metacommentary about their language use. One key teaching strategy was to use translingual mentor texts in different varieties of English, all of high literary quality, and in different modalities, creating a wide range of models for students to relate to and affiliate with. This diversity in literary texts was important for this school in a working-class neighborhood, where students labeled 'English language learners' made up 19% of the population. The largest racial/ethnic group was Hispanic (71%), followed by African American (26%), but there were also students who spoke Arabic, French, Albanian, Urdu and Fula. Importantly, students who supposedly came from the same group were diverse: Spanish speakers represented different diasporas and differed in their families' histories of migration (students from Mexico and Honduras felt minoritized by Dominican and Puerto Rican peers), and Black students who were not African American came from Africa, Jamaica or Haiti. Many students were of mixed heritage.

Ms Winter herself was white, upper middle class and had graduated from an Ivy League University. Her father had immigrated from Italy as an adult, but she did not identify as bilingual and spoke English as her L1. She appears to have approached the English language arts curriculum with a willingness to explore various definitions of verbal artistry in English beyond those she had grown up with, as Seltzer (2019b) explains:

> These details about Ms Winter's background speak to the common disconnects that exist between teachers and language-minoritized students of color. For students, teachers like Ms Winter are often the embodiments of those whom Flores and Rosa (2015) call white listening subjects, who hear deficiency in the language practices they perceive as deviating from an assumed (white) norm. Throughout the year, Ms Winter worked to hone her translanguaging stance [an attitude that valued and invited bi/multilingualism] (García et al., 2017) and raciolinguistic literacies (Seltzer & de los Ríos, 2018), becoming attuned to her own deeply held ideologies and more aware of how they contributed to the marginalization of her students. (Seltzer, 2019b: 994)

The data Seltzer collected – student and teacher work, interviews with Ms Winter and 14 students and approximately 100 hours of audio recordings – showed how Ms Winter implemented a critical translanguaging pedagogy with three components: translanguaging stance, translanguaging design and translanguaging shifts (García *et al.*, 2017). Ms Winter began the school year by telling students that they did not always have to speak English, much less 'standard English', in her classroom – her translanguaging *stance*. From the beginning of the semester, she told and continued to remind students that they could communicate their understanding in whatever style of language or language practices they saw fit during the process of learning. Using real-world examples as objects of literary study in the class, Ms Winter drew students' attention to the fact that it is possible to have serious discussions about subjects in vernacular English, or in multiple languages, and that experts and authorities did so all the time in the media.

In her translanguaging *design*, or lesson planning, Ms Winter included different varieties of English – white, African American and postcolonial literature – in the syllabus, and taught a variety of forms of literature that were all of a high standard. She also pointed out how the authors used their integrated language repertoires to make meaning, drawing on resources from different languages, dialects and modalities to achieve the rhetorical whole. Ms Winter put students in groups and then assigned each group an author whose work they would study over the course of five weeks for the author's influences, voice, linguistic choices, engagement with audience, censorship and critique. Students read and shared excerpts of their authors' works, biographical readings, articles and criticisms and interviews (if available). According to Seltzer and García (2020: 34), 'the combination of the authors' writing and writing *about* their writing provided models of both translingual text production and critical metacommentary about language'. It is important to highlight that Ms Winter did not speak any language and dialect but 'white' American English – her students, who were mainly Latinx and African American, acted as language brokers for her and for one another.

As for translanguaging *shifts*, these are 'the "moves" that teachers make that respond to students' language, questions, and critique, none of which can be predicted' (Seltzer & García, 2020: 36), which Ofelia García has sometimes referred to as 'la corriente', the current, in her scholarship (e.g. García *et al.*, 2017). At times, Ms Winter used a language of solidarity that positioned herself as a co-learner: 'I've learned a lot with you guys about the history of different language practices and how people who have power determine what language is considered good or valid and people who don't have power, their languages—or language practices— are considered inferior. But that's not actually the case' (Seltzer & García, 2020: 37). She drew connections between the varied literature and the high-quality works in her class that were likewise linguistically varied. This led one student to reflect that 'if we always adjust our language practices [in academic settings], then we perpetuate, we keep up, the idea that there are certain ways of speaking that are good and certain ways that are bad. So let's not change, let's use our language practices and resist the ideas of what's good and what's bad that society has' (Seltzer & García, 2020: 37).

Through their teacher's translanguaging stance, translanguaging design and translanguaging shifts, students developed (critical) language awareness, including an ability to dissect and analyze language – in terms of linguistic features used in different communicative settings, and in developing awareness of negotiable norms and how these can be challenged to resist deficit positionings in schools. This kind of learning does not need to exclusively happen in an English language arts class; for example, science teachers can also invite a variety of ways of speaking in scientific inquiry, and this more inclusive talk (beyond academic science registers) has been shown to lead to wider student participation beyond the most confident students (Rymes, 2015). Of course, time should be spent on teaching the 'academic' registers, e.g. to provide such language in worksheets for students to take up in group presentations. Teachers must take a translanguaging stance as students are in the process of learning, showing students that experts in every field can be multilingual or use a mix of academic and vernacular language when discussing concepts among themselves or addressing the public. Teachers must also position themselves humbly in interaction, not 'talking above' students (even as they model discipline-specific communication). Seltzer and García (2020: 39) conclude that (critical) language awareness 'will find students much success outside the classroom', whether they choose to momentarily align with standard language ideologies in a setting to achieve specific goals, or find ways to subvert them (for an investigation and discussion of these agentive choices, see Seltzer, 2019b).

Therefore, even at the level of a single class, a teacher can adapt a statewide curriculum to intentionally bring forth students' translanguaging and critical metalinguistic awareness, fostering the skills of linguistic deconstruction and critical appropriation. Instead of being stuck with dichotomies of home/school language, educators can re-see and re-hear what their students are doing and saying about their language practices. They can also help students to see these language practices from a more asset-oriented light, and in all their complexity. In learning to translanguage and engage in metalinguistic commentary while doing academic inquiry, students can position themselves in equal conversations with 'scholars, popular media figures, authors, and artists who live and create amid ideological tensions about language, power, and identity' (Seltzer, 2019b: 1005).

7.5 Empowering Teachers to Implement the Strategies

'Pedagogical strategies' go beyond the teaching–learning cycle of curriculum/materials design, instruction and assessment to include deliberate shaping of the sociocultural experiences and ideologies that directly or indirectly influence education. As shown by Faltis, Hélot, Young, Seltzer, García and other researchers, teachers should be *leaders* rather than followers when it comes to implementing joinfostering, lingua franca norms and CLA. Experienced and reflective teachers know what a translanguaging *stance*, *design* and *shifts* mean in their school and classroom contexts, and all they need is the time and agency to plan and act upon this knowledge – starting with being given enough autonomy to design their own classes, as Ms Winter did, and to collaborate with colleagues to promote CLA at the school level, as did the teachers in the Didenheim Project in Alsace. However, in an age of educational accountability, such time and autonomy are scarce (Gonzalez, 2021).

That said, teachers may still need to develop increased CLA – not necessarily increased technical training – regarding their sociolinguistic contexts and when it comes to language hierarchies in general. They must realize that the *forms of social organization* and the *sense of selves* that we take for granted in education can be reshaped in intentional and perceivable ways, which Kumaravadivelu (2001) calls a 'pedagogy of possibility'. In the plurilingual ELF classroom, English L1 students do not have to dominate discussion; it may be common but should not be seen as natural or inevitable. Languages that are minoritized in the class and/or the wider society can be prioritized by teachers and students. Less multilingual students who speak English as an L1 may feel their limitations, and admire the language skills of classmates who are more bi/multilingual, making linguistic desire run in both directions (Janks, 2004), and this kind of tension (e.g. between Jhon and Kix) can be addressed with sensitivity to the needs of both kinds of students (Woodley & Brown, 2016). L1 and HL speakers of a language should form connections instead of separate communities of practice. Finally, students cannot lead the class in reinstituting these alternative forms of organization that run counter to what is expected; only the teacher, with a *teacher's* authority, can explicitly and implicitly indicate that this is the way the class community will run. Otherwise, it will be assumed to run in default ways.

Doing things differently therefore requires critical social restructuring, which, though collaborative, is often led by the teacher. Empowering teachers is necessary for empowering students. Teachers must understand and transform sociolinguistic possibilities in their classes as active agents, in order to lead students to do the same and potentially extend the transformative strategies to new contexts beyond the class. However, the more teachers themselves are labeled from a deficit- rather than asset-based perspective – 'second language English speaker', 'monolingual English speaker who doesn't have much multilingual/multicultural knowledge', 'person from a working-class background who doesn't belong in the academy', 'intellectual with no life skills', not to mention outsiders to educational and applied linguistics theories – how can they emancipate students to take on new possible identities if they themselves cannot grapple with and transcend their own vulnerabilities and negative identity positionings in bi/multilingual education research and societal discourses?[8] Anxiety and defensiveness on the part of one classroom participant breeds more anxiety and defensiveness on the part of others, especially if they are coming from the teacher as the head of the class. In contrast, when the teacher takes charge to implement joinfostering, lingua franca norms, bridging pedagogy and CLA, the teacher enables students to enable each other academically, linguistically and culturally.

If, in a pedagogy of possibility, the forms of social organization and the sense of selves that we take for granted are changed in an intentional and perceivable way, this critical social restructuring is necessarily distributed across social actors, but is at the same time often led by the teacher – since students look to the teacher to determine what social norms will play out in the classroom's 'small culture' (Holliday, 1999). However, a teacher cannot implement joinfostering through translanguaging and code-switching without student uptake, and this requires the teacher's nuanced understanding of individual students' linguistic positionalities and the different language hegemonies on different scales that must be recognized and channeled in positive directions to create a translanguaging space that is reflective, equitable, inclusive and critical.

Notes

(1) We see this situation in Excerpt 19 when the experienced ESL head Kaori spontaneously takes over from the student teacher Rayna.

(2) We can equate L2 with English here, for simplicity's sake, although it can be an L3 or L4 for many students who are linguistic minorities in their country of origin, such as Skusta and Kok in this study.

(3) In Chapter 4 of Jacobson and Faltis (1990), Faltis describes code-switches in teacher speech that cause subtle but perceptible breaks in different parts of an utterance (see also Excerpt 1 in this study).

(4) The high school ESL teacher in Linares (2019), Ms Rosewall, responded to students' work in languages she did not understand through contextual cues and images they included in their writing journals – knowing she would read them in earnest – and by using Google translate and her basic knowledge of Spanish.

(5) In this study, I was struck by how these practices that develop language awareness were most evident in English 9 Ilokano L1 students' exploration of Korean, even though they lacked an expert in Korean to answer many of the questions they raised. This group of students also applied the same strategies of inquiry to academic literary analysis tasks in English, suggesting that their identities as competent and curious bi/multilingual language explorers transcended specific languages and tasks, partially enabled by the valued models of bi/multilingualism that were available (i.e. Kix and Juan).

(6) I put the word 'foreign' in quotation marks because in fact, there are many people in the country who speak the languages, some in communities that have lived in the country for generations.

(7) Nearly 40% of the children spoke home languages other than French (Arabic: 10.7%, Turkish: 9.5%, Polish: 4.7%, Portuguese: 2.4%, Italian: 2.4%, Other: 4.7%, plus another 4.7% who came from homes that spoke the regional language, Alsatian).

(8) I have deliberately created 'opposite' hypothetical examples to show that *no matter what the teacher's background*, they are vulnerable to deficit positionings. English L1 teachers who speak no other language to any great degree can still have cultural knowledge encompassing a rich collage of books, films, songs, etc., in different genres, registers and varieties of English, influenced by other languages, dialects and cultures from across time and space. These teachers would also have knowledge of English vernacular and bits and pieces of other languages to draw on for interpersonal purposes, which helps them create a classroom community (see e.g. the teachers in studies by Haneda, 2009; Linares, 2019; Seltzer, 2019a, 2019b, 2020; Woodley & Brown, 2016; Yoon, 2008).

8 Conclusion

This book investigated language use in the plurilingual, English as a lingua franca (ELF) classroom in terms of how translanguaging, code-switching, stylization and ELF contribute to identity positioning in classroom interactions. While it is widely accepted in sociolinguistics that a person's identity as a language user varies across time and space, for example in terms of socially constructed competence across more or less welcoming social environments (Norton, 2000), it is also evident that people negotiate linguistic competencies, with identity positions at stake, in unfolding dialogue within a setting, a process that can be studied through linguistic ethnography and other methods of classroom discourse analysis (Rymes, 2015). This final chapter summarizes the findings of the book, then outlines theoretical contributions, study limitations and directions for future research.

8.1 Summary of the Study

In this section, I summarize the main findings with regard to language identities in the plurilingual ELF classroom. Four types of positionality are examined: majority–minority relations, peer-to-peer relations, teacher–student relations and discourse relations.

8.1.1 Majority–minority relations

The translanguaging of the majority language group (i.e. speakers of the classroom majority language apart from English) impacts the potential translanguaging of other students. For example, in ESL 9/10, the more freely the 'loud' Filipino-speaking students translanguaged, thus displaying their language being in the majority, the more inhibited linguistic minority students seemed to become, preventing them not only from translanguaging but also from speaking altogether. In English 9, the productive use of Ilokano to do academic work in English caused the English-dominant Jhon and the singleton Fetu to support a 'speak English' classroom language policy that ostensibly would give them more access and less minoritized linguistic identity positionings. While the normalization of Ilokano use in small-group course-related work also paved the way for the Ilokano first language (L1) students to express themselves frequently in stylized phrases from their language of affinity, Korean, other students who cleaved more strongly to a 'speak English so everyone understands' classroom language policy largely avoided translanguaging throughout the study, except for a stylized, tongue-in-cheek parody of peers' translanguaging on the last day, as the pro-translanguaging researcher who aligned with their pro-translanguaging teacher was saying goodbye (Excerpt 7).

For these reasons, we can assume that translanguaging is different for students in the classroom linguistic majority and classroom linguistic minorities/singletons, as well as for students who are more or less recently arrived and are dominant in different languages, even if they appear to be from the same ethnolinguistic group. Ultimately, teachers need to direct attention to strategies that allow classroom linguistic minorities and singletons to translanguage in ways that put their languages on equal footing, and allow everyone to access their whole language repertoire to engage in academic work – even if (1) different languages have different interactional affordances in the classroom ecology, being more/less widely understood by the class as a whole; and (2) different individuals have varying proficiencies in their languages in terms of listening/speaking, reading and writing skills and domains of acquisition. This is because individuals do not tend to optimize the potential of translanguaging unless they can present their language and literacy repertoires in a pragmatically felicitous and asset- rather than deficit-oriented light. Their ability to do so is socially constructed through task design and others' unfolding reactions to their linguistic output.

8.1.2 Peer-to-peer relations

This study has highlighted the important role that peers play in positioning each other as linguistically competent in the language of instruction and other languages (including some peer group codes that involve much hybridity, defying the conventional boundaries between named languages; see Rampton, 1995). These positionings have an impact on student engagement, belonging and opportunities to participate fully in the academic and social life of the class. As I have discussed, students position one another through their language use as tutees (Excerpt 1), confident and cosmopolitan speakers of a language of affinity (Excerpts 3–4), 'one of the gang' (Excerpts 10–12), competent speakers of a heritage language (HL) (Excerpt 16), academically incompetent (Excerpt 17), language insiders/outsiders (Excerpt 18) or linguistically overreaching (Excerpt 19).

I have also argued that students who have a lot of linguistic capital in academic literacies in English *and* in the majority non-English language *and* in peer-group ludic translanguaging practices, such as Kix and Flow-G, have the fewest linguistic vulnerabilities and thus the most authority to determine relevant language standards in the classroom ecology – which Blommaert (2007; Blommaert *et al.*, 2005) called the 'order of indexicality' or the context-specific norms against which others' language production is implicitly or explicitly evaluated. Such students have this authority in the class whether they consciously wield it or not. It is important for teachers to pay attention to these context-specific orders of indexicality and take action to shape them in equitable and inclusive ways, preferably by recruiting students who are linguistically privileged in the class to help shape the sociolinguistic environment in positive ways so that others follow suit.

The bottom line is this: teachers need to get students to work together across linguistic and cultural knowledge asymmetries as generously as people are apt to do in self-chosen and low-stakes intercultural environments (such as extracurricular culture clubs or online fan communities), and regardless of the degree to which students in a working group affiliate with groupmates, the task type or the subject matter. If this were not a tall order in itself, all this must occur when

> students are acutely aware of asymmetries in language proficiency, on which they are continually assessed by both standardized and classroom tests, and in the informal judgment of their peers and adults at home and at school (with respect to the official classroom language(s), heritage languages, and peer groups' languages of affinity). (Mendoza, 2020b: 13)

This suggests that the ideal translanguaging pedagogy is bound up with other issues such as classroom management, needs analysis and culturally relevant curricula as well as material that broadens the cultural horizons of all classroom participants, encouraging them to learn from one another's linguistic backgrounds and affiliations (Gutiérrez, 2012; Hélot & Young, 2002).[1] No classroom participant can retreat into cultural solipsism (self-centeredness or building the curriculum only around one's own interests), nor should they have to 'just suck up' whatever the official curriculum hands them; instead, they must contribute to a class community that explores diverse funds of linguistic and cultural knowledge and forms of knowledge display. Some experienced teachers have managed to integrate this kind of curriculum with the 'official' curriculum (see Chapter 3, Section 3.2 in this study; Chapter 4, Table 4.1; and the literature reviewed in Chapter 7).

8.1.3 Teacher–student relations

Although translanguaging research often presents teachers drawing on students' linguistic and cultural funds of knowledge as critical educators concerned with social justice, little research explores the potential vulnerability of the teacher, especially if they do not share the same funds of knowledge as many of the students. Genuine empathy and interpersonal adeptness on the part of the teacher is needed to blend 'official' curricular knowledge with students', families' and communities' funds of knowledge (Linares, 2019; Seltzer, 2019a, 2019b, 2020), and these are qualities of the experienced and reflective rather than the novice teacher. However, research has shown that not only novice but also experienced teachers can avoid doing this, not because they fail to realize it is important, but because they feel unsafe, daunted by how little they know about students' languages and cultures (Beiler, 2021; Birello *et al.*, 2021). Teacher education that focuses on practical strategies for implementing all five principles of joinfostering, lingua franca norms and critical language awareness *as part of regular classroom activities* is much needed (e.g. Faltis, 2001; Woodley & Brown, 2016) so that teachers see these pedagogical strategies as a 'normal' everyday practice, a disposition anyone can have, and which matters more than knowledge they lack access to and will *never* have – and they will naturally react to this lack of access by saying such knowledge is unnecessary.

Ultimately, it is not necessary for teachers to know everything about students' languages and cultures to build bridges between students' funds of knowledge and the 'official' curriculum. As I discuss in Chapter 7, what teachers need to know and model for students is the *bridging* between academic literacies and everyday language practices that they share with students, in addition to fostering critical language awareness and an inclusive classroom community. When students see what teachers are doing, they understand that these inclusive and equitable values are the norms of the class, and will continue the bridging pedagogy to help each other learn in small-group work, using the funds of linguistic and cultural knowledge that the teachers do not know in order to literally 'loop everyone in' (i.e. to joinfoster while translanguaging; Faltis, 2001; Menken & García, 2010).

8.1.4 Discourse relations

One last type of relation worth investigating, one that is not so obvious, has to do with the marshalling of wider linguistic discourses in identity construction (Bucholtz & Hall, 2005). This study has shown that an essential aspect of getting *any* student to translanguage is an activity that allows that student to present their language repertoire in an asset-oriented rather than a deficit-oriented light. Since there is much variation between individual repertoires, the enabling models will differ from student to student. Juan was a role model for his translanguaging Ilokano L1 students in English 9 and for He and Fetu, who were also engaged in exploring coming of age in Sherman Alexie and Shakespeare; visiting actor Mr Nick was a role model for Jhon; Sandra Cisneros (or at least her poetry) was a role model for Aliah. Each of these role models evoked a particular discourse, e.g. that one could be a competent English student *and* a multilingual, that drama was just as intellectual as text-based literacy or that written translanguaging/stylization was as legitimate as generative translanguaging in oral speech.

These findings may have implications for diversifying the teacher profession and decolonizing the curriculum, suggesting that *it is not just about providing enabling models by hiring racially, culturally and linguistically diverse educators, as important as that is, but training ALL education professionals to provide a variety of models, shaping academic discourses in ways that further critical language awareness rather than just advantageous identity positionings for all* (see hooks, 1989; Seltzer, 2019b; Zavala, 2015). *We do not decolonize by seeing everyone represented in the curriculum; we decolonize by recognizing our responsibility to work toward the well-being of others besides ourselves.* For example, in Mortimer and Wortham's (2015) study, the rise of the bilingual Guarani–Spanish academic in the public imagination offered a more positive linguistic identity for students who were educated L1 speakers of the indigenous Paraguayan language Guarani, but the model still subscribed to one-language-at-a-time language use and professional-class language and literacy practices. Thus, this still had the effect of promoting some linguistic identities at the expense of others, rather than empowering all students regardless of their linguistic profiles. Furthermore, in some cases, the model assumed to be 'empowering' may have the opposite effect as that which was intended: for example, a 'whitewashed' African American male with a string of degrees may be institutionally positioned as the primary enabler of Black male students at risk of dropping out of postsecondary education, when in fact that instructor and his students have to navigate substantial face threats from each other (Young, 2004). When it comes to the relations constructed through discourses about certain types of people (models, prototypes, archetypes and stereotypes), there is a need for more research as well as more professional development to understand how teachers and students gain awareness of themselves as *influencers* of sociolinguistic discourse and prefabricated identities and learn to shape those discourses and images of people in ways that transcend *their own* individual identity positioning to further both equality and equity.[2]

8.2 Theoretical Contributions

This study has investigated a type of classroom that is understudied in the translanguaging literature. In this type of classroom, students and teacher are not part of the same bi/multilingual imagined community, but multiple overlapping ones. One thing they all share is the language that is the official medium of instruction and the dominant language in their society. In the learning context described in this study, a high school in Honolulu, Hawai'i, that language is English. In another context, it could be another nationally dominant language that is being used to instruct students from a diverse range of language backgrounds, such as Dutch in Belgium (e.g. Jaspers, 2011) or Nepali in Nepal (Sah & Li, 2020). I call this classroom context the *plurilingual ELF classroom* or the *plurilingual, Language X as a lingua franca classroom*. Many students in the plurilingual ELF classroom speak 'immigrant' languages; some of these are less commonly taught languages (LCTLs) that have never been offered in formal education settings in the students' adopted country (some of them having been born in that country) or even their parents' country of origin (e.g. Kok's Ilonggo in this study). Even when one of these immigrant languages is taught in a formal education setting (e.g. Arabic, Spanish), it tends to be taught in its 'standard' foreign form rather than in terms of the diasporic dialects spoken by students and their families, making them feel 'incompetent' in their own languages (Hélot, 2003; Valdés, 2001).

When these students are in an English-medium class, they are often studied from an English-speaking lens, described as 'English language learners' (ELLs) or 'emergent English speakers'. Their identities as English users and their English proficiencies are key research foci, but there is less attention to how they use their whole language repertoire (Tian *et al.*, 2020), especially in terms of their identity positioning and its impact on other class members. I hope that this book has shed light on these research participants in more multilingual terms, demonstrating that *the same social mechanisms* apply across all the languages, or across the whole language repertoire as translanguaging researchers would say: everyone wants to be able to claim multiple group identity belongings, and to have their language practices legitimized and bestowed with authority. To create a classroom community or 'critical translanguaging space' (Hamman, 2018) in which those identity positionings are possible for everyone, all classroom participants have to recognize how their reciprocal interactions and identity bids shape that space for one another.

In making such an observation, I wish to point out that translanguaging is indeed an instinct, but that different forms of translanguaging are not. They reflect patterns of language acquisition and domains of literacy development that some researchers have called 'translanguaging constellations' (Duarte, 2019; Rajendram, 2021). Different people may be more or less well versed in different types of translanguaging due to their social networks and life experiences: the 'learner-contingent soundscapes and textscapes that feed into bottom-up processes of item-based learning' (Ortega, 2014: 43). For example, some people may be used to using their L1 to 'language around' other languages, as the Ilokano L1 students did with English and Korean in English 9. Other people may translanguage more integratedly, within the same phrase or clause, or even at the morphosyntactic level, coining new words with features of two or more languages (e.g. Li, 2011). These students might be able to create works of art characterized by very dynamic translanguaging across multiple languages (Seltzer, 2020). Yet others may translanguage more dialectically, for instance between different varieties of English, such as Jhon in this study. Because one individual's or group's type of translanguaging in the plurilingual ELF classroom can create challenges of understanding or participation or deficit identity positionings for another individual or group, intentional or not, people must not only feel free to flex their whole language repertoires in translanguaging, but must also be willing to build bridges across different individuals' ways of translanguaging, and see/hear one another from asset-based perspectives, particularly with an eye to including linguistically minoritized students in the class: *those whose plurilingual repertoires look quite different from most others' plurilingual repertoires*. This also requires us to decenter our understandings of translanguaging, which are inevitably rooted in our own translanguaging practices and lived experiences as teachers and researchers (Mendoza & Parba, 2019).

By studying translanguaging, code-switching, stylization and ELF use together, I have illustrated that seeing the individual language repertoire as integrated and transcending the boundaries of named languages (Otheguy *et al.*, 2015) does not yield the only affordances for critical language pedagogy. To recognize distinct codes as social constructions negotiated *in situ* is to recognize one's responsibility to ratify different ways of speaking the same language – or to ratify different ways of translanguaging.[3] When understanding translanguaging at the individual or group level, we would do well to remember a pronoun invented by Gloria Anzaldúa: 'nos/otras' (Gutiérrez, 2012: 34–35). 'Nosotras' means 'us', while 'otras' means 'others', so 'nos/otras' with the slash in the middle allows us to see ourselves alongside others, connected, yet recognizing our differences. As a lesbian Chicana writer, Anzaldúa often felt both solidarity and lack of belonging among white feminists and the Chicano community that typically casts out gays and lesbians. Translanguagers can erase the '/otras' in 'nos/otras', ignoring the diversity within their community[4] – or they can keep the '/otras', acknowledging that translanguaging communities are necessarily made up of diverse individuals who are all legitimate representatives of the languages they speak and may translanguage in different ways. This view is necessary to recognize second language (L2) and HL speakers of Language X on equal footing as L1 or 'native' speakers, and different (diasporic, regional, etc.) varieties of socially constructed languages as legitimate varieties. *When all the languages in one's repertoire are legitimized, and one's ways of speaking those languages are legitimized, and one's ways of translanguaging are legitimized, only then would one be comfortable drawing on one's whole language repertoire (i.e. translanguaging) in any situation, including a classroom situation.*

On a related note, I caution against the idealization of children and youth as naturally translanguaging in ways that are socially affiliative and that flout language hierarchies, rather than ways that are exclusive toward others or at the very least maintain language hierarchies in education. It is our instinct to position ourselves positively, sociolinguistically and otherwise; it is not as instinctive to create a critical translanguaging space where everyone can do so. Although researchers must portray research participants sensitively and make empathetic attempts to understand their language choices and social behavior, it is brutally honest and complex portraits of young people's language practices and interactions that often yield the most useful findings for teacher development (e.g. Fordham, 1993; Jaspers, 2011; Rampton, 2006; Talmy, 2008; Wortham, 2006). We must know where students' academic, linguistic and cultural insecurities lie before we can even begin to consider how to foster a classroom culture where people raise one another up.[5]

Additionally, because the building of a classroom culture that raises everybody up hinges so much on the ability of the teacher to cultivate joinfostering, lingua franca norms and critical language awareness – not on the side but in the day-to-day teaching of the regular curriculum – teachers of plurilingual ELF classrooms need more time in their day to create or collaborate on deliberate translanguaging design in lesson planning (García *et al.*, 2017), as well as time to recycle previous lessons: in plain English, in students' languages, in oral translanguaged form, in multimodal ways, in translingual notes and finally in a monolingual assessed product, in addition to alternative final formats such as multilingual poetry (e.g. Allard *et al.*, 2019; Lin, 2016; Seltzer, 2020; Woodley & Brown, 2016; see also Figure 7.2 in Chapter 7, and the student poetry in this study). This has to do with not 'packing' the curriculum with too much material, or holding teachers and students accountable to rigid and demeaning 'target-language-only' classroom observations or standard monolingual assessments (García, 2009; García & Li, 2014; Shohamy, 2011). Following the massive strides made by researchers to legitimate translanguaging in plurilingual ELF classrooms (e.g. García & Kleyn, 2016), what remains is for teachers to have the autonomy and time to implement the best practices that are coming to light.

8.3 Study Limitations

This linguistic ethnography was unusual in that it investigated bi/multilingual practices in two high school English classes where there were no white L1 English speakers among the teachers, the students and the researcher. The researcher passes for a native speaker in English, her dominant L2, and speaks her HL (Filipino) and an additional language (French) at an intermediate level. The participating teachers Juan, Kaori and Rayna were academically fluent English users who had lived in the

US for a long time and spoke one or two other languages to an advanced degree. The students were all multilingual; most had been born outside the US, the majority from the Philippines and the minority from Micronesia – both of which are far more linguistically diverse than the US – with singletons from China, the Marshall Islands, Samoa and Vietnam. The study contributes to translanguaging research by illustrating how LCTLs were used alongside ELF in two high school English classes in an Inner Circle English-speaking country.

Despite this relatively novel contribution to the translanguaging literature, the study was limited in several ways. First, there were some sampling limitations. I visited the classes on the same day each week, observing roughly 20% of the lessons between January and May. Coming on Thursdays may have led to sampling bias, as I tended to observe mid-week activities. I also did not collect nearly as much interview data as I had originally planned because of the relatively low number of students who agreed to be interviewed individually about moments in the audio-recorded data that were interesting. More comprehensive and systematic data collection in this area could have allowed me to observe longitudinal patterns of language use for different individuals. Even the 60–70 hours of classroom talk I collected in both classes cannot compare to the number of hours in multi-year school-based ethnographies (e.g. Talmy, 2008). I also did not follow students out of class to document their social practices during recess and lunch, or after school, focusing only on the 'small culture' (Holliday, 1999) of each classroom.

The second limitation of the study is that it only involved English classes. There is still much work to be done on translanguaging in classes that are not seen as language oriented (even though discipline-specific language is still important), such as math, history, science, fine arts, tech, physical education, and health. One large-scale ethnography across various subject areas at a California school (Enright & Gilliland, 2011) found that in elective courses, there is greater curricular flexibility, no standardized testing and increased opportunity to design curricula around students' interests and needs, which in turn facilitates more student engagement and ironically leads to the development of higher-order academic skills than subjects steeped in rigorous standardized testing. This finding aligns with research indicating that curricula in which teachers have more autonomy to draw on students' funds of knowledge or teach (critical) language awareness may be that of electives or extracurricular programs rather than courses at school (e.g. Hélot & Young, 2005; Higgins *et al.*, 2012; Lin & Man, 2011).

Thirdly, I realize that my researcher positionality contributed to ethnolinguistic biases in my data collection. In Chapter 3, I have discussed how my positioning as an ethnically Filipino researcher and Filipino speaker studying translanguaging may have given the impression that it was Filipino language use or ethnically Filipino students, rather than translanguaging, that I was interested in, leading more Filipino than non-Filipino students to participate in all aspects of the study, including recordings and interviews. While all the teachers equally supported my research, I was only able to find a translator for Ilokano: a Filipino student at the university where I was doing my PhD and a former student of Juan's. Thus, my linguistic and cultural positioning was a double-edged sword, drawing in some participants and allies but potentially repelling (or at least making it harder to recruit) others. I wish I had compensated for this more by actively investigating why the Chuukese-speaking boys in English 9 did not translanguage in their classroom talk, even though there were a few of them who sat together. I could also have tried ways to get all students' feedback on what translanguaging they did after every lesson – including silent or individual translanguaging – by handing out a blank cue card ('please write all the translanguaging you remember doing during the lesson'), having explained to them what translanguaging is in a way they could understand. As I explain in Chapter 3 (the methods chapter), these were lost opportunities to study the language practices of non-Filipino students who may not have consented to be audio-recorded and/or interviewed, but might have shared more about their translanguaging with me, *if I had been more active in inviting them to do so*. I urge all translanguaging researchers of the same linguistic/ cultural background as the majority of research participants in a setting (or who are socially constructed as such) to be aware of this bias and to take action to correct it.

8.4 Directions for Future Research

I conclude with five directions for future research. First, this study has suggested the need for clearer distinctions between various types of 'mixed' language use, hopefully counteracting the universalizing tendencies of theories emphasizing the integratedness of the linguistic repertoire and the fluid boundaries between named languages as the sole key to linguistic and social justice in educational settings and beyond. Researchers must also investigate social positioning through the use of distinct codes (as they are defined, or socially constructed, in context) and how such positioning affects opportunities to learn. Additionally, more research is needed on how teachers not only learn to embrace translanguaging but also learn to shape classroom language practices *intentionally* to foster more equitable participation in day-to-day learning activities (Allard et al., 2019; Hamman, 2018), exploring social justice issues, including difficult or uncomfortable topics (Charalambous et al., 2016) and alternative forms of knowledge display (Hornberger & Link, 2012), some of which necessitate recognition of named languages to combat the hegemony of 'official' languages and 'standard' dialects (Flores & Rosa, 2015; Sah & Li, 2020).

Secondly, future research must be aware of linguistic hegemonies operating on multiple levels and timescales, not just the hegemony of 'white L1 English speakers' but also those of cultural and economic elites from a range of ethnic backgrounds who often use English in 'standard' ways, or in this study, the hegemonies of a working-class neighborhood which has majority and minority groups, the language majority in a class and the cultural/linguistic resources and positionalities of the teacher(s) and researcher(s). We have to understand what all the linguistic hegemonies are in a classroom or research setting to restructure all of them effectively. Thirdly, it is worth investigating how to create an inclusive, equitable classroom community given different class compositions, such as (1) the almost-bilingual class where most but not all students speak the same non-English language as their L1 (see Allard *et al.*, 2019, and both classes in this study); (2) the 'split' class where there are two main L1s, one of which is English (Duff, 2002); (3) the English-dominant class where L2 English speakers are a small minority (Yoon, 2008); and the (4) heterogeneous class with no clear linguistic majority, which seems to elicit the most courteous sociolinguistic dispositions (Matsumoto, 2018; Woodley & Brown, 2016).

Fourthly, studies might examine how a *plurilingual, Language X as a lingua franca* classroom can be created for languages other than English, and what role translanguaging plays. Quite often in these contexts, the main language resources used in translanguaging alongside Language X resources are those from English because English is the classroom participants' other shared language (e.g. Mendoza & Parba, 2019; Wang, 2019), again pointing to the need to develop ELF dispositions alongside translanguaging dispositions by drawing on the commonalities between ELF and translanguaging, that is, the critical orientations to language learning, teaching and use inherent in both areas of study. Moreover, it is worth examining how critical translanguaging pedagogy in *plurilingual, Language X as a lingua franca* classrooms might be different for colonial languages that more frequently serve as national languages or global lingua francas compared to LCTLs typically only learned by heritage speakers.

Finally, academics must always start with the day-to-day realities of teachers, and prioritize the issues that challenge teachers most – especially the interpersonal issues that come with class participants' individually different language repertoires and sometimes conflicting needs. Teachers of plurilingual ELF classes must first and foremost be given sufficient autonomy to experiment with deliberate translanguaging designs to implement joinfostering, lingua franca norms and critical language awareness, continually improving these designs based on their professional judgment. Teachers must also have the time to collaborate in feasible initiatives with colleagues at the school level and family/community members, to build an institutional culture where people have internalized the message that they have to learn *with* one another (inclusively) and *from* one another (reciprocally) (Faltis, 2001). The 'official' curriculum must somehow be transformed into 'windows and mirrors' learning (Gutiérrez, 2012) in which students and teachers see their communities' linguistic and cultural funds of knowledge (González *et al.*, 2006) and their other cultural affinities reflected, while having the opportunity to explore those of others, or those that are new to everyone, including knowledge that is part of the 'official' curriculum, as it is acquired with curiosity *and* critically re-appropriated by class participants. While everyone plays a role in these practices, the orchestration ultimately comes down to teachers. What translanguaging looks like in the plurilingual ELF classroom is, and should be, in the critical educator's hands.

Notes

(1) In other words, there are systemic structures that hinder teachers from engaging in such ideal pedagogies, due to lack of curricular freedom and preparation time.

(2) Equality means treating everyone the same; equity means treating people differently to enable equal opportunity. Both of these are integral to social justice in different situations.

(3) For example, it is impossible to recognize someone as a legitimate English user without sincerely recognizing (implicitly or explicitly) what they have said or written as a perfectly good instantiation of the language called 'English' (see a similar discussion in Lee, 2019).

(4) This can be an imagined community, which does not really function as a community but has imagined connections between individuals, such as the members of a nation or diaspora speakers of Language X (Anderson, 1983). Alternatively, it can be a 'small culture' (Holliday, 1999) or a community of practice (Lave & Wenger, 1991), a group of people who truly function as a community and meet regularly to get things done, such as the members of a class.

(5) Even among well-meaning people, the hardest thing to face are potential *conflicts of interest* between individuals and groups. As a settler of color raised in Canada and living in the US, I live and work with settlers (Anglophone, Francophone, kama'āina, Black, Latin@/x, Middle Eastern, Asian and others) and indigenous peoples. Not only must I avoid seeing place as something I can exploit for social, economic or cultural capital (Bourdieu, 1991), but I must also be careful about disregarding differences between others and myself in favor of superficial similarities (e.g. multilingualism), especially if unequal educational and socioeconomic circumstances are involved. As Trask (1991) points out, we can form diverse coalitions if we have a concrete social justice goal to work toward, but admitting irreconcilable differences in people's situations, wants and needs is a key aspect of meeting the goal.

Appendix 1: Language Questionnaire

Name: _____

(1) How often do you use another language in English class? (Choose one)
   (A) Never
   (B) Rarely
   (C) Sometimes
   (D) Often
   (E) All the time
       If your answer is (A), skip to Question 3. If your answer is (B), (C), (D) or (E), answer Questions 2 and 3.

(2) Please write the name of the language(s) here: _____
Now, check all the ways in which you use that language. (You can check more than one answer.)

   _____ I think to myself in the language.
   _____ I talk aloud in the language.
   _____ I write notes to myself in that language.
   _____ I translate to/from the language using a dictionary.
   _____ Other: _____

(3) If you sometimes/often/always use another language in English class, how is it helpful to you? If you rarely/never use another language in English class, why not?

_____
_____

Appendix 2: Interview Questions

Individual Student Interviews

Background

(1) What are some of the things you have learned (or are learning) in the class?
(2) How much do you hear languages other than English in the class? From you? From your peers?
(3) How many languages do you know? Can you describe how well you know each? (e.g. speaking, understanding, reading and writing)
(4) (referring to background questionnaire) Why do you use languages other than English in class? or Why do you use only English in class?
(5) Why do you think students use other languages in English class? How do you feel about this?

Retrospective
(with reference to data)

(1) Can you remember what's going on here and try to describe it for me?
(2) Do you think you would have been able to do these activities using English only? Do you think your work would have turned out just as well, or not?
(3) How do you think your language use affected your classmates' language use?
(4) Is there anything about your peers' use of different languages that is interesting or stands out to you?
(5) Do you think there should be any rules for what languages people can use in class?

* Probing questions are unique to each interview and are not listed here.

Teacher Interviews

Background

(1) Tell me the story of how you became a teacher and came to teach this class.
(2) What are the course outcomes? What do you think the students take away from the class?
(3) How much use of languages other than English takes place in the class? Do some students use LOTEs (languages other than English) more than others?
(4) Why do you think students use other language(s)? Why do you think others use English only?
(5) What would you like to know about students' use of other language(s)?

Retrospective
(with reference to data)

(1) Do you recognize this dialogue? What do you think is going on here?
(2) What do you think mixed language use is doing for the students here?
(3) Based on this data, do you think translanguaging is helping them complete the task?
(4) Based on this data, what social dynamics are emerging through the use of the languages?
(5) What else would you like to find out about students' multilingual practices?

Appendix 3: Data Handout

(1) **Code-switching to talk to different friends in the class (Jan. 17)**

There was one day at the start of the semester when you were juggling Ilokano and English to talk to two different seatmates – Kleo and Clara. During this class, Mr [Ed] was substituting for Juan and you needed to draw an illustration of a metaphor... 'life for me is a ___'.

You asked Clara, 'What you gonna put?'. There was a resulting conversation between you and Clara in Ilokano.

A few minutes later, you said life for you is a Mario game: obstacles to tackle, mushrooms to find, friends to accompany you and a princess to save. [You said this in English.] Then you asked Eufia (at another table) in Ilokano: 'What do you call (.) didiay kalaban dat diay Mario Bro. (.) dagitay mushroom nga babassit nga kulay brown?' [What do you call the thing (.) the enemies in the Mario Bros. (.) those tiny brown mushrooms?]

Later during the lesson, Kleo asked, 'What is that for?', meaning the recorder. You said, 'Recording'. She said, '=Oh'. And after that, you both started singing in English, almost to the recorder; in fact, she was tutting a harmony to your singing: '*Some people want it all...*'.

Throughout this class, you alternately chatted with Clara in Ilokano and sung along with Kleo to different English songs.

Question: How conscious are you of communicating with Clara mainly in Ilokano, Eufia in a mix of Ilokano and English, Kleo through *singing* in English, Mr [Ed] in English and Mr [Juan] in a mix of Ilokano and English? Why these language choices for these people?

(2) **Stylized use of Korean as cultural capital (Jan. 31 and Mar. 7)**

Jan. 31

Kix: (sings in falsetto) "*You are the damsel*—di ba kasdiay? [Is this how?] I like the EXO better than BTS. (raps four words in Korean) *You are the damsel I adore* (.) didiay kanta ni Guk (.) tapos 'Promise' by Jimin. Tapos 'Scenario' by TaeYoung. Hala dika agdengdenggek, saan ka nga talaga updated—" [You don't listen that's why you are not updated—]

Mar. 7

Kix: (to Konan) "Oppa?"
Konan: "Oppa?"
Kix: "Ilang taon ka na? [Ilang taon ka na?"
Konan: "[Hyu:::ng. Why Oppa?"
Eufia: "[Hyung. Oppa is older than you—"
Konan and Eufia: "Hyung."
Kix: "How old are you?"
Konan: "I'm more comfortable—"
Kix: How old are you?"
Konan: "Fifteen."
Kix: "O di I'm fourteen." (Pointing out to Eufia that he's right, as Konan is older than him.)
Konan: "So why do you—why do you—why do you call me 'oppa'? When you're a man."
Kix: "Oh right." (Eufia chuckles; apparently it isn't just about age but also about gender.)
Konan: "Call me oppa when you're a girl."

Why do you guys like Korean music and dramas? Why do you often ask Ms Rayna about Korean words or how to say things in Korean? Would you like to increase your Korean ability more than it currently is, and if so, how?

(3) I know you help others who are less proficient in English. I see though, that some of your classmates annoy you (e.g. Jhon) and it's sometimes hard to help them, right, while others also need help (Eufia, Clara, Rizze), and you help them with less annoyance. Why is that?

(4) Background question I forgot from last time: What else are you taking right now? What subjects do you find easy/hard?

References

Al-Bataineh, A. and Gallagher, K. (2021) Attitudes towards translanguaging: How future teachers perceive the meshing of Arabic and English in children's storybooks. *International Journal of Bilingual Education and Bilingualism* 24 (3), 386–400. https://doi.org/10.1080/13670050.2018.1471039

Allard, E.C. (2017) Re-examining teacher translanguaging: An ecological perspective. *Bilingual Research Journal* 40 (2), 116–130. https://doi.org/10.1080/15235882.2017.1306597

Allard, E.C., Apt, S. and Sacks, I. (2019) Language policy and practice in almost-bilingual classrooms. *International Multilingual Research Journal* 13 (2), 73–87. https://doi.org/10.1080/19313152.2018.1563425

Anderson, B. (1983) *Imagined Communities: Reflections on the Origin and Spread of Nationalism*. London: Verso.

Androutsopoulos, J. (2015) Networked multilingualism: Some language practices on Facebook and their implications. *International Journal of Bilingualism* 19 (2), 185–205. https://doi.org/10.1177/1367006913489198

Appadurai, A. (1996) *Modernity at Large: Cultural Dimensions of Globalization*. Minneapolis, MN: University of Minnesota Press.

Appleseed Center for Law and Economic Justice (2011) *Broken Promises, Shattered Lives: The Case for Justice for Micronesians in Hawai'i*. https://evols.library.manoa.hawaii.edu/bitstream/10524/23158/CaseForJustice_MicronesiansInHawaii.pdf (accessed 1 January 2022).

Asker, A. and Martin-Jones, M. (2013) 'A classroom is not a classroom if students are talking to me in Berber': Language ideologies and multilingual resources in secondary school English classes in Libya. *Language and Education* 27 (4), 343–355. https://doi.org/10.1080/09500782.2013.788189

Auer, P. (1996) From context to contextualization. *Links & Letters* 3, 11–28.

Auer, P. (ed) (1998) *Code-switching in Conversation: Language, Interaction, and Identity*. London: Routledge.

Baker, C. and Wright, W.E. (2017) *Foundations of Bilingual Education and Bilingualism* (6th edn). Bristol: Multilingual Matters.

Bakhtin, M. (1981) *The Dialogic Imagination: Four Essays* (ed. M. Holquist, trans. C Emerson & M. Holquist). Austin, TX: University of Texas Press.

Bamberg, M. (1997) Positioning between structure and performance. *Journal of Narrative and Life History* 7 (1–4), 335–342.

Beiler, I.R. (2021) Marked and unmarked translanguaging in accelerated, mainstream, and sheltered English classrooms. *Multilingua* 40 (1), 107–138. https://doi.org/10.1515/multi-2020-0022

Bickerton, D. and Wilson, W.H. (1987) Pidgin Hawaiian. In G. Gilbert (ed.) *Pidgin and Creole Languages: Essays in Memory of John E. Reinecke* (pp. 61–76). Honolulu, HI: University of Hawai'i Press.

Birello, M., Llompart-Esbert, J. and Moore, E. (2021) Being plurilingual versus becoming a linguistically sensitive teacher: Tensions in the discourse of initial teacher education students. *International Journal of Multilingualism* 1–15. https://doi.org/10.1080/1479 0718.2021.1900195

Blackledge, A. and Creese, A. (2017) Translanguaging and the body. *International Journal of Multilingualism* 14 (3), 250–268. https://doi.org/10.1080/14790718.2017.1315809

Block, D. (2018) The political economy of language education research (or the lack thereof): Nancy Fraser and the case of translanguaging. *Critical Inquiry in Language Studies* 15 (4), 237–257. https://doi.org/10.1080/15427587.2018.1466300

Blommaert, J. (2007) Sociolinguistics and discourse analysis: Orders of indexicality and polycentricity. *Journal of Multicultural Discourses* 2 (2), 115–130. https://doi. org/10.2167/md089.0

Blommaert, J. (2010) *The Sociolinguistics of Globalization*. Cambridge: Cambridge University Press.

Blommaert, J. and Horner, B. (2017) Mobility and academic literacies: An epistolary conversation. *London Review of Education* 15 (1), 2–20.

Blommaert, J., Collins, J. and Slembrouck, S. (2005) Spaces of multilingualism. *Language & Communication* 25 (3), 197–216. https://doi.org/10.1016/j.langcom.2005.05.002

Bonacina-Pugh, F. (2012) Researching 'practiced language policies': Insights from conversation analysis. *Language Policy* 11, 213–234. https://doi.org/10.1007/ s10993-012-9243-x

Borg, S. (1994) Language awareness as methodology: Implications for teachers and teacher training. *Language Awareness* 3 (2), 61–71. https://doi.org/10.1080/09658416.1994.99 59844

Bourdieu, P. (1991) *Language and Symbolic Power*. Cambridge, MA: Harvard University Press.

Bourdieu, P. (2000) *Pascalian Meditations*. Stanford, CA: Stanford University Press.

Brenzinger, M. and Heinrich, P. (2013) The return of Hawaiian: Language networks of the revival movement. *Current Issues in Language Planning* 14 (2), 300–316. https://doi. org/10.1080/14664208.2013.812943

Bucholtz, M. (1999) 'Why be normal?': Language and identity practices in a community of nerd girls. *Language in Society* 28 (2), 203–223. https://doi.org/10.1017/ S0047404599002043

Bucholtz, M. and Hall, K. (2005) Identity and interaction: A sociocultural linguistic approach. *Discourse Studies* 7 (4–5), 585–614. https://doi.org/10.1177/1461445605054407

Byram, M. (2000) *La diversité linguistique en faveur de la citoyenneté démocratique en Europe*. Strasbourg: Editions du Conseil de l'Europe.

Canadian Centre for Studies and Research on Bilingualism and Language Planning (CCERBAL) (2021) Translanguaging II (Mod: N. Slavkov): J. Cenoz, J. Cummins, N. Flores, D. Gorter, A. Lin, K. Seltzer. https://youtube.com//watch?v=fMMH2Y_Il08 (accessed 1 January 2022).

Canagarajah, S. (2011) Codemeshing in academic writing: Identifying teachable strategies of translanguaging. *The Modern Language Journal* 95 (3), 401–417. https://doi. org/10.1111/j.1540-4781.2011.01207.x

Canagarajah, S. (2012) Styling one's own in the Sri Lankan Tamil diaspora: Implications for language and ethnicity. *Journal of Language, Identity & Education* 11 (2), 124–135. https://doi.org/10.1080/15348458.2012.667309

Canagarajah, A.S. and Wurr, A.J. (2011) Multilingual communication and language acquisition: New research directions. *The Reading Matrix* 11 (1), 1–15.

Cenoz, J. and Gorter, D. (2020) Teaching English through pedagogical translanguaging. *World Englishes* 39 (2), 300–311. https://doi.org/10.1111/weng.12462

Chan, J. (2014) An evaluation of the pronunciation target in Hong Kong's ELT curriculum and materials: Influences from WE and ELF? *Journal of English as a Lingua Franca* 3 (1), 145–170. https://doi.org/10.1515/jelf-2014-0006

Chan, J.Y.H. (2016) Contextualising a pedagogical model for English-language education in Hong Kong. *World Englishes* 35 (3), 372–395. https://doi.org/10.1111/weng.12184

Charalambous, P., Charalambous, C. and Zembylas, M. (2016) Troubling translanguaging: Language ideologies, superdiversity and interethnic conflict. *Applied Linguistics Review* 7 (3), 327–352. https://doi.org/10.1515/applirev-2016-0014

Chun, E.W. (2009) Speaking like Asian immigrants: Intersections of accommodation and mocking at a US high school. *Pragmatics* 19 (1), 17–38. https://doi.org/10.1075/prag.19.1.02chu

College Board (2017) *English Language Arts Grades 6–12*. See https://springboard.collegeboard.org/ela/6-to-12-grade (accessed 1 January 2022).

Cook, V.J. (1992) Evidence for multicompetence. *Language Learning* 42 (4), 557–591. https://doi.org/10.1111/j.1467-1770.1992.tb01044.x

Copland, F. and Creese, A. (2015) *Linguistic Ethnography: Collecting, Analysing and Presenting Data*. London: Sage.

Coste, D., Moore, D. and Zarate, G. (2009) *Plurilingual and Pluricultural Competence*. Strasbourg: Council of Europe.

Coupland, N. (2003) Dialect stylization in radio talk. *Language in Society* 30 (3), 345–375. https://doi.org/10.1017/S0047404501003013

Creese, A. and Blackledge, A. (2010) Translanguaging in the bilingual classroom: A pedagogy for learning and teaching? *The Modern Language Journal* 94 (1), 103–115. https://doi.org/10.1111/j.1540-4781.2009.00986.x

Creese, A. and Blackledge, A. (2015) Translanguaging and identity in educational settings. *Annual Review of Applied Linguistics* 35, 20–35. https://doi.org/10.1017/S0267190514000233

Creese, A., Blackledge, A. and Takhi, J.K. (2014) The ideal 'native speaker' teacher: Negotiating authenticity and legitimacy in the language classroom. *The Modern Language Journal* 98 (4), 937–951. https://doi.org/10.1111/modl.12148

Creese, A., Blackledge, A., Bhatt, A., Jonsson, C., Juffermans, K., Li, J., Martin, P., Muhonen, A. and Takhi, J.K. (2015) Researching bilingual and multilingual education multilingually: A linguistic ethnographic approach. In W.E. Wright, S. Boun and O. García (eds) *The Handbook of Bilingual and Multilingual Education* (pp. 127–144). Hoboken, NJ: John Wiley & Sons.

Cummins, J. (2005) A proposal for action: Strategies for recognizing heritage language competence as a learning resource within the mainstream classroom. *The Modern Language Journal* 89 (4), 585–592.

Cummins, J. and Man, E.Y.-F. (2007) Academic language: What is it and how do we acquire it? In J. Cummins and C. Davison (eds) *International Handbook of English Language Teaching* (pp. 797–810). Boston, MA: Springer.

Cummins, J. and Early, M. (2010) *Identity Texts: The Collaborative Creation of Power in Multilingual Schools*. Stoke-on-Trent: Trentham Books.

Davies, B. and Harré, R. (1990) Positioning: The discursive production of selves. *Journal for the Theory of Social Behaviour* 20 (1), 43–63.

De Costa, P.I. (2014) Making ethical decisions in an ethnographic study. *TESOL Quarterly* 48 (2), 413–422. https://doi.org/10.1002/tesq.163

Dewey, M. (2012) Towards a post-normative approach: Learning the pedagogy of ELF. *Journal of English as a Lingua Franca* 1 (1), 141–170. https://doi.org/10.1515/jelf-2012-0007

Dovchin, S., Pennycook, A. and Sultana, S. (2017) *Popular Culture, Voice and Linguistic Diversity: Young Adults On- and Offline*. Cham: Springer.

Duarte, J. (2019) Translanguaging in mainstream education: A sociocultural approach. *International Journal of Bilingual Education and Bilingualism* 22 (2), 150–164. https://doi.org/10.1080/13670050. 2016.1231774

Duff, P.A. (1995) An ethnography of communication in immersion classrooms in Hungary. *TESOL Quarterly* 29 (3), 505–537. https://doi.org/10.2307/3588073

Duff, P.A. (2002) Pop culture and ESL students: Intertextuality, identity, and participation in classroom discussions. *Journal of Adolescent & Adult Literacy* 45 (6), 482–487.

Eckert, P. (2008) Where do ethnolects stop? *International Journal of Bilingualism* 12 (1–2), 25–42. https://doi.org/10.1177/13670069080120010301

Enright, K.A. (2011) Language and literacy for a new mainstream. *American Educational Research Journal* 48 (1), 80–118. https://doi.org/10.3102/0002831210368989

Enright, K.A. and Gilliland, B. (2011) Multilingual writing in an age of accountability: From policy to practice in US high school classrooms. *Journal of Second Language Writing* 20 (3), 182–195. https://doi.org/10.1016/j.jslw.2011.05.006

Faltis, C. (1990) New directions in bilingual research design: The study of interactive decision making. In R. Jacobson and C. Faltis (eds) *Language Distribution Issues in Bilingual Schooling* (pp. 45–57). Clevedon: Multilingual Matters.

Faltis, C. (2001) *Joinfostering: Teaching and Learning in Multilingual Classrooms* (3rd edn). Upper Saddle River, NJ: Merrill Prentice Hall.

Filipi, A. and Markee, N. (eds) (2018) *Conversation Analysis and Language Alternation: Capturing Transitions in the Classroom*. Amsterdam: John Benjamins.

Fishman, J.A. (1967) Bilingualism with and without diglossia; Diglossia with and without bilingualism. *Journal of Social Issues* 23 (2), 29–38.

Flores, N. and Schissel, J.L. (2014) Dynamic bilingualism as the norm: Envisioning a heteroglossic approach to standards-based reform. *TESOL Quarterly* 48 (3), 454–479. https://doi.org/10.1002/tesq.182

Flores, N. and Rosa, J. (2015) Undoing appropriateness: Raciolinguistic ideologies and language diversity in education. *Harvard Educational Review* 85 (2), 149–171. https://doi.org/10.17763/0017-8055.85.2.149

Fordham, S. (1993) 'Those loud Black girls': (Black) women, silence, and gender 'passing' in the academy. *Anthropology & Education Quarterly* 24 (1), 3–32. https://doi.org/10.1525/aeq.1993.24.1.05x1736t

Friedrich, P. and Matsuda, A. (2010) When five words are not enough: A conceptual and terminological discussion of English as a lingua franca. *International Multilingual Research Journal* 4 (1), 20–30. https://doi.org/10.1080/19313150903500978

Fujikane, C. (2005) Foregrounding native nationalisms: A critique of antinationalist sentiment in Asian American studies. In K.A. Ono (ed.) *Asian American Studies After Critical Mass* (pp. 73–97). Malden, MA: Wiley-Blackwell.

Fujikane, C. and Okamura, J.Y. (2008) *Asian Settler Colonialism: From Local Governance to the Habits of Everyday Life in Hawai'i*. Honolulu, HI: University of Hawai'i Press.

Galla, C.K. (2009) Indigenous language revitalization and technology from traditional to contemporary domains. In J. Reyhner and L. Lockard (eds) *Indigenous Language Revitalization: Encouragement, Guidance, & Lessons Learned* (pp. 167–182). Flag staff, AZ: Northern Arizona University.

Ganassin, S. (2020) *Language, Culture and Identity in Two Chinese Community Schools: More Than One Way of Being Chinese?* Bristol: Multilingual Matters.

García, O. (2009) *Bilingual Education in the 21st Century: A Global Perspective*. Malden, MA: Wiley-Blackwell.

García, O. and Kleifgen, J.A. (2010) *Educating Emergent Bilinguals: Policies, Programs, and Practices for English Language Learners*. New York: Teachers College Press.

García, O. and Li, W. (2014) *Translanguaging: Language, Bilingualism, and Education*. Basingstoke: Palgrave Macmillan.

García, O. and Kleyn, T. (eds) (2016) *Translanguaging with Multilingual Students: Learning from Classroom Moments*. New York: Routledge.

García, O. and Kleifgen, J.A. (2020) Translanguaging and literacies. *Reading Research Quarterly* 55 (4), 553–571. https://doi.org/10.1002/rrq.286

García, O. and Otheguy, R. (2020) Plurilingualism and translanguaging: Commonalities and divergences. *International Journal of Bilingual Education and Bilingualism* 23 (1), 17–35. https://doi.org/10.1080/13670050.2019.1598932

García, O., Ibarra Johnson, S. and Seltzer, K. (2017) *The Translanguaging Classroom: Leveraging Student Bilingualism for Learning*. Philadelphia, PA: Caslon.

García, O., Flores, N., Seltzer, K., Li, W., Otheguy, R. and Rosa, J. (2021) Rejecting abyssal thinking in the language and education of racialized bilinguals: A manifesto. *Critical Inquiry in Language Studies* 18 (3), 203–228. https://doi.org/10.1080/15427587.2021.1935957

Georgakopoulou, A. (2006) The other side of the story: Towards a narrative analysis of narratives-in-interaction. *Discourse Studies* 8 (2), 235–257. https://doi.org/10.1177/1461445606061795

Goffman, E. (1981) *Forms of Talk*. Philadelphia, PA: University of Pennsylvania Press.

Gonzalez, A. (1980) *Language and Nationalism: The Philippine Experience Thus Far*. Quezon City: Ateneo de Manila/University of the Philippines.

Gonzalez, J. (2021) Teachers are barely hanging on. Here's what they need. *Language, Culture, and Identity in Two Chinese Community Schools*. See https://cultofpedagogy.com/barely-hanging-on

González, N., Moll, L.C. and Amanti, C. (eds) (2006) *Funds of Knowledge: Theorizing Practices in Households, Communities, and Classrooms*. New York: Routledge.

Grosjean, F. (1989) Neurolinguists, beware! The bilingual is not two monolinguals in one person. *Brain and Language* 36 (1), 3–15.

Gumperz, J. (1982) *Discourse Strategies*. Cambridge: Cambridge University Press.

Gumperz, J. (1992) Contextualization revisited. In P. Auer and A. Di Luzio (eds) *The Contextualization of Language* (pp. 39–54). Amsterdam: John Benjamins.

Gutiérrez, R. (2012) Embracing Nepantla: Rethinking 'knowledge' and its use in mathematics teaching. REDIMAT (Revista de Investigación en Didáctica de las Matemáticas) 1 (1), 29–56.

Hall, K. (2014) Hypersubjectivity: Language, anxiety, and indexical dissonance in globalization. *Journal of Asian Pacific Communication* 24 (2), 261–273. https://doi.org/10.1075/japc.24.2.06hal

Hamman, L. (2018) Translanguaging and positioning in two-way dual language classrooms: A case for criticality. *Language and Education* 32 (1), 21–42. https://doi.org/10.1080/09500782.2017.1384006

Haneda, M. (2009) Learning about the past and preparing for the future: A longitudinal investigation of a grade 7 'sheltered' social studies class. *Language and Education* 23 (4), 335–352. https://doi.org/10.1080/09500780902954265

Hawai'i Board of Education (2015) Policy E-3: NĀ HOPENA A'O (HĀ). *Language, Culture, and Identity in Two Chinese Community Schools*. See https://boe.hawaii.gov/policies/Board%20Policies/Nā%20Hopena%20A'o%20(HĀ).pdf

Hawai'i Department of Education (n.d.) Who are Hawai'i's English learners (ELs)? *Language, Culture, and Identity in Two Chinese Community Schools*. See https://www.hawaiipublicschools.org/DOE%20Forms/EL%20Infographic.pdf

Hawai'i P-20 Partnerships for Education (2018) Serving Hawai'i's English learners. *Language, Culture, and Identity in Two Chinese Community Schools*. See https://www.hawaiidxp.org/publications/serving-hawaiis-english-learners-a-report-on-education-outcomes-for-hawaii-public-school-students-who-are-identified-as-english-learners/

Hawai'i State Department of Education (2016) Multilingualism for equitable education, policy 105-14. See https://boe.hawaii.gov/policies/Board%20Policies/Multilingualism%20for%20Equitable%20Education.pdf https://boe.hawaii.gov/policies/Board%20Policies/Multilingualism%20for%20Equitable%20Education.pdf

Heath, S.B. (1983) *Ways with Words: Language, Life and Work in Communities and Classrooms*. Cambridge: Cambridge University Press.

Hélot, C. (2003) Language policy and the ideology of bilingual education in France. *Language Policy* 2 (3), 255–277. https://doi.org/10.1023/A:1027316632721

Hélot, C. and Young, A. (2002) Bilingualism and language education in French primary schools: Why and how should migrant languages be valued? *International Journal of Bilingual Education and Bilingualism* 5 (2), 96–112. https://doi.org/10.1080/13670050208667749

Hélot, C. and Young, A. (2005) The notion of diversity in language education: Policy and practice at primary level in France. *Language, Culture and Curriculum* 18 (3), 242–257. https://doi.org/10.1080/07908310508668745

Hepburn, A. and Bolden, G.B. (2013) The conversation analytic approach to transcription. In J. Sidnell and T. Stivers (eds) *The Handbook of Conversation Analysis* (pp. 57–76). Malden, MA: Blackwell Publishing.

Hesson, S., Seltzer, K. and Woodley, H.H. (2014) *Translanguaging in Curriculum and Instruction: A CUNY-NYSIEB Guide for Educators*. New York: CUNY-NYSIEB.

Higgins, C. (2009) *English as a Local Language: Post-colonial Identities and Multilingual Practices*. Bristol: Multilingual Matters.

Higgins, C. (2010) Raising critical language awareness in Hawai'i at Da Pidgin Coup. In B. Migge, I. Léglise and A. Bartens (eds) *Creoles in Education: An Appraisal of Current Programs and Projects* (pp. 31–54). Amsterdam: John Benjamins.

Higgins, C. (2015) Earning capital in Hawai'i's linguistic landscape. In R. Tupas (ed.) *Unequal Englishes: The Politics of English Today* (pp. 145–162). London: Palgrave Macmillan.

Higgins, C., Nettell, R., Furukawa, G. and Sakoda, K. (2012) Beyond contrastive analysis and codeswitching: Student documentary filmmaking as a challenge to linguicism in Hawai'i. *Linguistics and Education* 23 (1), 49–61. https://doi.org/10.1016/j.linged.2011.10.002

Holliday, A. (1999) Small cultures. *Applied Linguistics* 20 (2), 237–264. https://doi.org/10.1093/applin/20.2.237

hooks, b. (1989) *Talking Back: Thinking Feminist, Thinking Black*. Boston, MA: South End Press.

Hornberger, N.H. and Link, H. (2012) Translanguaging and transnational literacies in multilingual classrooms: A biliteracy lens. *International Journal of Bilingual Education and Bilingualism* 15 (3), 261–278. https://doi.org/10.1080/13670050.2012.658016

Hymes, D. (1974) *Foundations in Sociolinguistics: An Ethnographic Approach*. Philadelphia, PA: University of Pennsylvania Press.

Irvine, J.T., Gal, S. and Kroskrity, P.V. (2009) Language ideology and linguistic differentiation. In A. Duranti (ed.) *Linguistic Anthropology: A Reader* (5th edn, pp. 402–434). Chichester: Wiley-Blackwell.

Jacobson, R. and Faltis, C. (eds) (1990) *Language Distribution Issues in Bilingual Schooling*. Clevedon: Multilingual Matters.

Jaffe, A. (2003) Talk around text: Literacy practices, cultural identity and authority in a Corsican bilingual classroom. In A. Creese and P. Martin (eds) *Multilingual Classroom Ecologies: Inter-relationship, Interactions and Ideologies* (pp. 42–60). Clevedon: Multilingual Matters.

Janks, H. (2004) The access paradox. *English in Australia* 139, 33–42.

Jaspers, J. (2011) Talking like a 'zerolingual': Ambiguous linguistic caricatures at an urban secondary school. *Journal of Pragmatics* 43 (5), 1264–1278. https://doi.org/10.1016/j.pragma.2010.05.012

Jaspers, J. (2018) The transformative limits of translanguaging. *Language & Communication* 58, 1–10. https://doi.org/10.1016/j.langcom.2017.12.001

Jenkins, J., Cogo, A. and Dewey, M. (2011) Review of developments in research into English as a lingua franca. *Language Teaching* 44 (3), 281–315. https://doi.org/10.1017/S0261444811000115

Jetnil-Kijiner, K. (2011) Tell them. *Multilingual Classroom Ecologies: Inter-relationship, Interactions and Ideologie.* See https://www.kathyjetnilkijiner.com/tell-them/

Johnstone, B. (2013) *Speaking Pittsburghese: The Story of a Dialect.* Oxford: Oxford University Press.

Jones, S. (2013) Literacies in the body. *Journal of Adolescent & Adult Literacy* 56 (7), 525–529. https://doi.org/10.1002/JAAL.182

Kachru, B.B. (1986) *The Alchemy of English: The Spread, Models and Functions of Non-native Englishes.* New York: Pergamon.

Kapono, E. (1995) Hawaiian language revitalization and immersion education. *International Journal of the Sociology of Language* 112, 121–135. https://doi.org/10.1515/ijsl.1995.112.121

Keju-Johnson, D. (1998) For the good of mankind. In Z. de Ishtar (ed.) *Pacific Women Speak Out for Independence and Denuclearisation* (pp. 52–58). Christchurch: The Raven Press.

Kohn, K. (2018) MY English: A social constructivist perspective on ELF. *Journal of English as a Lingua Franca* 7 (1), 1–24. https://doi.org/10.1515/jelf-2018-0001

Kubota, R. (1998) Ideologies of English in Japan. *World Englishes* 17 (3), 295–306. https://doi.org/ 10.1111/1467-971X.00105

Kubota, R. (2016) The multi/plural turn, postcolonial theory, and neoliberal multiculturalism: Complicities and implications for applied linguistics. *Applied Linguistics* 37 (4), 474–494. https://doi.org/10.1093/applin/amu045

Kubota, R. and Lin, A. (eds) (2009) *Race, Culture and Identities in Second Language Education: Exploring Critically Engaged Practice.* New York: Routledge.

Kumaravadivelu, B. (2001) Toward a postmethod pedagogy. *TESOL Quarterly* 35 (4), 537–560. https://doi.org/10.2307/3588427

Lam, W.S.E. and Warriner, D.S. (2012) Transnationalism and literacy: Investigating the mobility of people, languages, texts, and practices in contexts of migration. *Reading Research Quarterly* 47 (2), 191–215. https://doi.org/10.1002/RRQ.016

Lamb, G. (2015) 'Mista, are you in a good mood?': Stylization to negotiate interaction in an urban Hawai'i classroom. *Multilingua* 34 (2), 159–185. https://doi.org/10.1515/multi-2014-1008

Lave, J. and Wenger, E. (1991) *Situated Learning: Legitimate Peripheral Participation.* Cambridge: Cambridge University Press.

Lee, J.W. (2019) Translingualism as resistance against what and for whom? In T.A. Barrett and S. Dovchin (eds) *Critical Inquiries in the Sociolinguistics of Globalization* (pp. 102–118). Bristol: Multilingual Matters.

Leonet, O., Cenoz, J. and Gorter, D. (2020) Developing morphological awareness across languages: Translanguaging pedagogies in third language acquisition. *Language Awareness* 29 (1), 41–59. https://doi.org/10.1080/09658416.2019.1688338

Leung, C., Harris, R. and Rampton, B. (1997) The idealised native speaker, reified ethnicities, and classroom realities. *TESOL Quarterly* 31 (3), 543–560. https://doi.org/10.2307/3587837

Lewis, G., Jones, B. and Baker, C. (2012) Translanguaging: Origins and development from school to street and beyond. *Educational Research and Evaluation* 18 (7), 641–654. https://doi.org/10.1080/13803611.2012.718488

Li, W. (2011) Moment analysis and translanguaging space: Discursive construction of identities by multilingual Chinese youth in Britain. *Journal of Pragmatics* 43 (5), 1222–1235. https://doi.org/10.1016/j.pragma.2010.07.035

Li, W. (2014) Negotiating funds of knowledge and symbolic competence in the complementary school classrooms. *Language and Education* 28 (2), 161–180. https://doi.org/10.1080/09500782.2013.800549

Li, W. (2018) Translanguaging as a practical theory of language. *Applied Linguistics* 39 (1), 9–30. https://doi.org/10.1093/applin/amx039

Li, W. and Zhu, H. (2013) Translanguaging identities and ideologies: Creating transnational space through flexible multilingual practices amongst Chinese university students in the UK. *Applied Linguistics* 34 (5), 516–535. https://10.1093/applin/amt022

Lin, A. (2013) Classroom code-switching: Three decades of research. *Applied Linguistics Review* 4 (1), 195–218. https://doi.org/10.1515/applirev-2013-0009

Lin, A.M.Y. (2016) *Language Across the Curriculum & CLIL in English as an Additional Language (EAL) Contexts: Theory and Practice*. Singapore: Springer.

Lin, A. and Man, E. (2011) Doing-hip-hop in the transformation of youth identities: Social class, habitus, and cultural capital. In C. Higgins (ed.) *Identity Formation in Globalizing Contexts: Language Learning in the New Millennium* (pp. 201–209). Berlin: Walter de Gruyter.

Lin, A.M. and He, P. (2017) Translanguaging as dynamic activity flows in CLIL classrooms. *Journal of Language, Identity & Education* 16 (4), 228–244. https://doi.org/10.1080/15348458.2017.1328283

Linares, R.E. (2019) Meaningful writing opportunities: Write-alouds and dialogue journaling with newcomer and English learner high schoolers. *Journal of Adolescent & Adult Literacy* 62 (5), 521–530. https://doi.org/10.1002/jaal.932

Lippi-Green, R. (2012) The standard language myth. In R. Lippi-Green (ed.) *English with an Accent: Language, Ideology, and Discrimination in the United States* (pp. 55–65). New York: Routledge.

Liu, J.M., Ong, P.M. and Rosenstein, C. (1991) Dual chain migration: Post-1965 Filipino immigration to the United States. *International Migration Review* 25 (3), 487–513. https://doi.org/10.1177/019791839102500302

Long, M.H. (1983) Linguistic and conversational adjustments to non-native speakers. *Studies in Second Language Acquisition* 5 (2), 177–193. https://doi.org/10.1017/S0272263100004848

Lupenui, C.K., Sang, D.K., Seward, H., Lee, H., Walk, K., Benioni, K., Kawai'ae'a, K., Albert, L., Paishon Duarte, M., Zeug, M., Morris, M. and Kahumoku, W. (2015) Nā ahopena a'o statements: HĀ: BREATH. *Critical Inquiries in the Sociolinguistics of Globalization*. See https://www.hawaiipublicschools.org/DOE%20Forms/NaHopenaAoE3.pdf

MacSwan, J. (2000) The threshold hypothesis, semilingualism, and other contributions to a deficit view of linguistic minorities. *Hispanic Journal of Behavioral Sciences* 22 (1), 3–45. https://doi.org/10.1177/0739986300221001

MacSwan, J. (2017) A multilingual perspective on translanguaging. *American Educational Research Journal* 54 (1), 167–201.

MacSwan, J. (ed.) (2022) *Multilingual Perspectives on Translanguaging*. Bristol: Multilingual Matters.

Makoni, S. and Pennycook, A. (eds) (2007) *Disinventing and Reconstituting Languages*. Clevedon: Multilingual Matters.

Malsbary, C.B. (2012) 'Assimilation, but to what mainstream?': Immigrant youth in a super-diverse high school. *Encyclopaidea* 16 (33), 89–112.

Malsbary, C.B. (2013) *'It's not just learning English, it's learning other cultures'*: Belonging, power and possibility in an immigrant contact zone. *International Journal of Qualitative Studies in Education* 27 (10), 1312–1336. https://doi.org/10.1080/09518398.2013.837210

Marshall, S. and Moore, D. (2018) Plurilingualism amid the panoply of lingualisms: Addressing critiques and misconceptions in education. *International Journal of Multilingualism* 15 (1), 19–34. https://doi.org/10.1080/14790718.2016.1253699

Martin-Jones, M. (1995) Code-switching in the classroom: Two decades of research. In L. Milroy and P. Muysken (eds) *One Speaker, Two Languages: Cross-Disciplinary Perspectives on Code-Switching* (pp. 90–111). Cambridge: Cambridge University Press.

Martin-Jones, M. and Saxena, M. (2003) Bilingual resources and 'funds of knowledge' for teaching and learning in multi-ethnic classrooms in Britain. In A. Creese and P. Martin (eds) *Multilingual Classroom Ecologies: Inter-relationship, Interactions and Ideologies* (pp. 107–122). Clevedon: Multilingual Matters.

Matsuda, A. (2018) Is teaching English as an international language all about being politically correct? *RELC Journal* 49 (1), 24–35. https://doi.org/10.1177/0033688217753489

Matsumoto, Y. (2018) 'Because we are peers, we actually understand': Third-party participant assistance in English as a Lingua Franca classroom interactions. *TESOL Quarterly* 52 (4), 845–876. https://doi.org/10.1002/tesq.430

McFarland, C.D. (2009) Linguistic diversity and English in the Philippines. In M.L.S. Bautista and K. Bolton (eds) *Philippine English: Linguistic and Literary Perspectives* (pp. 131–156). Hong Kong: Hong Kong University Press.

Mendoza, A. (2020a) A linguistic ethnography of laissez faire translanguaging in two high school English classes. PhD dissertation, University of Hawai'i at Mānoa.

Mendoza, A. (2020b) What does translanguaging-for-equity really involve? An interactional analysis of a 9th grade English class. *Applied Linguistics Review* 1–21. https://doi.org/10.1515/applirev-2019-0106

Mendoza, A. and Parba, J. (2019) Thwarted: Relinquishing educator beliefs to understand translanguaging from learners' point of view. *International Journal of Multilingualism* 16 (3), 270–285. https://doi.org/10.14790718.2018.1441843

Menken, K. and García, O. (eds) (2010) *Negotiating Language Education Policies: Educators as Policymakers*. New York: Routledge.

Menken, K. and Kleyn, T. (2010) The long-term impact of subtractive schooling in the educational experiences of secondary English language learners. *International Journal of Bilingual Education and Bilingualism* 13 (4), 399–417. https://doi.org/10.1080/13670050903370143

Menken, K. and Sánchez, M.T. (2019) Translanguaging in English-only schools: From pedagogy to stance in the disruption of monolingual policies and practices. *TESOL Quarterly* 53 (3), 741–767. https://doi.org/10.1002/tesq.513

Menken, K., Kleyn, T. and Chae, N. (2012) Spotlight on 'long-term English language learners': Characteristics and prior schooling experiences of an invisible population. *International Multilingual Research Journal* 6 (2), 121–142. https://doi.org/10.1080/19313152.2012.665822

Mercer, N. (1997) Socio-cultural perspectives and the study of classroom discourse. In C. Coll and D. Edwards (eds) *Teaching, Learning and Classroom Discourse: Approach to the Study of Educational Discourse* (pp. 13–21). Madrid: Fundación Infancia y Aprendizaje.

Mignolo, W.D. (2003) *The Darker Side of the Renaissance: Literacy, Territoriality, and Colonization* (2nd edn). Ann Arbor, MI: University of Michigan Press.

Mirvahedi, S.H. (2021) What can interactional sociolinguistics bring to the family language policy research table? The case of a Malay family in Singapore. *Journal of Multilingual and Multicultural Development* 1–16. https://doi.org/10.1080/0143463 2.2021.1879089

Mori, J., and Sanuth, K.K. (2018) Navigating between a monolingual utopia and translingual realities: Experiences of American learners of Yorùbá as an additional language. *Applied Linguistics* 39 (1), 78–98. https://doi.org/10.1093/applin/amx042

Mortimer, K.S. and Wortham, S. (2015) Analyzing language policy and social identification across heterogeneous scales. *Annual Review of Applied Linguistics* 35, 160–172. https://doi.org/10.1017/S0267190514000269

Norton, B. (2000) *Identity and Language Learning: Gender, Ethnicity and Educational Change*. Harlow: Longman.

Okamura, J.Y. (2008) Ethnic boundary construction in the Japanese American community in Hawai'i. In C. Fujikane and J. Okamura (eds) *Asian Settler Colonialism: From Local Governance to the Habits of Everyday Life in Hawai'i* (pp. 233–255). Honolulu, HI: University of Hawai'i Press.

Ortega, L. (2014) Ways forward for a bi/multilingual turn in SLA. In S. May (ed) *The Multilingual Turn: Implications for SLA, TESOL, and Bilingual Education* (pp. 32–53). New York: Routledge.

Otheguy, R., García, O. and Reid, W. (2015) Clarifying translanguaging and deconstructing named languages: A perspective from linguistics. *Applied Linguistics Review* 6 (3), 281–307. https://doi.org/10.1515/applirev-2015-0014

Palmer, D.K., Martínez, R.A., Mateus, S.G. and Henderson, K. (2014) Reframing the debate on language separation: Toward a vision for translanguaging pedagogies in the dual language classroom. *The Modern Language Journal* 98 (3), 757–772. https://doi.org/10.1111/modl.12121

Pennycook, A. and Otsuji, E. (2014) Metrolingual multitasking and spatial repertoires: 'Pizza mo two minutes coming'. *Journal of Sociolinguistics* 18 (2), 161–184. https://doi.org/10.1111/josl.12079

Perez Hattori, M.T. (2020) Ta nå'i i fino-ta hinagong – Giving breath to our words: Empowering multilingual learners through the arts. Keynote speech at the Hawai'i Department of Education Multilingualism and Arts Symposium, 11 January, McKinley High School, Honolulu, HI.

Perez-Milans, M. (2013) *Urban Schools and English Language Education in Late Modern China: A Critical Sociolinguistic Ethnography*. Abingdon: Routledge.

Piccardo, E. (2013) Plurilingualism and curriculum design: Toward a synergic vision. *TESOL Quarterly* 47 (3), 600–614.

Pinker, S. (1994) *The Language Instinct: How the Mind Creates Language*. New York: HarperCollins.

Poza, L. (2017) Translanguaging: Definitions, implications, and further needs in burgeoning inquiry. *Berkeley Review of Education* 6 (2), 101–128.

Rajendram, S. (2021) Translanguaging as an agentive pedagogy for multilingual learners: Affordances and constraints. *International Journal of Multilingualism* 1–28. https://doi.org/10.1080/14790718.2021.1898619

Rampton, B. (1995) Language crossing and the problematisation of ethnicity and socialisation. *Pragmatics* 5 (4), 485–513. https://doi.org/10.1075/prag.5.4.04ram

Rampton, B. (2002) Ritual and foreign language practices at school. *Language in Society* 31 (4), 491–525. https://doi.org/10.1017/S0047404502314015

Rampton, B. (2006) Talk in class at Central High. In B. Rampton (ed.) *Language in Late Modernity: Interaction in an Urban School* (pp. 41–93). Cambridge: Cambridge University Press.

Rampton, B. (2011a) From 'multi-ethnic adolescent heteroglossia' to 'contemporary urban vernaculars'. *Language & Communication* 31 (4), 276–294. https://doi.org/10.1016/j.langcom.2011.01.001

Rampton, B. (2011b) Style contrasts, migration and social class. *Journal of Pragmatics* 43 (5), 1236–1250. https://doi.org/10.1016/j.pragma.2010.08.010

Rampton, B., Maybin, J. and Roberts, C. (2015) Theory and method in linguistic ethnography. In J. Snell, S. Shaw and F. Copland (eds) *Linguistic Ethnography: Interdisciplinary Explorations* (pp. 14–50). London: Palgrave Macmillan.

Ratliffe, K.T. (2011) Micronesian voices: Culture and school conflict. *Race Ethnicity and Education* 14 (2), 233–252. https://doi.org/10.1080/13613324.2010.519971

Reinecke, J. (1969) The historical background of makeshift language and regional dialect in Hawai'i. In J. Reinecke (ed.) *Language and Dialect in Hawai'i: A Sociolinguistic History to 1935* (pp. 23–82). Honolulu, HI: University of Hawai'i Press.

Roberts, S. (2019) Uncovering the early history of Pidgin through archival research. Lecture, 19 February. University of Hawai'i at Mānoa, Honolulu, Hawai'i.

Ruiz, R. (1984) Orientations in language planning. *NABE Journal* 8 (2), 15–34. https://doi.org/10.1080/08855072.1984.10668464

Ruuska, K. (2016) Beyond ideologies and realities: Multilingual competence in a languagised world. *Applied Linguistics Review* 353–374. https://doi.org/10.1515/applirev-2016-0015

Rymes, B. (2014) Marking communicative repertoire through metacommentary. In A. Blackledge and A. Creese (eds) *Heteroglossia as Practice and Pedagogy* (pp. 301–316). Dordrecht: Springer.

Rymes, B. (2015) *Classroom Discourse Analysis: A Tool for Critical Reflection* (2nd edn). Abingdon: Routledge.

Rymes, B. and Smail, G. (2021) Citizen sociolinguists scaling back. *Applied Linguistics Review* 12 (3), 419–444. https://doi.org/10.1515/applirev-2019-0133

Sah, P.K. and Li, G. (2020) Translanguaging or unequal languaging? Unfolding the plurilingual discourse of English medium instruction policy in Nepal's public schools. *International Journal of Bilingual Education and Bilingualism* 1–20. https://doi.org/10.1080/13670050.2020.1849011

Sánchez, M.T. and Menken, K. (2019) Ofelia García and the CUNY-NYSIEB community: Symbiosis in furthering translanguaging pedagogy and practice. *Journal of Multilingual Education Research* 9 (1), 157–173.

Sandhu, P. (2015) Stylizing voices, stances, and identities related to medium of education in India. *Multilingua* 34 (2), 211–235. https://doi.org/10.1515/multi-2014-1012

Saranillo, D.I. (2008) Rethinking Filipino and 'American' settler empowerment in the U.S. colony of Hawai'i. In C. Fujikane and J. Okamura (eds) *Asian Settler Colonialism: From Local Governance to the Habits of Everyday Life in Hawai'i* (pp. 256–278). Honolulu, HI: University of Hawai'i Press.

Sato, C. (1985) Linguistic inequality in Hawai'i: The post-creole dilemma. In N. Wolfson and J. Manes (eds) *Language of Inequality* (pp. 255–272). Berlin: Mouton.

Sato, C. (1994) Language change on a creole continuum: Decreolization? In K. Hyltenstam and Å. Viberg (eds) *Progression and Regression in Language* (pp. 127–147). Cambridge: Cambridge University Press.

Saxena, M. and Martin-Jones, M. (2013) Multilingual resources in classroom interaction: Ethnographic and discourse analytic perspectives. *Language and Education* 27 (4), 285–297. https://doi.org/10.1080/09500782.2013.788020

Sayer, P. (2010) Using the linguistic landscape as a pedagogical resource. *ELT Journal* 64 (2), 143–154. https://doi.org/10.1093/elt/ccp051

Sayer, P. (2013) Translanguaging, TexMex, and bilingual pedagogy: Emergent bilinguals learning through the vernacular. *TESOL Quarterly* 47 (1), 63–88. https://doi.org/10.1002/tesq.53

Schleppegrell, M.J. (2004) *The Language of Schooling: A Functional Linguistics Perspective*. New York: Routledge.

Seltzer, K. (2019a) Performing ideologies: Fostering raciolinguistic literacies through role-play in a high school English classroom. *Journal of Adolescent & Adult Literacy* 63 (2), 147–155. https://doi.org/10.1002/jaal.966

Seltzer, K. (2019b) Reconceptualizing 'home' and 'school' language: Taking a critical translingual approach in the English classroom. *TESOL Quarterly* 53 (4), 986–1007. https://doi.org/10.1002/tesq.530

Seltzer, K. (2020) 'My English is its own rule': Voicing a translingual sensibility through poetry. *Journal of Language, Identity & Education* 19 (5), 297–311. https://doi.org/10.1080/15348458.2019.1656535

Seltzer, K. and de los Ríos, C.V. (2018) Translating theory to practice: Exploring teachers' raciolinguistic literacies in secondary English classrooms. *English Education* 51 (1), 49–79.

Seltzer, K. and García, O. (2020) Broadening the view: Taking up a translanguaging pedagogy with all language-minoritized students. In Z. Tian, L. Aghai, P. Sayer and J.L. Schissel (eds) *Envisioning TESOL through a Translanguaging Lens* (pp. 23–42). Cham: Springer.

Shohamy, E. (2011) Assessing multilingual competencies: Adopting construct valid assessment policies. *The Modern Language Journal* 95 (3), 418–429. https://doi.org/10.1111/j.1540-4781.2011.01210.x

Short, D.J., Echevarría, J. and Richards-Tutor, C. (2011) Research on academic literacy development in sheltered instruction classrooms. *Language Teaching Research* 15 (3), 363–380.

Sifakis, N.C. (2019) ELF awareness in English language teaching: Principles and processes. *Applied Linguistics* 40 (2), 288–306. https://doi.org/10.1093/applin/amx034

Skutnabb-Kangas, T., Phillipson, R., Mohanty, A.K. and Panda, M. (eds) (2009) *Social Justice through Multilingual Education*. Bristol: Multilingual Matters.

Storch, N. (2002) Patterns of interaction in ESL pair work. *Language Learning* 52 (1), 119–158. https://doi.org/10.1111/1467-9922.00179

Strauss, A. and Corbin, J.M. (1997) *Grounded Theory in Practice*. Thousand Oaks, CA: Sage.

Sultana, S. (2021) Regionalism, nationalism, and ethnicism in the digital translingual spaces. Online lecture, 27 May. Akal University.

Svalberg, A.M. (2007) Language awareness and language learning. *Language Teaching* 40 (4), 287–308. https://doi.org/10.1017/S0261444807004491

Swain, M. (2006) Languaging, agency and collaboration in advanced second language proficiency. In H. Byrnes (ed.) *Advanced Language Learning: The Contribution of Halliday and Vygotsky* (pp. 95–108). London: Continuum.

Swain, M. and Watanabe, Y. (2012) Languaging: Collaborative dialogue as a source of second language learning. In C.A. Chapelle (ed.) *The Encyclopedia of Applied Linguistics*. Wiley Online Library. https://doi.org/10.1002/9781405198431.wbeal0664.pub2

Talmy, S. (2008) The cultural productions of the ESL student at Tradewinds High: Contingency, multidirectionality, and identity in L2 socialization. *Applied Linguistics* 29 (4), 619–644. https://doi.org/10.1093/applin/amn011

Teodoro, L.V. (ed.) (2019) *Out of This Struggle: The Filipinos in Hawai'i*. Honolulu, HI: University of Hawai'i Press.

Tian, Z., Aghai, L., Sayer, P. and Schissel, J.L. (eds) (2020) *Envisioning TESOL through a Translanguaging Lens: Global Perspectives*. Cham: Springer.

Trask, H.K. (1991) Coalition-building between natives and non-natives. *Stanford Law Review* 43 (6), 1197–1213. https://jstor.org/stable/1229037

Trask, H.K. (2000) Settlers of color and 'immigrant' hegemony: 'Locals' in Hawai'i. *Amerasia Journal* 26 (2), 1–24. https://doi.org/10.17953/amer.26.2b31642r221215k7k

Trask, H.K. (2004) The color of violence. *Social Justice* 31 (4), 8–16. https://jstor.org/stable/29768270

Trinidad, C. (2005) The vanishing Filipinos. *Honolulu Star Bulletin*. See http://archives .starbulletin.com/2005/12/11/editorial/myturn.html (accessed 1 January 2022).

Tupas, R. and Lorente, B.P. (2014) A 'new' politics of language in the Philippines: Bilingual education and the new challenge of mother tongues. In P. Sercombe and R. Tupas (eds) *Language, Education, and Nation-Building: Assimilation and Shift in Southeast Asia* (pp. 165–180). Basingstoke: Palgrave Macmillan.

Tusting, K. and Maybin, J. (2007) Linguistic ethnography and interdisciplinarity: Opening the discussion. *Journal of Sociolinguistics* 11 (5), 575–583. https://doi.org/10.1111/j.1467-9841.2007.00340.x

Valdés, G. (2001) Heritage language students: Profiles and possibilities. In J.K. Peyton, D.A. Ranard and S. McGinnis (eds) *Heritage Languages in America: Preserving a National Resource* (pp. 37–77). Washington, DC: Center for Applied Linguistics.

Valdés, G. (2020) Sandwiching, polylanguaging, translanguaging, and codeswitching: Challenging monolingual dogma in institutionalized language teaching. In Z. Tian, L. Aghai, P. Sayer and J.L. Schissel (eds) *Envisioning TESOL through a Translanguaging Lens: Global Perspectives* (pp. 114–147). Cham: Springer.

Van Dyke, J.M. (2007) *Who Owns the Crown Lands of Hawai'i?* Honolulu, HI: University of Hawai'i Press.

Vertovec, S. (2007) Super-diversity and its implications. *Ethnic and Racial Studies* 30 (6), 1024–1054. https://doi.org/10.1080/01419870701599465

Vettorel, P. (2016) WE- and ELF-informed classroom practices: Proposals from a pre-service teacher education programme in Italy. *Journal of English as a Lingua Franca* 5 (1), 107–133. https://doi.org/10.1515/jelf-2016-0005

Vygotsky, L.S. (1980) *Mind in Society: The Development of Higher Psychological Processes*. Cambridge, MA: Harvard University Press.

Wa-Mbaleka, S. (2014) English teachers' perceptions of the mother tongue-based education policy in the Philippines. *European Journal of Research and Reflection in Educational Sciences* 2 (4), 17–32.

Wang, D. (2019) *Multilingualism and Translanguaging in Chinese Language Classrooms*. Cham: Springer.

Warren, C.A. (2015) Conflicts and contradictions: Conceptions of empathy and the work of good-intentioned early career white female teachers. *Urban Education* 50 (5), 572–600. https://doi.org/10.1177/0042085914525790

Watson-Gegeo, K.A. (1988) Ethnography in ESL: Defining the essentials. *TESOL Quarterly* 22 (4), 575–592. https://doi.org/10.2307/3587257

Williams, C. (1994) *Arfarniad o ddulliau dysgu ac addysgu yng nghyd-destun addysg uwchradd ddwyieithog* [An evaluation of teaching and learning methods in the context of bilingual secondary education]. PhD dissertation, University of Wales, Bangor.

Willis, P. (1981) *Learning to Labour: How Working Class Kids Get Working Class Jobs*. New York: Columbia University Press.

Wong, S. (1979) *Homebase*. New York: Penguin.

Wong Fillmore, L. (1997) *Authentic Literature in ESL Instruction*. Glenview, IL: Scott Foresman.

Woodley, H. and Brown, A. (2016) Balancing windows and mirrors: Translanguaging in a multilingual classroom. In O. García and T. Kleyn (eds) *Translanguaging with Multilingual Students: Learning from Classroom Moments* (pp. 83–99). New York: Routledge.

Wortham, S. (2006) *Learning Identity: The Joint Emergence of Social Identification and Academic Learning*. Cambridge: Cambridge University Press.

Wortham, S. (2008) Linguistic anthropology of education. *Annual Review of Anthropology*, 37 (1), 37–51. https://doi.org/10.1146/annurev.anthro.36.081406.094401

Wortham, S. and Reyes, A. (2017) Discourse analysis across events. In S. Wortham, D. Kim and S. May (eds) *Discourse and Education* (pp. 71–84). Cham: Springer.

Yoon, B. (2008) Uninvited guests: The influence of teachers' roles and pedagogies on the positioning of English language learners in the regular classroom. *American Educational Research Journal* 45 (2), 495–522. https://doi.org/10.3102/0002831208316200

Young, V.A. (2004) Your average nigga. *College Composition and Communication* 55 (4), 693–715. https://doi.org/10.2307/4140667

Zavala, V. (2015) 'It will emerge if they grow fond of it': Translanguaging and power in Quechua teaching. *Linguistics and Education* 32, 16–26. https://doi.org/10.1016/j.linged.2015.01.009

Zimmerman, D.H. (1998) Discoursal identities and social identities. In C. Antaki and S. Widdicombe (eds) *Identities in Talk* (pp. 87–106). London: Sage.

Index

Page number in italic type refer to tables and figures. Those followed by 'n' refer to notes.

Printed in the USA
CPSIA information can be obtained
at www.ICGtesting.com
JSHW011107020724
65693JS00029B/127